ORACLES OF NOSTRADAMUS

BY

CHAS. A. WARD.

"Gentem quidem nullam video, neque tam humanam atque doctam, neque tam immanem tamque barbaram, quæ non significari futura, et à quibusdam intelligi prædicique posse censeat."—CICERO, *De Divinatione*, i. 2.

SUN BOOKS

Sun Publishing Company
Santa Fe, N.M.

"Quorum potentia intellectualis immediate à Deo agitata creditur, prophetæ dicuntur; quorum voluntas heroës; at quorum intellectus et voluntas censetur agitata à potentiis invisibilibus dependentibus, appellantur magi." — CHRIST. THOMASIUS, *in Brunck, Hist. Phil.* v. 512.

THE LEADENHALL PRESS, LONDON, E.C.
(T. 4543)

"Tu te mocques aussi des prophètes que Dieu
Choisit en tes enfants et les fait au milieu
De ton sein apparoître, afin de te prédire
Ton malheur à venir ; mais tu n'en fais que rire.
Ou soit que le grand Dieu l'immense éternité
Ait de Nostradamus l'enthousiasme excité,
Ou soit que le démon bon ou mauvais l'agite . . .
Comme un oracle antique, il a de mainte année
Prédit la plus grand part de nostre destinée."
RONSARD, *To Nostradamus.*

Printed in the United States of America
Sun Publishing Company
P.O. Box 5588, Santa Fe, N.M. 87502-5588

TO MY MOTHER.

Οὐδὲν ἐν ἀνθρώποισι πατρὸς καὶ μητρὸς ἄμεινον
Ἔπλετο, τοῖς ὁσίη, Κύρνε, μέμηλε δίκη.

THEOGNIS, p. 16, ed. 1766.

" But higher far my proud pretensions rise,—
The son of parents passed into the skies."

COWPER, On My Mother's Picture, line 110.

IF THERE CAN BE ANYTHING IN A BOOK LIKE
THIS WORTHY OF DEDICATION TO A BEING SO
NOBLE AS THOU IN LIFE WERT ' VER. A BEING
NOW MORE ENNOBLED STILL BY THE HEAVEN-
BLEACHED RAIMENT OF IMMORTALITY PUT ON ;
TO THEE, PURE SOUL SERENE ! TO THEE DOES
THY STILL LOVING SON, EARTH-HAMPERED, DEDI-
CATE THIS THE BEST LABOUR OF HIS HEART AND
HEAD AND YEARS. THE BEST OF IT IS THINE
INDEED ALREADY ; AND WERE THE REST WORSE
HARVESTED THAN PERHAPS IT IS,—MORTALITY
BEING ALLOWED FOR DULY,—THY SOUL RECEIVING
MUST BE MUCH CHANGED BY EXALTATION, IF
QUEEN-LIKE, IT CANNOT MAKE A SORRY LOVE-
GIFT RICH BY GOLDEN WELCOME GIVEN IT.

IF THINGS OF KITH BE KIN, GOD WILLING, WE
SHALL MEET AGAIN ERE LONG. TILL WHEN,
FROM THIS BARE HEATH TERRENE AND HOME-
LESS, I SPEED THE WORD ADIEU. DEAR ONE !
FOR A LITTLE WHILE ADIEU.

THY SON,
C. A. W.

THREE PROPHECIES OF OLD TIME.

That Troy should triumph in Rome—

> Νῦν δὲ δὴ Αἰνείαο βίη Τρώεσσιν ἀνάξει,
> Καὶ παίδων παῖδες, τοί κεν μετόπισθε γένωνται.
>
> *Iliad*, xx. 306.

That America should be discovered—

> " Venient annis
> Sæcula seris, quibus Oceanus
> Vincula rerum laxet, et ingens
> Pateat Tellus, Tiphysque novos
> Delegat orbes ; nec sit terris
> Ultima Thule."
>
> SENECA.

French Revolution, 1788-89, predicted in 10th Century.

" Des le X⁰ siècle, Albumasar avait calculé que l'année *mil sept cent quatre-vingt-neuf* serait féconde en révolutions sociales, à cause de l'une des grandes conjonctions de Saturne. L'astrologie est vanité, erreur, mensonge, tout ce que vous voudrez ; mais enfin voilà une prédiction d'une authenticité irrécusable."—ALBUMASAR, *De Magnis Conjunctionibus Tract.* ii., *Different.* 8. *Vide* MIGNE, *Dict. des Prophéties*, ii. 339.

PREFACE.

———◦◦◦———

THIS is no doubt a strange book. An attempt to gather a meaning out of a few of the involved, crabbed, and mystical quatrains of the great seer of France, the greatest perhaps that the world has ever seen, must of necessity be strange. My treatment, too, may possibly seem to many no less strange than the subject-matter itself. I will speak specially as to this latter point towards the close of the preface.

In last December, treating upon Nostradamus in the *Gentleman's Magazine*, I had occasion to remark that every honest man of awakened powers is a kind of prophet, and has to do with the future, or eternity, as it is usually styled. Since then I have come upon the same idea in the writings of Philo Judæus. He thinks that the Scriptures testify in some sort that every good man is a prophet :

" For a prophet says nothing of his own, but everything that he says is strange, and prompted by some one else ; and it is not lawful for a wicked man to be an interpreter of God, as also no wicked man can be properly said to be inspired ; but this statement is only appropriate to the wise man alone, since he alone is a sounding instrument of God's voice."—PHILO, *Heir of Divine Things*, § 52, Bohn, ii. 146.

Again, at page 32 of this book, it will be seen that I have described the faculty of anticipating the future, a thing so remarkably developed in Nostradamus, as being, if once we admit its existence in him, a perceptive endowment of the whole human race, that must be classified as a sixth sense. I have since found, with no little delight, that Coleridge, in his "Table Talk" (ed. 1836, p. 19), designated such faculty as "an inner sense," for, speaking of ghosts and dreams, he says ;

"It is impossible to say whether an inner sense does not really exist in the mind, seldom developed, indeed, but which may have a power of presentiment. All the external senses have their correspondents in the mind ; the eye can see an object before it is distinctly apprehended ; why may there not be a corresponding power in the soul? The power of prophecy might have been merely a spiritual excitation of this dormant faculty." *

* This noble and enlarged thought is worthy of Coleridge, who is the greatest thinker of our century, whether you take him as poet or philosopher. Nobody has yet claimed for him the pre-eminence which, I believe, to be his. The peculiar, nay, unique frailties of the man have blinded the men of his own time to the super-eminent, intellectual, *practical*, and imaginative endowments with which he was so affluently furnished. By the middle of next century, some hundred or so years from his death, the fact will have dawned upon the world, if not before. It will then be recognized that such a personality as his, was "a great birth of time," and to be registered as such in the death-less calendar of genius. Saint, seer, and sage was that man. Not "spoilt in the making," as the witty Lamb put it, with all

In the matter of prophecy, Photius says, in his "Amphilochia," that prophecy is by no means the lambent malice of a friend jocose. We must admit, of course, some damage that hindered general currency, as also the attainment of such now worthless cash-results as fell to beings distinctly inferior to himself, such as Byron, Southey, Wordsworth, Moore, great as some estimate them to be ; and this failure shut Coleridge out from social success,—that success which most of us so ignorantly and greedily covet here, because it makes the present comfortable. But the chief reason, of any shortcoming hurtful to success, that may be observable in Coleridge, 'no doubt arose from his being far too great to be adequately measured by any of his fellow-men. Many of them were, it is true, highly capable men as the world goes. Even Carlyle, however, who has disparaged him, when placed beside him, dwarfs to a man of Lilliput. We have to bear in mind always that excellent remark of La Bruyère, "Celui qui ne prévoit rien, est souvent dupe ; celui qui prévoit trop, est toujours malheureux." This is true of all prophets, and especially true of Coleridge.

But, another thing there is that helps to diminish Coleridge in the general estimation. He has not completed work enough, in well set and fixed form, for posterity to be quite able to render him adequate, that is to say, resplendent justice. His unexampled conversational gifts have somewhat barred the way to a due appreciation of his equally unexampled literary potentialities. His conversational aptitudes have perished in the moment of their triumphant display. Being without record in this respect, he suffers precisely as the greatest actor does. Triumphs of the table and the salon are like the triumphs of the stage, we can only revive them in spirit, on the basis of some felicitously appreciative sentence, chance embalmed in print, that some competent contemporary has ejaculated. I, for instance, know the overwhelming power of Kean only through my mother, and the burning phrases left behind by Byron and Coleridge. But the next generation can have no cognizance of him beyond those phrases. It is for this precise reason I indite so long a note as this on Coleridge, out of the pure respect I bear necessarily connected with virtue : for that Herod pre-announced, as it were, that the Gentile magi, Judæa, and the world were about to recognize Christ for King, and so he desired to make away with him. In this way he played the part of prophet to the whole human race. Caiaphas, he thinks, was not conscious of what he said ; in the mania of a desire to kill, his lips prophesied that it was right that one should die to save the whole world. " Let his blood be upon us and upon our children," is a foreboding instinct of the same description. In the council of the Pharisees (John xi. 48), it was prophetic, " If we let him alone, the Romans will come and take away our place and nation ; " and though *they* followed out their own counsel, this is just what happened. "And see," he adds, "the ass in the Old Testament could forecast future things." He was an heretical writer, Photius, but he was evidently not so far away, as the world is now, from believing that prophetic endowment is a sense widely distributed to humanity in

him for his stupendous intelligence and incommensurable soul. I have, indeed, tried to put on record elsewhere my impression of his poetry ; but, I have not yet been able to get it printed. Should it ever be so, it would at least acquire some value from the fact of its representing, in a limited and qualified degree, Coleridge's vivid influence upon one who may partially stand on the footing of a contemporary. Coleridge is a spirituality in the world, and his modes of revealing himself are such as lead the run of mankind to esteem him visionary ; but it will be found that it is they, not he, that must be reckoned " such stuff as dreams are made of."

general. These hints alone may furnish us with food
for useful meditation.

Now, with all this a reader will very likely say,
Supposing we grant you the prophetic as a sixth
sense, to be henceforth reckoned as a permanent
though generally latent endowment of the race, what
is the good of such a sense, supposing, with you, that
your prophet can never be understood till after the
event has taken place, and then only when some
drudging interpreter has untwisted his tortuous
language and thrown it into the intelligible vernacular?
There are several ways of replying to this. First,
are there not thousands of objects in the domain of
nature that man has not yet discovered the use of?
Anatomists are still at a stand to tell us what is the
use of the spleen. What naturalist can say for what
reason the noxious serpent is sent into the world?
Why the Georgium Sidus was only discovered by
Herschel in 1781, instead of by Pythagoras, a much
greater man? Sensible men have commonly to content themselves with simply ascertaining the existence
of a fact, and they have to rest all the while in total
ignorance of why this fact exists. Again, suppose
you believe, as the majority do, in the Christian
revelation; how can you account for the multiplicity
of sects who read the Bible each in its own way?
Can you account for a divine revelation that reveals
one thing to one man and a contrary thing to another?
Obviously, then, there are many things that exist as

facts, and yet no man living can assign the reason of them. With regard to any fact that can be asserted, the first thing to establish is, Is it a fact? That once settled, you may wait for the rest of it until you can get it.

But again, and with special regard to Nostradamus, you will see (and by referring to the index you may find the various places at which I treat of it) that he must have had the whole sequence of visions passing clearly before his eyes, with some vocal utterances occasionally accompanying them, by which the names of men and places and things were announced to him. His method was to set this down in prose narration, either during the sitting or instantly afterwards. On inspection, at cooler intervals, and when he had descended from the heat and ecstasy of fatidical rapture, he would discern at once that the sequence must be broken and the names concealed. If, as it stood in prose, it had been understood by the world, it would have fallen not as a prophecy but as a thunderbolt; not as a thing in book-form, but as an earthquake, that must have changed or shaken the face of Europe, and so have interfered perpetually with its own realization.

Seeing this, he followed the practice of the elder oracles of Delphi, Dodona, and the rest. He broke up the sequence, threw the utterances into metre, mingled much learning linguistic to darken them, and obscured the names, of the great men introduced, under the impenetrable mask of the anagram. Thus regarded, it is not a subject for wonder that he did this: it would have been akin to madness to have done anything else.

It now becomes desirable that I should furnish some clue to enable a reader to arrive rapidly at the pith of this book and its oracular forecasts, so that he may discern for himself in a few minutes, whether, or whether not, the topics treated of have for him a sufficient interest to lead him on to make a thorough study of the book, or to decline it altogether. There is a huge prejudice in this our day that sets in strongly with the multitude against anything that endeavours to deal seriously, or by mystical insight, with things occult, spiritual, or future.

The reader, first of all, should glance over the life of Nostradamus. It will be for him to determine whether my vindication of his name from imposture be adequate or not. Dr. Cobham Brewer is the most recent writer who asperses him as a " charlatan " (see his " History of Germany," p. 164). The reader will see that Nostradamus is of Jewish birth. Coleridge remarks (" Table Talk," p. 31) that all other nations

" Seem to look backwards, and also to exist for the present ; but in the Jewish scheme everything is prospective and pre- paratory ; nothing, however trifling, is done for itself alone, but all is typical of something yet to come."

Further than this, Thomas Burnet, in his eloquent Latinity, tells us (" Archæ. Philos," Book I. chap. vii.

p. 59, ed. 1727) that Apollonius said bitterly of the
Jews that they were the most inept of barbarians, and
never invented a single thing useful to mankind.
That they were what Bacon would call a people of
" no fruit." They taught nothing in their schools, says
Burnet, of the circle of the sciences, " ad encyclopædiæ
studia," as we do now, but that no race in the world
so abounds with prophets, and men endowed with the
celestial spirit, as " the Jews."

Those who care anything for the occult processes,
that incite to prophetic utterance, would now do well
to read the chapter on magic, commencing at p. 75.
It gives a few hints as to the practices of adepts, and
of the Roman superstitions about tripods, alphabetic
interrogatories, and so forth ; and it becomes tolerably
clear from all this, that Nostradamus was skilled in
all the known methods of incantation, astral, pharma-
ceutic, or electrical, and that he practised them in all
their fulness, though with reticent circumspection, and
very reluctant and enigmatic avowal. The account
of the conspirators against Valens (p. 86) strongly
resembles the modern table-turning. But, as this
chapter is more curious by far than necessary, it may
be passed over by all those who merely wish to
appraise quickly the value of Nostradamus as a figure
in history with claims to prophetic faculty hanging on
to it.

From the Historical Fragments, commencing at
p. 89, it will be seen that he clearly prophesied the

violent death of Henri II., to whom he dedicates his
" Luminary Epistle." The historical context is very
interesting, as showing not only the exact fulfilment
of the forecast of Nostradamus ; but, that another
astrologer, who was consulted by the king, had fore-
warned him in almost the same words of the same
danger threatening, that he should die " in duel." We
see the king adhering to the literal word *duel*, and
out of court etiquette feeling the manifest impos-
sibility of the prophecy being fulfilled. We get also
the gossip of the court about it, and about the value
of horoscopes, from the Princesse de Clèves ; further-
more, we learn about the obstinate blindness with
which the king forced on his own destruction at the
very close of the day and tournament, by the indul-
gence of a pure whim against the advice and wish of
everybody around him. The murder of Henri III.,
in like manner, is announced, together with the death
of his father, at p. 99 ; at p. 124 it is foreshadowed
again as proceeding from the hand of a young monk ;
and at p. 125 the name of Clément is hinted by a
play upon the French words signifying mild and
clement. The massacre of St. Bartholomew's Day, at
p. 106, stands out in all its vivid horror, and as proceeding from the very hands of *le roi farouche ;* but,
compressed into four lines only.

The coming of Henri IV. to the French throne is
introduced with the very name of his family, Vendôme,
figured in the anagram Mendosus. Here we find

also (p. 132) the execution of the Marshal de Biron ; his name is actually given as Robin, which yields it letter for letter in anagram. This, too, is concerning a man not probably born when the stanza was devised. The name of the marshal is disguised, because it would have marked him out too distinctly when he came upon the stage of public life ; but, the name of Lafin is given, the subordinate individual who betrayed Biron to the King. It occupies pages to describe this event, but with the terseness, reappearing constantly, which is so remarkable a feature in the style of Nostradamus, he compresses the whole event, and all that he has to say upon it, into six lines.

The chapter on Louis XIV. (p. 150) teems with curiosities of the same inscrutable order ; though less startling than what we have already pointed out, yet is it quite sufficient to have made the reputation of an ordinary man.

We may now pass to England (p. 166), and the quatrain relating to its seven governmental changes, throughout a period of two hundred and ninety years ; this is as startling as anything of the kind can well be. The next instance, that on the Stuart Dynasty (p. 170), conveying, as it does, the struggle between Charles I. and Cromwell, is simply miraculous ; and it should challenge the attention of a listening world. This would seem to·be the inevitable result, unless the learned of all orders and degrees can, singly or combined, do away with the interpretation put upon it. *Lonole* is now for the first time pointed to as being the anagram of *Old Noll,* or Oliver Cromwell. But before this transpired, M. le Pelletier had none the less applied the quatrain to Charles and Cromwell. If this fails to convince a reader that he is in the presence of a seer and worker of wonders, I do not know what can bring recognition home to him. The single line (p. 173)—

"Senat de Londres mettront à mort leur Roy."

has, as presenting the execution of Charles I., made, in former but forgotten days, the round of the world, and from time to time has served to keep alive a sort of dumb admission that there had once been a fatidical diviner of note called Nostradamus. Burns remarks, what we all know, that "the passion of prying into futurity, makes a striking part of the history of human nature." It does not look much like it, though, when such a prophecy as this has been allowed to pass out of memory ; so that few even of educated men could re-syllable it to you, or furnish you with any better criticism on the man who penned it, than that he was an old French impostor and astrologer. They know ten times as much about Mother Shipton, concerning whom little or nothing is authentic ; whilst Nostradamus's book has been probably in print for nearly three hundred and fifty years.

The next is a quatrain on Cromwell exclusively

b

(p. 177), "more butcher than king," as Nostradamus calls him ; and he will be found to regard Napoleon (p. 236) in very much the same light. He gives England an ascendancy of the seas (p. 181) for a stretch of more than three hundred years,—a term which, I think, will be found to be on the point of expiring now. Of course his quatrains relating to England are, on the whole, much inferior in interest to those relating to France. What stands collected under the heading of "England" will, nevertheless, well repay persual. The Battle of Dunbar, for instance (p. 205) is in its way as vivid, though conveyed in but four lines of verse, as Carlyle's famous account of the engagement which is given in the Cromwell Letters. He prophesies the death of Cromwell (p. 210) to fall on the 3rd of September, seven years later than the battle of Worcester. It is true we gather this by implication, but with all the other wonders duly weighed, a candid reader will admit this to be the probable intention and true meaning here. The Fire of London is given as falling out in 1666 (at p. 214).

His name for the French Revolution is *Le Commun Advenement,* which I render The Vulgar Advent. This, right up to the very end, is the most astounding part of all that has been recorded by Nostradamus, or brought into intelligibility by his commentators. This preface would run to far too great length were I to attempt even to touch upon all of the points of interest, that we here find to be so strangely dealt with.

Take merely the first stanza (p. 227). Napoleonism is spoken of, almost before it has been announced, as proscribed ; and, to spring up again as it did in 1848 ; and then to sink finally seventy-three years after. At that passage (at p. 227) the reader may see how, out of the mouth of Napoleon himself, the exact term of seventy-three years proves to be the correct period. This has never been so much as hinted before. If anything be miraculous, in the accuracy of prevision, I think this may,—and with but little superstition,— be deemed to be so.

There is a remark to be made of some importance, to my thinking, because it establishes the subtle analogy that sometimes subsists in the relation between things, that are not generally reckoned to have any connection one with the other. Now, the Vulgar Advent, of course, is signalized by the usurpation of government by the people ; but is it not highly significant that, out of the natural fountain of speech, and with no particular or conscious intention accompanying, the low proletarian rabble, that bring it about in blood, are spontaneously designated by themselves and others as the *Rouges?* The abhorrent many, when they play the despot, don the colour *red*, and doff for ever, as they hope, the royal *purple.* They may hope what they please ; but, when their vices ripen, they *must* fall under the empire of one,—who is iron-shod, sword-girt, and rat-eaten as to the heart,—who will trample them into order. Call him Lonole, Olestant,

or clement Cæsar, which you will ; a beast from the
abyss must arise to rule the bestial. This is the
truly representative man who emerges at the epochs.
Rousseau, the red-head, with the curse of Iscariot
upon him, may begin the series. A red philosopher
first introduces his Pandemonium as order ; secondly,
Les rouges rouges le rouge assomeront (p. 274); and
thirdly, the destroyer, the Napoleon, or Apollyon, introduces and then crowns himself with his own hand.
A red series in a red sequel so sealed, so shuts the same.

As we are upon analogies, another curious one may
here be noted. The colours of the tricoloured flag
symbolize revolution by the reversal of the order of
nature. The primary colours in the solar spectrum
are, as well as in the primary arc of the rainbow, red,
yellow, blue (p. 331); whilst in the tricolour the succession is blue, white, red. Out of this flag, or bow,
in the political heavens there is no hope to come,
for it yields no promise but that of a deluge,—*rouge.*

The sanguinary death of Louis XVI. is foreshown
at p. 241. In the "Luminary Epistle" to Henri II.
(p. 69) the very year is given (1792) to which the
quatrain of Louis's death refers. Take next the
arrest at Varennes (p. 243), and then another miracle
of precision shines forth ; for Saulce, the grocer's
name in that little town, is pregiven (p. 248). The
Tuilleries are mentioned by name,—a place where
burnt a tile-kiln, when Nostradamus was inditing for
us the prophecy.

Now refer to the Napoleonic rule (p. 286). See Napoleon born in the west of Europe, and the way he could seduce, in a language not his own, is pointed out to you ; and, his name is to be a name that the Fates know (p. 287).

Take, again, that strange identification of the Gallic Hercules with his analogue Napoleon. How, as a jay taught by Talma, he at the Tuilleries apes the fine birds and court splendour of the old *régime* (p. 294). Then read the quatrain at p. 297, where the simple soldier reaches empire, and so strikes close analogy again with Cromwell. Then read (p. 300) that awful curse fulminated, when counsel shall die out of the shaven head ; see Sclavonia gather (p. 303), and old Moscow burn, whilst the eagle (p. 304) is beaten back with a swarm of birds, and hovers to its fall at Leipsic.*

---

* Touching this curse to fall on Napoleon, a somewhat singular analogy arises in comparing with it the axiom laid down by Thomasius, quoted in Bruncker's "Hist. Crit. Philos.," v. 488. He says that the spirit is, as it were, resident in the centre of all bodies, and thence emits rays, so extending matter. But where it draws back the rays from the circumference of the material to the centre, it soon dissolves and corrupts the body. *Si vero radios ex circumferentia materiæ spiritus attrahat ad centrum, resolvitur corpus et corrumpitur.* If we suppose this to have taken place at the epileptic seizure of Napoleon, the mental attack becomes an image or antitype of the battle of Leipsic, when the swarm of birds beat back the eagle. An interpreter, such as Joseph, could have told him the meaning of the dream or swoon. The defeat was first of all rehearsed in the soldier's own brain.

I do not deem it necessary to particularize any further; for if all this gathered into one conspectus is not enough to carry conviction home to the mind of any one; and, make the reader know that at Salon, three hundred and odd years since, there lived a Frenchman, who saw all this in visions of the night, interpretative speech accompanying, and set it down at first in too clear prose, and secondly in rythmic riddles afterwards; why, then, I think that fifty times more evidence, thrown in upon the top, could carry no conviction with it.

I have said many things about science and its modern tendencies that will be deemed foolish by some, and by others undeservedly severe, so that a few words upon it seem necessary here. If the word "science" merely means the study of nature, it has my admiration as a pursuit. But if it means *knowledge*, I say it is an absolute misnomer. There is no true knowledge out of wisdom, and all that is wisdom in man is comprised in his veneration of Deity. "The fear of the Lord is the beginning of wisdom." It is evident, that what we call science in this day, does not tend that way at all.

But, to take it briefly another way, if you do not know the *first cause* of anything, you can only attain to a knowledge of relativities, but never of anything as it is in itself. Your methods can have neither beginning nor end. Hence a man can only attain to relative knowledge which, in the strict meaning of words, is not knowledge at all. Thus science is impossible.

Those, who pretend to science, talk much now about an Atomic Theory. They speak of their atom, contrary to its etymology, as being a thing infinitely divisible. This they adopt as a subterfuge, that no one may be able to drive them home. But if you leave them to their own devices,—their own chemical analyses, quantitative and qualitative, when they get beyond vapour, leave them in possession of a *nothing* to divide. It is then they approach Deity *in minimis;* but for the cloud upon their sight they cannot see Him. Such men apprehend nothing except through the intellect ; but the perfect intellect yields only half the man. It can only deal with the subject-matter furnished to it by the senses. There is, high-placed above it, the spirit of life ; which possesses a sense of its own, and by this the heart and head are interlinked. When the ideas (for lack of a better word) of these two are thought into harmony,—or, what Coleridge would call "unity,"—then, and then only, is the comment of the whole man perfect. Take this for an axiom : If you believe your sense, you may be right ; if you believe your senses, you are out of them.

Cogito ergo sum ("I think therefore I am") has been accredited to Descartes as wisdom for a long time. It is nonsense. It is a proof gathered from the action of the intellect alone, and is a *critique* physical, rather than metaphysical, and here can afford no proof of anything.

Another word about *Atoms*, and I must have done, or this will not be a preface, but a metaphysical treatise; and though that may be greatly wanted, this is not the place for it. Yet, as I have arraigned science, it becomes advisable that I should furnish to the competent reader a spot or foothold, where being placed, he may, if he will, command my meaning. In the Chaldaic oracles there occur two curious lines; I quote them below that there may be no equivocation possible.* "Now, these fabricate individual things (τὰ ἄτομα, atoms), and sensible objects, and corporeal things, and things classed under matter." The Neoplatonists said that ideas were an emanation of the divine fire. Plato said very much the same thing of the human soul itself. An atom thus becomes a fiery *individuality* (atomic); not, observe, what the nonsensical chemist of to-day calls it,—when by his terrene fire he has reached vapour,—an infinitely divisible atom, but a particle indivisible; that, having traversed all the forms, goes out at the other end of matter; or back again in a chariot of fire to the idea it started from. The world's Opifex made it by fire, and the tradition of Elias is that it will be dissolved by fire at last; but what, friend, should it prove that

---

* Οἱ δὲ τὰ ἄτομα καὶ αἰσθητὰ δημιουργοῦσι:
Καὶ σωματοειδῆ καὶ κατατεταγμένα εἰς ὕλην.
                STANLEY'S "Hist. Chald. Phil.," p. 43.

it is every day doing so always? A fiery idea began it, and in an idea of fire it ends. Also man's life is nothing but a leap through matter from fire to fire. The ordeal by fire was a type of this.

The professional critic and expert must, after this sketch, be left to himself to judge of everything here set down according to the established rules of art, and the interests multifarious of the special literary organ he may write for and derive emolument from. I expect but little recognition from such criticism ; yet, as it is often the result of a life devoted to study and of wide learning, its indifference, or even its hostility, is likely to prove useful,—whether by its fault-finding or in its discovery of actual error. Whatever its sagacity may in this way show to be wrong, I hope to receive with equanimity and thankfulness, and to put right should a second edition be asked for. So much for the professional critics.

What remains to be said touching my method of treatment will probably have no interest whatever for such critic, nor yet for the general reader. It purely, and I think solely, concerns the thoughtful and capable reader. The exceptional man, who finally, and all the world over, is the best friend of the true writer ; and who, banded with others like himself, determines solidly the value of, and ultimate position to be given to, every new book, that is a book at all, born into the world of letters.

Such a reader I would only forewarn against two

preliminary objections, that might at a hasty first glance tend to excite some prejudice in his mind. The episodes indulged in, and the apparent self-sufficiency of utterance exhibited on questions of moment, that seemingly wise men are divided upon still ; or that men of supposed authority have in general estimation settled long ago. Many such things will here be found to have been laid bare again to the very roots, and challenged to show a reason. This is absolute arrogance everywhere in the estimation of the multitude, learned and un-learned. Reader, gentle and capable, let me give you my view on these two points : could I make it also your view, how well rewarded should I be.

As to episodes : my own view of a book is this, that it should furnish a stimulus to thought if possible at every page ; that nothing should enter into it for the sake of book-making ; and that, so long as the subject of the book is clearly and consecutively advanced, anything else, that can vitally be thrown in without interruption, is so much the more gained to the world in the study of itself, or, in other words, in the study of man ; this Pope has, I incline to think rightly, ruled to be his proper vocation here. Very close and consecutive treatment of a difficult matter must always, when long continued, weigh down the spirits, and somewhat fatigue the attention of the reader. At such a time an interesting episode happily intro-duced will rally the spirits ; and, by a momentary diversion, will renew the attention, enabling the reader to attach himself again with vigour to the main thread. There are episodes of course, as there are other things, good and bad. The episode that is dull in itself and distracts attention is bad ; that which is in itself interesting and relieves fatigue, carrying the mind back to the main subject refreshed, is entirely good. The episodes in the following pages the reader will judge to be good or bad as they fall under the rule given above or transgress it.

The charge of arrogancy is a little more difficult to deal with, and also to rebut. But even here I do not despair of being exonerated by the capable reader, whom alone, on this point, it is requisite to address. Many years ago I came upon a passage in Coleridge to the effect that he had always pursued light, be-lieving that it must lead to truth, and truth to happi-ness ; but that, let it consummate in joy or not, follow it he would, for truth's sake. Truth attracted, and he, in fact, must draw to it. I shut the book up, and said, So will I ; and, with certain failures, much inter-ruption by necessary duties, and innumerable personal shortcomings, so I have. The result has been an ever-increasing solitude,* until at last no eremite of

---

* To get one thing, one must always forego some other. Jupiter did not give prescience to Tiresias till Juno had struck him blind. And for our own great Milton it was necessary he should have wisdom at one entrance quite shut out, before, in " Paradise Lost," he could make men's memory |a prisoner to his name for ever, in a willing though perpetual serfdom.

the desert is more alone than I for years have been. Thus placed, I have thought on many questions, with books and without them, caring but little what the greatest said, so only I kept moving onward towards that spot where the light of morning dawned, or where the still rathelier twilight promised dawning. My attention always lay between things and thoughts, keeping clean aloof from vain opinion, which leads to nothing, though she be, according to Pascal, *Regina del mondo.* As no renown of genius could bring me to respect any man's opinion ; so I strove that no self-seeking, nor hope out of some novelty or strangeness to win originality, might bring me to adopt any principle soever that fell short of justness in the least, or of sacred truth anyhow attainable by man. As I sank others, so have I sunk myself and all personal belongings, striving, if I might, to make myself a trumpet of smooth passage or clear mouthpiece to the truth that lies behind us all,—behind every man that cometh into the world,—though haply there be but few who can allow it free enough scope and exit through them. As in this way I have grown nearly dead both to myself and others, and want little of emolument and less of glory (accurrent from without), it seemed not unlikely that so epurated a voice-piece might utter more of less adulterate truth, than it falls in common to the lot of most to do. So much am I a mere person (*persona*), mask, thing sounded through, as that the voice at last seems scarcely to be mine at all, but something larger, higher, better much, than I pretend to be. I do not even claim a perfect utterance, or out-put, for what remains of me,—call it trumpet, mask, person, or what not,—must remain, I know, always beset with some earth and earthiness that mars a pure transmission. Yet, weak as it may be and is, the weak things of the world are those that most confound the mighty ones established of authority by man. Where is any boasting, I ask, in this; or what of arrogance is here? Will any man spend thirty years thus to become a voice-tube merely? None the less is it at last a voice crying in the wilderness, "Desolate are those who in the earth lack vision of wisdom, or call gold wealth." Capable and gentle reader, test this prologue, and try it, believing, that if there be any good thing in it, solitude and The Alone have wrought it. With them, as by seraphic marshalling,—with tent pitched, or travelling on, under the night-star or by day,—you may safely thread the pages following, assured that nothing but good can issue or accrue therefrom to you. Most excellent reader, let *Vale Valete!* fall as the benediction of an eremite upon your ear to-day; as also upon your pilgrimage hereafter, till the hour vespertine of sleep drop down, that closes all for each.

WALTHAMSTOW, E., 1891.

" Quelle physique corpusculaire, quels atomes déterminent ainsi leur nature ? vous n'en savez rien ; la cause sera éternellement occulte pour vous. Tout ce qui vous entoure, tout ce qui est dans vous, est une énigme dont il n'est pas donné à l'homme de deviner le mot."—VOLTAIRE, *Dict. Phil.*, s.v. *Occultes.*

CONTENTS.

———◦◦◦———

> "In Nature's infinite book of secrecy
> A little can I read."
>
> *Anthony and Cleopatra*, i. 2.

"I am Isaiah,—be it spoken with all humility,—to the advancement of God's glory."—LUTHER'S *Table Talk*, Bohn, p. 12.

Yes, indeed, Luther, with quite Lutheran humility !

> " Canys gwn a fydd rhag llaw."
> "For I know what has been, and will be hereafter."
>
> TALIESSIN.

" Prophetia est solum futurorum contingentium, quia longe distant ab humana cognitione ; sed secundario ad eam pertinent præterita et præsentia."—ST. THO. AQUINATIS, *Summa*, p. 409.

ORACLES OF NOSTRADAMUS.

LIFE OF NOSTRADAMUS.

MICHEL DE NOSTREDAME was born in Provence, in the town of St. Remy, in the year 1503, upon a Thursday, the 14th of December, about noon. Tycho Brahe (1546), D'Herbelot (1625) the great Orientalist, and Bruce (1730) the Abyssinian traveller, were all born on the same day of the month. Coincidences such as these are, perhaps, not worth much; yet, do they interest us less than the rainfall of a month, or the precise pressure of the wind on Cleopatra's needle?—which goes by the name of Cleopatra because Cleopatra had nothing whatever to do with it. Robert Étienne, the great printer, was also born in 1503. What would, however, more have affected the family of Nostradamus is the expulsion of the French from Naples on October 31, 1503, after the famous battles in April, fought on two consecutive Fridays with disaster to the French; the battles namely, of Seminara and Cerignola. Many have said that the evil omen attaching to Friday dates

B

from that period. If we had never heard of Good Friday we also might have been of their opinion.

His father, like Milton's, a notary, was James Nostradamus, a name which is equivalent to *de Nôtre Dame.** Moreri calls his family "*une famille noble ;* " † others say that he was of Jewish descent, but of a family that had been converted to Christianity, and that he claimed to be of the tribe of Issachar, deriving thence his gift of prophecy, for they were " men that had understanding of the times, to know what Israel ought to do " (1 Chron. xii. 32) ; or, as in Esther i. 13, " the seven wise men that knew the times." It is true that but few of the orthodox commentators interpret these passages as signifying astrological or prophetic forecast ; but that may be, nevertheless, the real meaning (vid. Poole's " Synopsis ").

How could Nostradamus be of Issachar, as that was one of the lost tribes ? would be a natural inquiry enough ; and one could only answer it, as the wit did, in a case somewhat similar, that He could only resemble Issachar in being a great, " strong ass " (Gen. xlix. 14).

His mother's name was Renée de Saint Remy.

---

* The facts for this life are taken, where no other reference is given, from a scarce work, entitled, " La première face du Janus François, par Jean Aimes de Chavigny Beaunois, 1594." It is found in the Library at Paris ; but not in the British Museum. Fortunately M. le Pelletier gives an almost literal transcript of this " Brief discours sur la vie de M. Michel de Nostredame."

† " Archives du Magnetisme Animal," vol. viii. " Tous deux " (*i.e.* father and mother) "appartenaient à une famille Juive," converted in the sixteenth century, and of the tribe of Issachar (" Nouvelle Biog. Générale " [Le Pelletier, i. 16 n.]).

Her ancestors by the father's and mother's side were men skilled in mathematics and medicine : one was physician to René, or Renatus, titular King of Jerusalem and Sicily, and Count of Provence ; whilst the other was physician to John, Duke of Calabria, who was the son of King René. Our author, in his Commentaries, says that a knowledge of mathematics had traditionally descended (*de main en main*) to him from his early progenitors ; and, in the Preface to his " Centuries," he adds : " *Que la parole héréditaire de l'occulte prédiction sera dans son estomac intercluse.*"

It was his great-grandfather * who gave him, almost as in sport, a first taste for the celestial sciences. After the death of this relative he was put to school at Avignon, to study his humanity courses, and thence he went to the university at Montpellier, to acquire philosophy and the theory of medicine.

Montpellier, the Mons Pessulanus of antiquity, contains the most famous school of medicine in all France. It is ancient, and is said to have been founded by Arabian physicians when forced to fly from Spain—Moreri says in the year 1196, by the disciples of Averroes and Avicenna. Its inhabitants are reputed to be witty and most polite. It once had numerous noble churches and many religious establishments, but since the Huguenots became masters of it, in 1561, they ruined all this, and made the city the headquarters of their party for a time. Louis XIII. besieged it in 1622, and took it. His first act was to rebuild the Cathedral of St. Peter and the other churches ; the desecration of all such edifices being the

* His grandfather, Moreri tells us.

Puritan and Huguenot fashion there and everywhere. The town seems always to have been a fief of the Crown of France. But a number of kinglets, such as the King of Aragon and the King of Majorca, appear at different times to have had seignorial rights in Montpellier ; and many church councils have been held there. All these matters are of some slight interest, as furnishing in a filmy fashion a notion of those influences, mental and physical, that would have been floating around Nostradamus when studying there. The seizure of the town by the Huguenots would have occurred some years before his death. As he was a true Churchman, their successes would have embittered his mind, and may have influenced some of the visions contained in the " Sixains" and " Présages."

It may interest us as Englishmen to know that in the extensive botanical garden at Montpellier lie the remains of Miss Temple, the Narcissa, whose death and funeral are so vividly recounted by Young in the " Night Thoughts." He appears to have considerably misrepresented the transaction ; but George Eliot has made up for it by a criticism upon him and his works, conceived, perhaps, in the grossest and worst taste that criticism from a woman's pen has ever fallen into. She grows so angry that she can hardly even see that Young is a poet in any sense of the word. She might easily have found out that he was, by comparing some of her own verses with his.

Another point of interest to us in regard to Montpellier is the reversal of public opinion touching the climate of the place. Brompton, sixty or

eighty years ago, was, from the mildness and salubrity
of its air, coupled with its then semi-rural aspect,
called " the Montpellier of London." The analogy
could never have been very remarkable, as Brompton
is about on a level with the River Thames, whereas
Montpellier's splendid promenade of the Place de
Peyron is 168 feet above the sea-level, whilst the whole
town runs up the hillside, as its name expresses.
Still, the phrase testifies to the opinion then prevalent. Owing to the brightness of its atmosphere
and the beauty of its suburbs, the town was long
recommended by British physicians as a health-resort
to patients suffering from pulmonary complaints ;
but the weather-vane of science has now reversed
that opinion entirely. Its climate is found to be
changeable, its sunshine is blazing, its atmosphere
is charged with dust that is impalpable, all the
while that it seems to be clear ; and its cold mistral
blasts do but portend a spot most singularly hurtful
to the lungs. The fashion varies in localities, drugs,
theories, and treatment, and as a health resort for
English people the reputation of Montpellier has
passed away ; but the " École de Médecine " still
retains its ancient renown as the central seminary of
medical instruction in France.

Learned and medical as it was in the days of
Nostradamus, it could not escape visitation by a great
plague,* and Michael Nostradamus had to retreat to
Narbonne, Toulouse, and Bordeaux. In these towns
he commenced practice, when about twenty-two years
of age, and four years later he bethought him of

* Moreri assigns this to the year 1525.

returning to Montpellier for refreshment, and to take his Doctor's degree. This he got through very quickly, and in a manner that won him the admiration and applause of the whole College. In returning to Toulouse he passed through Agen, a town on the Garonne, where he met with no less a person than the learned Jules César Scaliger,* with whom he entered at once into the most intimate familiarity. This induced him to take up his permanent residence in the town. But after a while their cordiality grew less, till rivalry and pique sprang up between them, and they thenceforth stood aloof from one another. Here he married a lady "*une fort honorable demoiselle,*" though history has not divulged her name. By her he had two children, who died young; she also died. Finding himself again companionless, he returned to his natal soil of Provence. When he reached Marseilles, he was invited by the Parliament of Provence to come to Aix, where he stayed three years, receiving a salary from the city from the time the plague broke out, in 1546. It seems to have raged fiercely, and it is said that he furnished to the Seigneur de Launay the reports which he has given in his book, "Le Théâtre du Monde."

After the contagion passed away, the town, Moreri records, voted him for several years following a considerable pension. His services must consequently have been recognized as valuable. He has left us the

---

* He calls Scaliger in the heyday of friendship "a Virgil in poetry, a Cicero in eloquence, a Galen in medicine," and declares that to him he is indebted for his scientific attainments ("Penny Cyclopædia," s.v. *Nostradamus*).

formula of his plague powder in Chapter VIII. of his treatise " Des Fards." As a curious instance of the modesty of the women of Aix, he records that they began to sew themselves up in their winding sheets, as soon as they were attacked by the contagion, that their bodies might not be exposed naked after death (" Penny Cyclopædia "). I suppose we may judge from this that the system of burial during the contagion was as gross and indecent as in the famous plague of London ; or is this only a fanciful imitation of the story of the women of Marseilles in classical times ?

He went thence to Salon de Craux, which lies midway between Avignon and Marseilles. Here he married for the second time. The lady's name is given by Garencières as Anna Ponce Genelle ; Anne Poussart, says Moreri ; others say Pons Jumel. (See the epitaph further on.) There is the same incertitude as to his family. Jean Aimes de Chavigny, whom we are following, makes it to consist of six children, three boys and three girls ; while Garencières says three sons and one daughter.

It was here, relates our memoir, that, foreseeing great mutations were about to affect all Europe, and that civil wars and troubles were so soon to come upon the kingdom of France, he felt an unnaccountable and new enthusiasm springing up uncontrollably in his mind, which at last amounted almost to a maddening fever, till he sat down to write his " Centuries " and other " Presages." The first of these " Presages " is dated 1555, and runs as follows :—

" D'Esprit divin l'ame presage atteinte,
  Trouble, famine, peste, guerre courir ;
  Eaux, siccitez, terre et mer de sang teinte,
  Paix, tresac à naistre, Prelats, Princes mourir ! "

He kept them by him for a long time, half afraid to
risk the publication ; he foresaw there was danger, and
that it would lead to infinite detraction, calumny, and
backbiting, as indeed it finally fell out. A thing like
this is like the fox stolen by the Spartan youth, that
eats the heart out, and is sure to get vent sooner or
later. His memorialist says, that at last, overcome
by a desire to be useful to the public, he produced
them. No sooner had he done so than the rumour
ran from mouth to mouth, at home and abroad, that
something marvellous and admirable had appeared.
One cannot see of what use they could be to the
public, as they could not possibly be understood till
they were interpreted after the event and by it. In
some of the quatrains he says as much himself. He
no doubt published them because he felt an intense
longing so to do ; and, when the mind of a man reaches
this stage of desire, it will not take him long to find
some excellent reason for carrying out the impulsion.
Public good, the advancement of religion, the sus-
tentation of faith, the psychological inference as to
the immortality of the human soul, or any other good
phrase, will serve a man as a sufficient reason for
doing what he wants to do. That man must be a
great searcher into his own consciousness, if he cannot
readily assume that the motive assigned in such a
case is the *causa causativa* of the act of putting forth.

Moreri's account is not exactly the same as that of

our memoir. Moreri describes him as being invited to Lyons in 1547, but as returning very quickly to Salon, only to find that his popularity at the latter place had greatly abated. The disappointment he experienced from this treatment made him withdraw a good deal from society, and commit himself the more to hard study. He tells us that he had for a long time previously practised divination; now he began to think himself to be directly inspired as to the future. From this time, as the lights occurred to his mind, he began committing them to writing at the moment. He set them down at first in plain prose, if you can call enigmatical sentences plain prose; at any rate, they were not written in verse.

Garencières' version varies again. With him it is, that Nostradamus found by experience that the perfect knowledge of medicine is unattainable without the aid of astrology, to which he now addicted himself. It is an alluring science, and one towards the pursuit of which his natural genius strongly disposed him, so that he made very rapid progress in it. His first publications in this line consisted of almanacs, according to the custom of the time, for profit and recreation's sake; and in these he so happily hit off the conjuncture of events that both he and his publications became greatly sought after. It is somewhat curious that so few of these almanacs appear to be now extant. One would have expected that documents of such interest, once in type, would not perish entirely from all households and libraries. It may, however, be taken as a proof of the maelstrom of time that engulfs everything, so that by the period

when posterity grows interested in any event, all its
belated questionings are presented with a universal
blank. The spirit of literary piracy, too, seems to have
been rife in those early days. The success of his
work soon became a cause of discredit to him, as it
led enterprising printers and booksellers to vend,
under his name, almanacs destitute of everything that
had constituted the merit of his.

When the work made its appearance, it divided the
public. Some called the prophet a simple visionary,
or, in coarser phrase, a fool; others accused him of
magic, and of being in too close treaty with the Devil
to be honest. A few held their judgment in suspense,
and would pronounce no opinion on the subject. A
vast number of the grandees and of the learned, both
at home and abroad, thought that he was endowed
with a gift supernatural; and amongst these were
Henri II. and Catherine de Medici. It remained to
the *esprits forts* and the ignorant public, who knew
nothing of him but his name, to pronounce him a
charlatan and impostor. There is one thing certain,
he felt much hesitation as to publishing at all; and,
when he took that step at last, he addressed the book
to his infant son, and not to any public character, in
the year 1555. At this period he would be fifty-two.
This is not a time of life at which men usually commence a course of imposture. When he is summoned
to the Court at Paris, loaded with honours and consulted on high matters (*de choses importantes*), he displays nothing but moderation and good sense, and
returns contentedly to his modest home at Salon.
Upon all ordinary lines of human judgment, such

conduct seems to indicate genuineness; and this is strengthened, if not established, by his genuine gravity of deportment and serious religious sentiments. Nobody has denied the purity of his life. Still, a certain Lord Pavillon, of his own day, wrote against him, or perhaps against this publishers' figment of a name, rather than his. Further, we find the book led to the bitter epigrammatic distich of the poet Jodele, or as others say, of Beza,—

" Nostradamus cum falsa damus, nam fallere nostrum est,
  Et cum falsa damus, nil nisi nostra damus."

This can very easily be turned against the piratical almanac makers, thus :—

" Vera damus cum verba damus quœ Nostradamus dat ;
  Sed cum nostra damus, nil nisi falsa damus."

In spite of piracy and obloquy, the repute of Nostradamus grew, as we have said, in influential quarters, until it came to the ears of Queen Catherine de Medici and Henri II., on the publication, in March, 1555, of the first seven Centuries of his " Prophecies." The remaining Centuries, the Sixains, and Presages, were not published till long after. In the following year, 1556, they sent for him to attend the Court in Paris: though Garencières says he left Salon on July 14, 1555, and reached Paris on August 15th, a particularity which seems to indicate special knowledge.* The Lord Constable Montmorency attended him at his inn, and presented him to the king in

* " That the great bulk of French society of his day was impressed by his effusions there can be no doubt " (Chambers' " Book of Days," vol. ii., p. 13).

person. The king showed him high favour, and
ordered him to be lodged at the palace of the
Cardinal de Bourbon, Archbishop of Sens, during his
stay in the capital.

When there a severe attack of gout seized him, that
lasted ten or twelve days. His majesty sent him two
hundred crowns in gold (two hundred écus d'or ; vid.
Moreri) in a velvet purse, and the queen one hundred
crowns (Le Pelletier, i. 92). They then despatched
him to Blois, to visit their children, the royal princes,
and give his astrological opinion. He repaired thither,
and seems to have acquitted himself to the satisfaction of the king. It is quite certain that he did not
tell them precisely what he thought,* for the princes
were Francis II., Charles IX., and Henri III., whose
tragical fates he has correctly set out, and with un-
mistakable clearness, as may be seen (at pp. 84, 86, 96)
by the forecasts in his strange book. He, however,
cast their horoscopes and acquitted himself in this, as in
all other transactions, *en homme d'esprit.* He returned
to Salon so much encouraged that he set to work
and completed his " Centuries," consisting of three
hundred more quatrains. These further quatrains he
appears to have printed in 1558, but Garencières says
that he dedicated them to the king in 1557. The
only thing that is certain is that the Texte-type dates
the epistle June 27, 1558. This " Luminary Epistle "
to the king, Garencières tells us, discovers future
events " from the birth of Louis XIV., now reigning,
till the coming of antichrist." †

---

* Moreri says that nobody knows what his report was.

† Garencières, as we have shown, says Nostradamus dedi-

Henri II. was killed the following year, 1559, at the tournament of St. Quentin, as we shall see it fully set forth at Quatrain 35 in Century I.

cated the "Luminary Epistle" to Henri II. in 1557. M. le Pelletier holds (i. 10) that Henri II. never knew of the dedicatory epistle written to him by name, and that, as the events referred to do not concern the House of Valois, they could have had no interest for him had he known of the epistle. M. le Pelletier adds a most singular note to this remark, that the epistle is dedicated "*A l'invictissime, très puissant, et très chrestien Henry Roy de France Second.*" This epigraph he maintains not to be addressed to Henri II., for he remarks that he was no longer alive when it made its appearance. Now, this is not so ; for the dedicatory letter was dated in print June 27, 1558, and the king's death only took place in 1559, so that the document was even in print before his death. But, had it not been so, there is no reason whatever why Nostradamus should not have have supplied the king with a copy of the letter and quatrains in manuscript long before either of them had been committed to type. Jean de Roux, Curé de Louvicamp, wrongly suggests that it was intended as a prophetical dedication to Louis le Grand or XIV. M. le Pelletier thinks it was not even dedicated to the great Henri Quatre, but to a "*Henry, Roy de France Second*"—*second* being the Latin *secundus*, or prosperous, *i.e.* some king not less illustrious than Henri Quatre, whose reign is to arise in the future. This it is which furnishes to the reader the secret purpose of Le Pelletier's book, which is to set forth the claims of the Duc de Bordeaux, who would have ascended the French throne as Henri Cinq. Accordingly, in the body of the book, he has interpreted five quatrains and one sixain of the prophecies of Nostradamus as referring to this glorious King *Henri Second*, who has never arrived, and who, being now some years dead, never can. We have seen that the Curé de Louvicamp could even suppose that Louis XIV. could stand for "Henry, Roy de France Second." M. F. Buget, in his "Étude sur Nostradamus," has the same idea, that he does not address Henri II., because he was not of a character sufficiently great to merit the attribution of such spiritual

He had now become quite a court favourite, for Emanuel, the Duke of Savoy, visited him at his house at Salon about this period, in the month of October ; and, in the December following, the Princesse Marguerite de France, sister of Henri II., who by the treaty of peace at Cambresis was to marry the duke, came also to Nostradamus, entertaining him very familiarly (Garencières and Moreri).

Charles IX. made a progress through the kingdom in 1564, to quiet the cities that had mutinied ; and

authority to him by our prophet, as if the flattery of a dedication was to be interpreted *au pied de la lettre.* It could only be addressed, he thinks, to a really great man, a saint. M. Buget, in his book of 1862, evidently was another of those who made the fatal error of interpreting Nostradamus out of the future, instead of carefully following the enigmas thrown out by him to find their fulfilment in the past. These gentlemen, if they had assiduously read the Epistle itself, instead of consulting their imaginative faculties, would have perceived plainly enough that Nostradamus was writing to the only king he knew, before whom he had personally presented himself, and whom, as he says, he had highly reverenced from "*iceluy jour que premierement devant icelle je me presentay.*" The concluding words of the Dedication are equally plain, and show that he is addressing a king whom he has individually seen with his own eyes : "*depuis que mes yeux furent si proches de vostre splendeur solaire.*" All the rest is to be set down to the strain of courtly flattery that was customarily addressed to kings, then and down to a period full two hundred years later, especially on occasion of penning royal dedications. The purpose of this long note is to establish, once and for all, I trust, that "*Henry, Roy de France Second,*" stands, without any subtlety at all, simply for King Henri II., and nothing more. It is vain to endeavour to make millstones transparent that we may shoot unexpected rays of light through them. They will answer their purpose by being left in the dark, and will grind grain the better for it. Transparency will in such cases represent frangibility.

when he came to Provence, on arriving at Salon, November 17th, he asked first of all for Nostradamus. Nostradamus was in the suite of magistrates around the king, so that he was presented on the instant, upon which the king made him his Physician in Ordinary, and honoured him with the title of Counsellor. He complained rather bitterly of the neglect with which his fellow-townsmen treated him. César Nostradamus reports this, saying, "*Et de ce, me souviens fort bien, car je fus de la partie*" (Moreri). On the return journey he again inquired for Nostradamus, and gave him two hundred écus. He was at this time over sixty, and with his health fast breaking under severe attacks of gout. He died within about sixteen months of this period, and the salary and profits of Physician in Ordinary must have greatly comforted the old man in his latter days. He enjoyed now the further satisfaction of being flocked to by learned men, grandees, and others, who resorted to him far and near, as to an oracle. "As St. Jerome remarks of Livy, so may we remark of him," says his biographer, Jean Aimes, "that those who came to France sought Nostradamus as the only thing to be seen there."

The closing scene is now drawing very near, and we find him much afflicted with his maladies, notably arthritic gout, as distinguished from podagra, which Dr. Cullen considers as the seat of idiopathic gout. He awaited with firmness his climacteric, as they used to designate a man's sixty-third year. He died on the 2nd of July, 1566, a little before sunrise, having all his senses yet about him, for the arthrisis turned to dropsy about eight days previously, and early on the second day of the month suffocated him. Jean Aimes says that Nostradamus was well advised of the time, even of the very day and hour, when his death must take place. The prophet reminded him frequently towards the close of the previous June that he had written with his own hand, in the Ephemerides of Jean Stadius, these words in Latin, *Hic prope mors est* ("Here is death at hand"). "The day," continues this friend, "before he exchanged this life for a better, after I had spent many hours with him, and late at night was taking leave of him until the following morning, he said, 'You will not see me alive at sunrise.'" M. le Pelletier gives (i. 91) Presage 141 as a stanza pointing to his own death ; but, as the "Presages" were not printed till 1568, their authenticity may or may not be accepted as the reader feels inclined. The lines run thus, and are remarkable enough, if we admit that they were a genuine forecast ; for, although they assign no specific date, yet they sum up the principal facts rather fully :—

> " De retour d'Ambassade, don de Roy mis au lieu ;
> Plus n'en fera ; sera allé à Dieu :
> Parans plus proches, amis, freres du sang,
> Trouvé tout mort près du lict et du banc."

The meaning given to this is, that on his return from Arles, whence he was sent for, in 1564, by Charles IX., to see him a second time, after he had safely put away the three hundred crowns given him by the king and queen, his last transaction would be concluded, and he would then render his soul to God. His nearest relatives, brothers, and friends would find him dead near his bed, seated, as was customary with him, on the bench at its foot, as he could there breathe more freely.

This is the interpretation put upon it by M. le Pelletier. As I understand César Nostradamus, the king did not send for him to Arles, but asked again for him on his majesty's return to Salon ; and I should think the word "ambassade" must refer to some private mission the king had sent him upon entirely apart from this, and for which he paid him. Be this as it may, the fact that Nostradamus assigns no date for his death, in this presage, goes to establish its authenticity, one would incline to say. For supposing it to have been foisted in, after his death, surely a fabricator of the marvellous would first of all have made it to show *trois vingts et trois bis*, and twisted that into some colourable shape. He would have been little likely to add as a prophetical feature that the king's present had been put away in a safe place, as to do so seems anything rather than a supernatural instinct. It is a touch of prose more than of the Python. On the whole, I should incline to take the verse for a genuine emanation from the pen of Nostradamus. Certainly he would recognize, even medically, that, as he found himself to be growing "*fort caduc et débile*" towards his climacterical year, he would know that his dissolution was at hand. A man's grand climacteric is generally considered to arrive at 63, though some place it at 81, that number being composed of 9 times 9. In either of these periods, if sickness occur, it is considered as especially likely to prove fatal.

C

There seems to be a diversity of opinion about this, for some say that the *annus climactericus* is 84, or 12 times 7. Aulus Gellius thinks the opinion to be of immense antiquity, running back to the Chaldeans ; and no doubt Pythagoras derived it from the East. Ficinus explains it by saying that the body of man is ruled over by each planet in turn for the space of one year, and, Saturn being the most maleficent, every seventh year falling to his presidency becomes extremely dangerous. This explanation would shut out the nines, except in the sixty-third and eighty-first year, but it would also vitiate the whole scheme of astrology, for the planet under which a man was born (say he were born under Saturn) would dominate his body at birth, and be, one must suppose, the ruling planet that year, and, if it were Saturn, would recur only on his eighth year. Eighty-four would not be in favour generally, as it consists entirely of even numbers, though divisible by seven. Many held that only a number produced by the multiplication of an odd number could be climacterical. Augustus thought it a subject of great rejoicing when he had passed over his sixty-third year.* Moreri will have eighty-one to be properly speaking the climacteric, and he notes that at this age died Plato, Diogenes, Eratosthenes the geometer, and many other illustrious personages. Some went so far as to say that political bodies had their climacterical periods ; and they certainly, judging from our own country, have periods of fatal folly, whether or no the nines and sevens collide, or the stars fight against

* Aulus Gellius, " Noctes Atticæ," xv. 7.

Sisera. But amongst other oddities of history may be chronicled the fact that Henri Quatre was the sixty-third King of France, which made Malherbe talk of—

> " La vaine étude s'applique,
> A trouver la climatérique,
> De l'éternelle fleur-de-lis "—

that *fleur-de-lis* whose terrible withering up in the fatal year of '93 Nostradamus so powerfully forecasts.

Suffice it to say that in this climacterical crisis Nostradamus succumbed in his sixty-third year to gout, which turned to dropsy.*

Nostradamus was interred at the church of the Franciscan Friars (Les Cordeliers) at Salon, as it is noted, on the left-hand side of the church door (Garencièies). His widow erected to him a marble tablet, "representing his figure to the life, and his arms above it." The epitaph is as follows, made, they say, in imitation of that great Livy aforenamed, the Roman historian :—

D. M.

CLARISSIMI OSSA

MICHAELIS NOSTRADAMI,

UNIUS OMNIUM MORTALIUM JUDICIO DIGNI,

CUJUS PENE DIVINO CALAMO TOTIUS ORBIS,

EX ASTRORUM INFLUXU, FUTURI EVENTUS

CONSCRIBERENTUR.

VIXIT ANNOS LXII. MENSES VI. DIES XVII.

OBIIT SALONE AN. CIƆIƆLXVI.

QUIETEM POSTERI NE INVIDETE. ANNA PONTIA GEMELLA

CONJUGI OPT. V. FELICIT.

---

* It was really in the sixth month of his sixty-third year that he died.

TRANSLATION.

" Here lie the bones of the illustrious Michael Nostradamus, whose almost divine pen alone, in the judgment of all mortals, was worthy to record, under the influx of the stars, the future events of the whole world. He lived 62 years, 6 months, 17 days. He died at Salon in the year 1566. Posterity, disturb not his sweet rest ! Anne Ponce Gemelle hopes for her husband true felicity."

The text of this epitaph is that given by Benoist Rigaud in the edition of Nostradamus published by him in 1568.

In stature he was somewhat undersized, of a robust body, sprightly, and vigorous. He had a broad and open forehead, a straight even nose, grey eyes, of kindly expression, but in anger capable of flashing fire. The general expression was severe, though pleasant, so that a grand humanity shone through the seriousness. Even in age his cheeks were rosy. He had a long thick beard, and excellent health till nearly the close of life ; he had his senses, being alert and keen, up to the very last moment. He had a good and lively wit, seizing with quick comprehension everything that he wished to acquire. His judgment was very penetrating, his memory happy and reten-tive. He was taciturn by nature, thought much and spoke little ; but at the right time and occasion he could discourse extremely well. He was quick, and sudden even to irascibility ; but very patient where work had to be done. He slept four or five hours only out of the twenty-four. He practised freedom of speech himself and commended it in others. He was cheerful and facetious in conversation, though in jesting a little given to bitterness. He was attached, so says De Chavigny, to the Roman Church, and held fixedly the Catholic faith ; out of its pale there was for him no salvation. Though pursuing a line of thought entirely his own, he had no sympathy with the Lutheran heretics of so-called Freethought. He was given to prayer, fasting, and charity. As far as outward observance was concerned, he might be classed with the highly respectable and decent. Le Pelletier says, " Sa fin fut Chrétienne ; " but he adds a little further on that his style is very much more like that of the Pagan oracles of Greece and Rome than of the canonical prophets of Hebrew inspiration. He was very generous to the poor, and held it as a sort of maxim that in this sense it was legitimate to make friends with "the mammon of unrighteousness."

Jean Aimes de Chavigny, who seems to have come over from Beaune to play the part of a Boswell to Nostradamus, and, after his friend's death, is said to have devoted twenty-eight years of his life to editing the " Centuries " with notes,* says that he collected twelve books of the " Centuries," of which vols. vii., xi., and xii. are imperfect. These are in quatrains, and are classified as *Prophéties*, and they extend to very remote ages. The *Presages*, we are told, were written between 1550 and 1567,† and were collected by Aimes and reduced into twelve books

---

* *Temple Bar*, xli. p. 87, authority for the term of years.

† How any could have been written in 1567, I know not, as Nostradamus died in 1566. But, however this may be, there are twelve *Presages*, or one for each month throughout the year 1567. The last one is that which we have already given, as relating to his own death.

in prose, as he thinks them worthy of the attention of posterity. The few *Presages* that are in print run to only one hundred and forty-three quatrains in verse ; so we must suppose that those written in prose have perished entirely.

Nostradamus left two brothers behind him : one named Bertrand ; the other, Jean, who was his junior, and proctor to the Parliament at Aix, composed a History of Provence, and also wrote the lives of the Poets of Provence.*

Moreri states that by his second wife he had six children, three boys and three girls. Of his sons, César, the eldest, was a person of demonstratively gay and kindly spirit. It was to him, when quite a child, that Nostradamus dedicated the first seven of the " Centuries " published by him. These are the most authentic of all, and Moreri remarks that, if you wish the quatrains to be without interpolation, you should secure early editions. The reader will understand that to be now unnecessary, inasmuch as we have all along been dealing with the *Texte-type.* César was born at Salon, 1555, and died 1629. He, like his uncle Jean, was an author, and wrote upon the same topics, leaving in manuscript a collection of the most re-markable things happening in Provence from the year 1080 to 1494. In this he included the lives of the poets of Provence. Many years after his death, his nephew and namesake, César Nostradamus, who was Governor of Provence and gentleman in waiting

---

* The book was entitled, " Les vies des plus célèbres et anciens poëtes provensaux, qui ont floury du tems des comtes de Provence " (Lyon, 1575) ; a book still sought for, and rather rare.

upon the Duc de Guise, found them, and himself
worked at them, till, in 1603, the Parliament of the
province voted him three thousand livres to encourage
him to complete the work, which he did ; and they
were finally printed in Lyons in 1614, under the title
of "Chroniques de l'Histoire de Provence." He com-
mences with the Celtic Gauls at the early date of the
Deluge. This is worthy of a true scion of the tribe
of Issachar. A very strange story is told of César by
La Motte le Vayer in his "Instruction pour Mon-
seigneur le Dauphin." He, like his father, Michel,
had a taste for forecasting the future, and had
ventured to predict that Pouzin, which was besieged,
would perish by fire ; but it was taken by *coup de
main.* Whilst the pillage was going forward, the
foolish prophet was, it is said, seen, match in hand,
endeavouring to set it on fire. He was caught ; and
Saint-Luc, the commander, asked him if he had
prophesied anything for himself that day. He replied,
"No!" on which the general rode at him with his
lance, and killed him on the spot. Moreri relates
this story somewhat differently. If either version
were true, it would be clear that César did not understand "*la parole héréditaire de l'occulte prédiction,*"
and that the lancehead instead was "*dans son
estomac intercluse.*" From other authorities, however,
it would seem that he was busy about his history
long after the date thus assigned for his death.
Charles, his brother, was very excellent in Provençal
poetry, and several pieces of his are still extant.
Michel's third son, whose name is not given us by
Moreri, became a Capuchin.

An anecdote is related by Garencières, which he throws out as "a merry passage" to recreate his reader. Nostradamus was with Lord Florinville in Lorraine, at the Castle of Faim. He was attending medically his lordship's mother. In the yard where they strolled there were two little pigs, one white and the other black. His lordship inquired of Nostradamus jestingly what would be the fate of those pigs. "We shall eat the black one, and the wolf shall eat the white," said he. Lord Florinville secretly ordered the cook to get ready the white one for supper. When it was spitted ready for roasting, the cook left the kitchen for something, and in his absence a young tame wolf came in and ate a part of it, so that it could not appear at table. The cook immediately killed the black one, and sent it up at the time appointed. His lordship, not knowing what had happened, said to Nostradamus, "Well, sir, we are now eating the white pig; how shall the wolf get it?" "I do not believe it," rejoined the prophet; "it is the black one that is upon the table." The cook was sent for, and by his confession the truth came out, much to the surprise of everybody present. Another story follows this, that Nostradamus had said that treasure was hidden in a little hill near Faim, that it would not be found if sought for, but that, if the ground was dug for any other reason, it would. Garencières adds that there is great probability about this, as it is the site of an ancient temple, and many times since antiquities have been unearthed here. He completes his cock-and-bull story by saying that many such tales are told of Nostradamus all over

France, but that he passes them by as being "unwilling to write anything without good warrant."

Amongst other nonsensical reports spread was one that he caused himself to be buried alive, and that he continued to write prophecies. This, no doubt, was set afloat by those honest publishers who in life had done him the honour to pirate his almanacs; at any rate, it made for their interest. It has also been pretended that so many in Salon regarded him as an impostor, that for security's sake he was buried in the Franciscan Church.

Those who desire the Bibliography of the editions of Nostradamus up to the year 1840 will consult that which has been admirably drawn up by Eugène Bareste, Paris, 1840, in his work upon "Nostradamus." Or they may find it copied textually, with all due acknowledgment of its excellence, in the first volume of Le Pelletier's edition of the "Oracles."

The works of Nostradamus, besides the "Prophecies," seem to have been—

Several Almanacs, two of which were translated at once into English, and are given by Watt, "Bib. Brit."

"Almanacke for 1559." London : 1559. 8vo.

"Almanacke et Prognostications." London : 1559. 8vo.

Moreri gives further an—

Almanac for country labourers, to mark the seasons favourable for their work. A true predecessor, this, of Moore's *Vox Stellarum*.

"Predictions before 1558." London : 1691. 4to. This is named by Watt, and may be a translation of the genuine first edition of the "Seven Centuries," but I have not met with it.

"Prophecies of the Kings and Queens of England." 1715. This is the work by D. D. that we have largely quoted from.

"An excellent Treatise on Contagious Infirmities in 1559-60.'
Translated into English.   London : 1559.

"Traité des Fardements."   Lyon : 1552.

"Des Confiteurs," etc.   Anvers : 1557.

"Opuscule de plusieurs exquises Receptes, divisé en deux parties."   Lyon : 1572.   16mo.   This contains both the above.

"La Remède très utile contre la Peste et toutes Fièvres pestilentielles."   Paris: 1651.   8vo.

"Paraphrase de Galien sur l'exhortation de Menodote aux Études des Beaux Arts."   Lyon: 1558.   8vo.

Touching the prophecies of Nostradamus, Théophile de Garencières gives us an interesting fact, that, after the primer, it was the first book at school in which he learnt to read.   It was the custom in France then (*i.e.* 1618) to initiate children by that book.   They thought the crabbed and obsolete words, such as long survived in the English law, would give the scholars some idea of the old French language ; so that the book got republished from year to year like an almanac.   He chronicles that many have run mad from overstudying the prophecies.   He dissuades readers from doing this, because interpretation must always be a little uncertain where, like an ancient oracle, the author indulges in a double sense, which he thinks Nostradamus often does.   Without a peculiar genius, he does not suppose it possible to get at a right understanding of the quatrain.   Even when the prophecy is quite plain, as that the Parliament should put King Charles to death, no reader, until it had happened, could tell when, or how, it would be brought about.   Even his astrological signs will not fix things, because the planets go and return again to the same bearings.   Some of his reasons are very peculiar, one being that it is not profitable for the *vulgar* to have knowledge of the future, that God reserves the knowledge of the times to Himself, and that it might trespass upon "business of State" to discover and lay open things which the prudent wish to conceal; and he concludes, oddly enough, that "for these reasons (dear Reader) I would not have thee entangle thyself in the pretentions of knowing future things."

He conceives that there are many concurrent causes tending to diminish the prophetic reputation of Nostradamus. The very ordinary manner in which he conformed to the rules and ritual of the Roman Catholic Church, would lead no one to infer that he enjoyed any extraordinary favour from the Almighty; his proficiency in judicial astrology would furnish matter of prejudice against him in the minds of many learned men; the very devout suspected him of necromancy, and familiarity with the Angel of Darkness; finally, the inherent obscurity of his style, has been rendered still more difficult by the interminable faults introduced by the copyists and the carelessness of printers. Now, it is admitted, he says, and by its ablest defenders, that judicial astrology cannot enable its professor to foretell such particularities as proper names and other circumstances that hang upon the freewill of men; and, as our author does foretell such things as these, he must have had recourse to the black art to obtain his results. Accordingly Lord Florimond de Raimond, in his "Birth of Heresies," makes this charge against him; also Lord Spond, in the third volume of his "Annals," in 1566, devised this epitaph for him. "Mortuus est hoc anno nugax ille toto orbe famosus *Michel Nostradamus*, qui se præscium et presagum eventuum futurorum per astrorum influxum venditavit, sub cujus deinceps nomine quivis homines ingeniosi suas hujus modi cogitationes protendere consueverent, in quem valde apposite lusit qui dixit : *Nostra damus* cum falsa damus," etc.*

Provoked thus, Garancières endeavours to prove Nostradamus to have been enlightened by the Holy Spirit. We shall not follow him in this matter any further than to avail ourselves of the facts we may light upon in the course of his arguments, and to record a few of the eulogies upon him that Garencières gathers from eminent authors in times past. To these we may add some authorities who in modern times have named him ; but these mostly sum up his forecastings as springing from venality, vanity, and imposture.

Of proper names, that Nostradamus has anticipated, the list is considerable. He names the Lord of Monluc ; Captain Charry ; Lord de la Mole, Admiral of the Galleys to Henri II. ; Entragues, beheaded by Louis XIII. ; Clarepegne, the headsman ; Sinan, the Pasha who destroyed Hungary ; Clément, who murdered Henri III. ; the Attorney David and Captain Ampus ; Rousseau, the Mayor of Puy ;

* " In 1566 died that trifler, so famous throughout the world, Michael Nostradamus, who boasted while he lived that he knew and could foretell future events by the influence of the stars, in whose name afterwards many ingenious men have put forth their imaginings, justifying him who said so aptly, ' Nostra damus,' etc."

Louis, Prince of Condé; Sixtus V., calling him son of Hamont; Gabrielle d'Estrée; Lord Mutonis; Anthony de Sourdis, Lord Chancellor of France; the Queen Louise; Antony of Portugal. Since Garencières' time other names have been identified: Narbon, the Minister of War; Saulce; Lethuille, for the Tuilleries; Lonole, for Old Noll, or Cromwell; Montmorency; Le Grand Chiren, anagram of Henri le Grand; Mendosus, anagram of Vendosme; Norlaris, anagram for Lorrains; Robin, anagram of Biron; Rapis, anagram for Paris; Esleu Cap, for Capet, or Louis XVI.; Varennes, the place where Louis was arrested; the play upon *bour* and *bon*, for Bourbon (Cent. vii. 44); Ergaste, anagram of Estrange for Marie Antoinette the Austrian; Mont Gaulfier, for Montgolfier, the æronaut; the island of Elba, mentioned as Æthalia, the ancient name of Elba; Sainct Memire, anagram for Sainct Meri; and the play on "dort leans" for Louis Philippe. This is a goodly list of names to guess at haphazard. Such chance as could so result would rival any prophecy in the miraculous nature of its elements.

Again, as regards the curious things he mentions, one might make out a long list. The date of the Fire of London. The five hundred Marseillais that led the attack upon the Tuilleries. The naming of the very year 1792 for the French Revolution; the 22nd of September in that year being the date from which the Republicans began to reckon anew their era. Many more might so easily be gathered as to even weary the reader with their enumeration.

He mentions the birth of persons that were born after his death. Now, judicial astrology could give no help in such cases, since to commence casting a nativity presupposes birth. In his epistle to his son César we shall see what he says of himself and the gifts he possessed ; but even there he was obliged to be somewhat obscure, to protect himself from the ridicule of the world on the one side, and from the severities of the Church on the other. He tells his son to eschew the study of the future astrologically, to avoid magic, as prohibited by the Church and Scripture, and that he himself had burnt some books that taught the art of prophesying, although it is pretty evident that he had first read them through very carefully himself. He relates that a mighty flame burst forth from them to the danger of his house, and this he interpreted to be the consequence of their falsity. But yet he seems to have gone through a good many of the magical forms when he was about to devote the night to prophetical studies. He holds that inspired Revelation is "*a participation of the Eternal Divinity,*" though he scarcely lays claim to being a prophet in this sense of the word ; in fact, he denies himself to be such a prophet. But, failing to claim inspiration, and denouncing the practice of astrology and the pursuit of magic, one is left somewhat in the dark as to what he really did profess to be the source of fatidical utterance possessed by him. That he had the gift in a marvellous potency this book will show ; and that he openly claimed to possess it his whole life proves. It is, in fact, from this I should desire to establish that at least he was no impostor, for he only told others what he began by implicitly believing himself.

As to his obscurity, he himself admits it as a thing to be cultivated both in the times he lived in and in those that were to follow. No one can truthfully deny that obscurity and prophecy seem to be almost interchangeable and convertible terms. The prophecies in Scripture are of such ambiguity that Whitby was commended by many for concluding his Commentary on the Bible with the General Epistle of Jude, without a word bestowed upon the Revelations of St. John. There are those who will hold that prophecies are useless, as they cannot generally be understood until they have been fulfilled. It is obvious that many prophecies are of such a nature as that, if they were clearly understood previous to the event, they would prevent their own fulfilment, and so cease to have been prophecies. What they foretold would never have occurred. The philosophy of history is supposed to show that Providence shapes the course of human events, how much soever humanity may seem at every instant to be following out its own collective will. This theory is most in favour amongst erudite modern thinkers, who incline very little towards acquiescence in the old Church doctrine of Predestination. Yet inspired prophecy is a collateral proof of the same principle as that which underlies the philosophy of history. Both of them depend on the finger of God shaping—first shaping chaos into things, and then things into their continuous courses. The shaping is not needed more at the first creation than it is at every successive stage, whether for preservation or for progression. Again, the interest of uninspired prophecy is for mortal man not much less vivid; for, if we have interpreted Nostradamus rightly, we find in him a man living three hundred years ago talking intelligibly, if not clearly, of things that are happening to-day. If there be a power in human nature,—latent in the generality, but in a few alert and quick,—to link far centuries together in anticipatory thought, I take it to be quite clear, that that one fact must revolutionize the whole scheme of human philosophy as accepted now, whether it relates to life, to death, or to futurity. The fatidical capacity implies a spirit of immortality in man. With that once established, we re-enter upon the domain of faith; we recognize that the earth is drossy and the body sin; we re-create the soul, and laugh at the fool (or the philosopher) who doubts, denies, and ridicules it. It gives new ground to teach the immortality of man; it lifts us above the dirt-doctrine of gold; it renders poetry once again possible to lips hallowed with Apollo's fire; it brings back a possibility of worship upon earth, and, with that, prayer, praise, and peace. Bates, the silver-tongued, says well, that for man "it is as natural to pray as to breathe."

Garencières is of opinion that the writings of our prophet were for a century allowed to "be in darkness," but we have seen that in his own day Nostradamus attracted the notice of the learned, of the nobility, and of the king himself. Garencières says that the first book they gave *him* at school after the primer was " The Centuries," so it was not neglected then; and M. le Pelletier remarks that Nostradamus's fame has now been before the world for three hundred years, with an always growing reception. Of course, as time wanes, and as fresh quatrains become interpreted after accomplishment, the series must shine with an ever augmenting brilliancy and splendour. The kings of France have never been quite indifferent to the Oracles, or at least to such of them as could be shown to refer to them individually. It is reported of Charles Edward Stuart, the Pretender, that he to the last conned * over the volume, anxiously hoping to find in it some stanza promising to his royal line restoration to the throne of England, but in vain (Chambers' "Book of Days," ii. 13).

In modern times prophecy is derided, and our seer, obscurely hinting his strange forecasts, is voted incoherent, rhapsodial, or an impostor. Almost every one has heard his name mentioned, but that is all. Few who come across his work accidentally on a bookshelf can make head or tail of his Provençal and half obsolete terms. Without special study you cannot understand him ; and to study a work that lies under a general ban of imposture, in a time when only lucrative study is pursued, is a thing not to be thought of by a *littérateur* of any intelligence. Consequently in England it is a name, floating far and wide it may be, that nevertheless remains but a name and nothing more. I hope, however, when this book comes to be read by the competent few, it will be seen that there exists far more than a mere name to be dealt with here ; that in Nostradamus we have the greatest fatidical seer, not divinely accredited,

---

* Bouys does the same for Napoleon I.

that the world has ever beheld; that if accepted as
being endowed with a rare and curious foresight,—
after the severest inquiry into what he has done
has been instituted by grammarians, historians, and
philosophic critics,—it will next become necessary to
try to look into the causes, and so ascertain how he
operated. If we cannot succeed in that, and yet
cannot deny his work, we must add the faculty, so
remarkably developed in him, to the perceptive
powers of the human race, as a sixth sense,—generally
latent but sometimes developed,—the faculty of anticipating the future. Science, so called, must enlarge
its narrow categories, and admit, though never so
grudgingly, that a new faculty of vast import must
henceforth be accedited to humanity; a faculty which
the superstitious and the profoundly religious alike
have immemorially admitted, but which philosophers,
as such, have as persistently ignored, denied, or even
ridiculed. It has often been said by troubled thinkers,
with a pretentious flourish of baffled profundity, that
"true philosophy begins in doubt." I would whisper
it down the wind, but not in Gath, that for the most
part there it also ends. Anatomy cuts up a dead
man to find life. Analysis reduces final investigation
to a *caput mortuum*. Philosophy begins in doubt,
and travels a wide circle to close in doubt again.
Perhaps, after all, the best basis might be faith.
Beginning with faith, haply a man might find God
accompanying investigation with him step by step
through life, even in this world and its miraculous
garden, till the hour come for him to step, through
the six-foot wicket, into the Paradise of that glorious

world that is adjacent to us but not seen, where sighs are not heaved, and whose glories are incorruptible.

When we come to enumerate some few of the opinions that have been expressed on the writings and character of Nostradamus, it will be seen that a vast number of them condemn him for charlatanry and imposture, especially as we approach our own day. For now what is denominated science accepts nothing for true but what is deducible from the reason ; it takes for granted that nothing can be known respecting the future, beyond what cultivated prudence can gather from a politic acquaintance with the past, coupled perhaps with a sagacious estimate of the principles new at work, and the fruit they are likely to engender. In fact, what the knowledge of a wise man can enable him to foresee, covers for such theorists the whole extent and province of all prophecy possible to man,—the sagacity of Mazarin, which detected the revolutionary element in the Cardinal de Retz whilst still a youth ; or the prediction of Bishop Butler, in 1741, that the *levelling spirit* then visible, under the direction of principles that were atheistic, threatened dangers that might menace Europe. But to call this prophecy is to be ignorant of what the word prophecy means. To state it thus, or so to limit it, is to deny the existence of the prophetic faculty altogether. A direct denial of the thing is better than a sceptical definition of it. Scepticism, then, in our day, not believing there can be such a thing as a true presage, concludes that Mother Shipton and Nostradamus stand on precisely the same footing. They read a quatrain of Nostradamus, only understand one line out of four, and say that, although that one may be intelligible, the Sphinx itself could make nothing of the others, and that out of a number of such verses it would be marvellous if something curious were not occasionally let fall. The next inference is that the author set up for a gift that he did not possess, and soon found the imposture was far more lucrative than the dull routine of medical practice, as in those times the superstition of the public was unlimited. The ignorance of the Middle Ages is pointedly contrasted for us now with the wisdom and knowledge of our own day. What, prejudice apart, does this mean, if briefly summed up in an aphorism? Only this: that the wisdom of to-day gives us the Nihilist of *no faith*, in place of the Astrologer of *too much*.

We ought to remember in all this that our author had reached the mature age of fifty-two before he printed one word of the work that we are spending time over. He tells us that for generations the family of Nostradamus had inherited and transmitted some share of the prophetic gift (Garencière's Preface, p. 16), that it came to him as a natural genius; in which it seems that his sons partially shared. He had cultivated it long for his private pleasure, and the request in which his almanacs stood seems to have first led him to think he might more largely utilize the faculty. He never appears to have made any large sum of money through it. He supported himself and brought up his family by steady work in his professional calling. On the very brink of publicity, anticipating malign influences, he still hesitated to take the final

plunge; and, when he did take it, he was in his
fifty-third year. Men seldom pass though life per-
forming all its duties with credit and decorum, earn a
competency, and at fifty-two enter upon a career of
contemptible imposture. No; this is not according
to human nature. We must acquit him of imposture.

Michel Nostradamus was one of the most learned
men of his day, the friend of Jules César Scaliger.
He knew many modern languages, and the Hebrew,
Greek, and Latin. He had followed medicine from
the age of twenty-two, took his Doctor's degree at
twenty-six, filled a professorial chair at Montpellier,
and late in life devoted himself to judicial astrology ;
in which, and in an intuitive forecast beyond what
that can bestow, he has distanced by far all other
competitors in the same line. Let a reader thoroughly
acquaint himself with all that is here set before him
as to Charles I. in England, and its bloody re-enactment
in the French Revolution, letting all the rest stand
aside ; and, if he can rise from the perusal, feeling that
there is any kind of imposture discoverable throughout those strange and wonderful revelations, then he
himself possesses so miraculous a form of judgment, as
to leave me without a word further to advance upon
the subject.

M. le Pelletier conceives that the *Commun Advéne-
ment*, or *l'avénement au règne des gens du commun*,
which I have rendered " The Vulgar Advent," extending from the death of Louis XVI. to the reign of
Antichrist, is the grand object of Nostradamus. It
is to paint this lurid epopee that he devotes three-
quarters at least of his quatrains, according to

le Pelletier. Myself, I think this proportion to be
overstated. But our prophet returns to it again and
again, elaborates the most minute details, and con-
centres upon it as in a focus the brightest rays of
his mystical genius. Some think that Catharine de
Medici was largely influenced in her firm and far-
seeing policy by the counsels of Nostradamus, whom
she visited expressly at Salon de Craux, in 1564, with
her son, Charles IX. This may have been so, but it
is a great question whether Nostradamus, for all his
visions, curiously as they realize themselves in time,
could advise the queen or anybody else at all better
than any other wise man of elaborate culture could.
His visions would come to him as verses to a great
poet, and when written down and the afflatus fled, he
would drop back to the ordinary condition of humanity.
He would drop back to the level of reason and the
discourse of science, with nothing to specially distinguish him from other men well placed to learn
such wisdom and knowledge as this world has to
bestow upon them. To expect more of him is to
expect with the commonalty that if you met Milton in
Bread Street he would address you in blank verse, and
strain "Good morning" into metre. Great men cut
very plain figures in common broadcloth. It is the
impostor who is magisterial, and puts on the airs of a
Cagliostro.

Nostradamus is sometimes a pillar of fire, but
oftener is he a pillar of cloud. He is a past master in
words, and depicts events with a terseness that almost
baffles parallel ; but still his employment of these
same words is more practical than artistic, for he

never rises to poetry. As an accepted visionary he
is perhaps less swayed by the imagination than any
man of at all kindred type that one can mention.
With him words are as often used to veil as to
unfold his meaning. His contempt for simple persons,
the ignorant, is very broadly marked. Men of knowledge are to constitute his audience ; the heaven of
prophecy is in his opinion a region unfit for children.
He, clean contrary to the example set forth in St.
Mark (x. 14), will suffer none such to approach him.*
He chiefly predicts the *evil* to come ; what is good
only figures in his pages incidentally, and at long
intervals. But here it is to be observed that the
staple of true prophecy must always run parallel with
that of history ; whilst, as to the latter, it has grown
into an axiom, "Happy is the country that has no
history." He fatigues while he fascinates us amid
the variety of his combinations ; yet a deeper examina-
tion will often end in clothing these riddling and vext
allusions in a magical and floating investment that
lifts them up into a calm sublimity.

Still he is clearly no prophet in the old and Hebrew
sense of the word—like Isaiah, Daniel, David, John,—
a man who neither respects his own person as regards
its safety, nor the person of other men as regards
their position. You cannot say of him : "*Scimus quia
verax es, non enim respicis personam hominum*" (St.
Matt. xxii. 16), which is the test-touch all the world
over of a true prophet. Le Pelletier's summing-up is :

---

* See the ban he utters in Century VI., at the close—
"*Barbari procul sunto.*" He shows a quite Horatian and
heathen antipathy to the *profanum vulgus.*

c'est un artiste en pronostics. There is a Pythic ring in all he writes and says; a sub-flavour, too, of cabalistic lore far gathered from those ancient compromising books which he saw fit to burn. The outward signs of his procedure and methods are palpably magical, as set forth in the stanzas that open his first Century to the reader. If we know that he professed Christian orthodoxy, equally we know that he practiced judicial astrology, and made unquestionable use of the Pagan ritual of incantation. These rites, uncomprehended by all the erudite in books who wrote about them, were by the divines and fathers of the early Church ignorantly attributed to prestidigitation, Toledan art, and fraudulent compact with the sable fiend. Perhaps they may turn out to have been merely natural excitations, empirically discovered, tending to enable the subject of them more fully to reach a state of semi-conscious ecstasy; to place the cerebral light in the current of latent light that pervades all space (if such an expression be permissible), and so elicit results that are ordinarily unattainable by man. Bouys, who wrote in 1806, plainly considers him to have been a clairvoyant. The animal magnetizers call him a *crisiaque.* Possibly all these processes only served to place him in a position favourable to clairvoyance; but on all this, respected and gentle reader, construct your own opinion. Let the man be to you prophet, sorcerer, or clairvoyant. Call him what you will, so you free him from the stigma of impostor. M. le Pelletier's judgment as to that ought to be regarded as final: "*L'ampleur de son génie, et la sureté inimaginable de son coup d'œil, ne permettent guère de la croire.*"

It has been well said that the man and his works
are an enigma. Everything in our author is
ambiguous : the man, the thought, the style. We
stumble at every step in the rough paths of his
labyrinth. Once we enter, jeering voices seem to
deride us from behind each stanza, strophe, word.
We try to interrogate, but grow silent before a man
of emotionless nerve and of impenetrable mask.
What are these "Centuries"? What is Nostradamus?
In them and him all may find something ; but no man
born of woman can find *all.* The Sphinx of France
is here before us ; a riddler, riddling of the fate of
men : a man at once bold and timid ; simple, yet
who can plumb his depth? A superficial Christian, a
Pagan perhaps at heart ; a man rewarded of kings :
and yet, so far as we can see, furnishing no one
profitable hint to them that could make their life run
smoother, or remove a single peril from their path.
He leaves a book of things malign, written by one
who, albeit, never spoke a word that *à tous ne seroit
agréable.* Behold this Janus of a double face ; his
very breath is double ; the essence of ambiguity lies
wrapped incarnate in him, and it moulds the man, the
thought, the style.

PRÉFACE À MON FILS.

THE PREFACE OF MICHAEL NOSTRA-DAMUS TO HIS PROPHECIES.

TO Cæsar Nostradamus his son, life and felicity. Thy late arrival,* Cæsar Nostradamus my son, has made me bestow much time, through nightly vigils, to leave you in writing a memorial to refer to, after the corporal extinction of your progenitor, that might serve for the common profit of mankind, out of what the Divine Being has permitted me to learn from the revolution of the stars. And since it has pleased the immortal God that thou shouldst come into the natural light of this terrene abode, and shouldst say that thy years are not yet calculated astronomically, and thy March months are incapable to receive in their weak understanding what I must necessarily record [as to happen] after my time :—seeing also that it is not possible to leave thee in writing what

* Cæsar Nostradamus was born at the beginning of 1555, so he was but a few weeks old when his father dedicated to him the first four " Centuries," published for the first time in 1555, by Macé Bonhomme, the printer at Lyons. In the name of this son the epistle is really a dedication to his spiritual sons ; that is, to his interpreters and students in all future ages.

might suffer injury and be obliterated by time ; for the inherited gift of occult prediction will remain confined to my own bowels :—considering that events of human proposal are uncertain, whilst all is governed and directed by the incalculable power of Heaven, guiding us, not by Bacchic fury, nor yet by Lymphatic * motion, but by astronomical assertion—" *Soli numine divino afflati præsagiunt et spirito prophetico particularia.*" †

Although for years past I have predicted, a long time in advance, what has afterwards come to pass, and in particular regions attributing the whole accomplishment to divine power and inspiration, also other unfortunate and fortunate occurrences have been pronounced with accelerated promptitude which

---

* Lymphatics, Garencières (p. 16) tells, were anciently those who were mad for love ; and he absurdly adds that the sign of it was, that such persons threw themselves into the water,— *lympha* meaning water. Varro says that in Greece those who were mad were called νυμφολήπτους, which means caught by nymphs. Festus, to fit this, thinks that men went mad by seeing the image of nymphs in the water fountains. Others have it that they were afraid of water, as if it were hydrophobia that possessed them. But *nympha* and *lympha* approach each other so nearly, that when a man is once caught by a nymph he is, for the time being, mad to all intents and purposes,—"it is not given to a man to love and to be wise." Leaving all this to be settled as it may, there is no question but in the medical technology of Nostradamus a deep melancholy is what was understood by the Lymphatic motion,—melancholy being the temperament most apt for study, poetry, and vaticination. Garencières invents a word for the occasion, or uses one that has since grown obsolete. He employs the verb *lymphatize.*

† "Such alone as are inspired by the divine power can predict particular events in a spirit of prophecy."

have since happened in other parts of the world,
—for I was willing to maintain silence and to pass
over matters that might prove injurious [if published]
not only as relates to the present time, but also for
the most part of future time, if committed to writing,
since kingdoms, sects, and religions will pass through
stages so very contrary, and, as regards the present
time, diametrically opposed,—that if I were to relate
what will happen in the future, governors, sectaries,
and ecclesiastics would find it so ill-accordant with
[*si*] their auricular fancy, that they would go near to
condemn what future ages will know and perceive to
be true.   Considering also the sentence of the true
Saviour, " *Nolite sanctum dare canibus neque mittatis
margaritas vestras ante porcos, ne forte conculcent eas
pedibus suis, et conversi dirumpant vos* " [Matt. vii. 6].

This it is which has led me to withhold my tongue
from the vulgar, and my pen from paper.   But, later
on, I thought I would enlarge a little, and declare in
dark and abstruse sayings in consideration of [*pour*]
the vulgar advent [vid. Le Pelletier, i. 163] the most
urgent of its future causes, as perceived by me, be the
revolutionary changes what they may, so only as not
to scandalize the auricular frigidity (of my hearers),
and write all down under a cloudy figure that shall
essentially and above all things be prophetical.
Although " *Abscondidisti hæc à sapientibus, et pruden-
tibus, id est, potentibus et regibus, et enucleasti ea exiguis
et tenuibus.* " * By the grace of God and the good

* " Thou hast hidden these things from the wise and prudent,
i.e. from the powerful and from kings, and hast revealed them
to the small and weak." This is Nostradamus's gloss upon
Matt. xi. 25.

angels, the Prophets have had committed to them the spirit of vaticination, by which they see things at a distance, and are enabled to forecast future events. For there is nothing that can be accomplished without Him, whose power and goodness are so great to all His creatures as long as they put their trust in Him, much as they may be [exposed] or subject to other influences, [yet] on account of their likeness to the nature of their good guardian angel [or genius] that heat and prophetic power draweth nigh to us, as do the rays of the sun which cast their influence alike upon bodies that are elementary and non-elementary. As for ourselves personally who are but human, we can attain to nothing by our own unaided natural knowledge, nor the bent of our intelligence, in the way of deciphering the recondite secrets of God the Creator. " *Quia non est nostrum noscere tempora, nec momenta,*" * etc. Although, indeed, now or hereafter some persons may arrive to whom God Almighty may be pleased to reveal by imaginative impression some secrets of the future, as accorded in time past to judicial astrology, when [*que* for *quand*] a certain power and volitional faculty came upon them, as a flame of fire appears.† They grew inspired, and were

---

* Acts i. 7.

† Nostradamus seems, whenever he alludes to this appearance of flame as preceding vaticination, to have in his mind the descent of tongues of fire at Pentecost (Acts ii. 3), διαμεριζόμεναι γλῶσσαι ὡσεὶ πυρός. A flame of fire, be it observed, conveys a double symbol : it resembles a tongue in form. Its luminousness and its purifying tendency express the celestial nature of spirit, as contrasted with matter, and also inspiration. So that intrinsically and extrinsically it represents prophetic utterance.

able to judge of all inspiration, human and divine, alike. For the divine works, which are absolutely universal, God will complete ; those which are contingent, or medial, the good angels direct ; and the third sort come under the evil angels.*

Perhaps, my son, I speak to thee here a little too occultly. But as to the hidden vaticinations which come to one by the subtle spirit of fire, or sometimes by the understanding disturbed, [it may even be, by] contemplating the remotest stars, as being intelligences on the watch, even to giving utterance to declarations [that] being taken down in writing declare, without favour, and without any taint of improper loquacity, that all things whatsoever proceed from the divine power of the great eternal Deity from whom all goodness emanates. Further, my son, although I have inserted the name of prophet, I do not desire to assume a title of so high sublimity at the present moment. For he who "*Propheta dicitur hodie, olim vocabatur videns;*"†

Grotius contributes an unusually good note upon this passage, pointing out that as in Genesis (xi. 9), confusion of tongues scattered mankind, so here (Acts ii. 3) the gift of tongues was to bring men again into one brotherhood.

* This passage is very difficult to bring to a clear sense in translation. Garencières has simply evaded it. It seems to mean that God operates all the great effects in the universe ; that, as He is the Maker, so is He the perpetual operator in the world,—its cause and life ; but that the guardian angels are good and bad, and are charged with some sort of duty and office, not as affecting the mechanic frame of the world, but in respect of mankind. This is in conformity with the Cabala and Hermetical teaching ; but what he precisely means cannot, I think, be quite absolutely stated.

† "He who is called prophet now, once was called seer."

for, strictly speaking, my son, a prophet is one who sees things remote from the knowledge of all mankind. Or, to put the case ; to the prophet, by means of the perfect light of prophecy, there lie opened up very manifestly divine things as well as human ; which cannot come about, seeing that the effects of future prediction extend to such remote periods. Now, the secrets of God are incomprehensible, and their efficient virtue belongs to a sphere far remote from natural knowledge ; for, deriving their immediate origin from the free will, things set in motion causes that of themselves could never attract such attention as could make them recognized, either by human augury, or by any other knowledge of occult power ; it is a thing comprised only within the concavity of heaven itself, from the present fact of all eternity, which comes in itself to embrace all time.

Still, by the means of some eternal power, by an epileptic Herculean agitation, the causes by the celestial movement become known. I do not say, my son, in order that you may fully understand me, that the knowledge of this matter cannot yet impress itself upon thy feeble brain, that very remote future causes may not come within the cognizance of a reasonable being ; if they are, notwithstanding, purely the creation of the intellectual soul of things present, future things are not by any means too hidden or concealed. But the perfect knowledge of causes cannot be acquired without divine inspiration ; since all prophetic inspiration derives its first motive principle from God the Creator, next from good fortune, and then from nature. Wherefore the independent causes being independently produced, or not produced, the presage partially happens, where it was predicted. For the human understanding, being intellectually created, cannot penetrate occult causes, otherwise than by the voice of a genius by means of the thin flame (vid. page 76) [showing] to what direction future causes incline to develop themselves. And further, my son, I implore you never to apply your understanding on such reveries and vanities as dry up the body and bring perdition to the soul and disturb all the senses. In like manner, I caution you against the seduction of a more than execrable magic, that has been denounced already by the sacred Scriptures, by the divine canons of the Church— although we have to exempt from this judgment Judicial Astrology. By the aid of this it is, and by divine revelation and inspiration, united with deep calculations, we have reduced our prophecies to writing. And, notwithstanding that this occult philosophy was *not* reproved by the Church, I have felt no desire to divulge their unbridled promptings. Although many volumes have come before me, which had laid hidden for many ages. But dreading what might happen in the future, after reading them, I presented them to Vulcan, and as the fire kindled them, the flame, licking the air, shot forth an unaccustomed brightness, clearer than the light is of natural flame, resembling more the explosion of powder, casting a subtle illumination over the house as if the whole were wrapped in sudden conflagration.—So that at last you might not in the future be abused by searching for the perfect transformation, lunar or solar, or incorruptible metals hidden under the earth, or the sea, I reduced them to ashes.—But as to the judgment which perfects itself by means of the celestial judgment, that I am desirous to manifest to you : by that method you may have cognizance of things future, avoiding all fantastic imaginations that may arise, and limiting the particularity of the topics by divine and supernatural inspiration ; harmonizing with the celestial figures these topics, and that part of time, which the occult property has relation to, by the potential virtue and faculty divine, in whose presence the three aspects of time are clasped in one by eternity —an evolution that connects in one causes past, present, and future—"*quia omnia sunt nuda et aperta,* etc." *—

From all which, my son, you can easily comprehend, notwithstanding your tender brain, the things that are to happen can be foretold by nocturnal and celestial lights, which are natural, coupled to a spirit of prophecy,—not that I would assume the name or efficacy of a prophet, but, by revealed inspiration, as a mortal man the senses place me no farther from heaven than the feet are from the earth. "*Possum non errare, falli, decipi,*" † (albeit) I am the greatest sinner in this world, and heir to every human affliction. But being surprised sometimes in the ecstatic work, amid prolonged calculation, and engaged in nocturnal studies of sweet odour, I have composed books of prophecies, containing each one hundred astronomic quatrains of forecasts, which I have tried to polish

---

* " For all things are naked and open."

† " I am able not to err, fail, or be deceived."

through obscurely, and which are perpetual vaticinations, from now to the year 3797. It is possible that this figure will make some lift up their forehead, at such a vast extent of time, and variety of things to take place under the concave journey of the moon ; and this universal treatment of causes, my son, throughout the earth, which, if you reach the natural age of man, you will see in your climate, under the heaven of your proper nativity, as things that have been foreseen.

Although the everlasting God alone knows the eternity of the light proceeding from Himself, I say frankly to all to whom He has decreed in long and melancholy inspiration to reveal His limitless magnitude, which is beyond both mensuration and comprehension, that by means of this occult cause divinely manifested, principally by two chief causes, comprised in the understanding of the inspired one who prophesies. One is that which comes by infusion, which clarifies the supernatural light, in him who predicts by astral process, or forecasts by inspired revelation, which is practically a participation in the divine eternity, by which means the prophet comes to judge of that which his share of divine spirit has given him, by means of communication with God the Creator, and the natural endowment accorded him. It is to know that what is predicted is true, and has had a heavenly origin ; that such light and the thin flame is altogether efficacious ; that it descends from above, no less than does natural clearness ; and natural light renders philosophers quite sure of their principles, so that by means of the principles of a first cause they have penetrated the profoundest abysses and attained the loftiest doctrines.

But to this end, my son, that I may not wander too profoundly for the future capacity of thy senses, and also because I find that letters shall suffer great and incomparable loss, and that I find the world before the universal conflagration, such deluges and deep submersion, that there will remain scarcely any land not covered with water, and that for so long a period, that everything will perish except Ethnographies and Topographies. Further, after and before these inundations, in many districts the rains will have been so slight, and there will fall from heaven such an abundance of fire and incandescent stones, that scarcely anything will remain unconsumed, and this will occur a short time before the last conflagration. Further, when the planet Mars completes its cycle, at the end of his second period, he will recommence his course. But some will gather in Aquarius through several years, and others in Cancer, which will be of still longer duration. Now that we are conducted by the moon, under the direction of the Creator, and before she has finished her entire circuit the sun will come, and then Saturn. Now, according to the celestial signs, the reign of Saturn shall come back again, so that, all calculated, the world is drawing on towards its anaragonic revolution.

From the time I am writing this, before 177 years 3 months and 11 days, by pestilence, long famine, and wars, and more still by inundations, the world between this day and that, before and after, shall be diminished, and its population so reduced that there will hardly be hands enough to attend to agriculture, and the lands will be left as long without culture as they have been under tillage. This, so far as celestial judgment manifests, that we are now in the seventh millenary, which completes all and introduces us to the eighth, where is the upper firmament of the eighth sphere, which, in a latitudinary dimension, is where the Almighty will come to complete the revolution, where the celestial figures will return to their courses, and the upper motion which renders the earth stable for us and fixed, "*non inclinabitur in seculum seculorum,*" * unless His will be accomplished, and no otherwise.

Although by ambiguous opinions exceeding all natural reason by Mahometical dreams, also sometimes God the Creator by the ministry of angels of fire, and missive flame, presents to the external senses, even of our eyes, the causes of future predictions, that indicate the future event which must manifest itself to him who presages anything. For the presage which is made by the exterior light comes infallibly to judge partly with and by means of the exterior flame ; although truly the part which seems to come by the eye of the understanding springs only from the lesion of the imaginative sense. The reason is too evident, the whole is predicted by the afflatus of divinity, and by means of the angelic spirit inspired to the man prophesying, rendering him [as it were] anointed with vaticinations, visiting him to illuminate him, and, stirring the forefront of his phantasy by divers nighty apparitions no less than daily certitude, he prophesies by astronomic administration conjoined with the

* "Whence it shall not deviate from age to age."

holiest future prediction, taking nothing into his consideration but the hardihood of his free courage.

Come at this hour to understand, my son, that I find by my revelations [astral], and which are in accordance with revealed inspiration, that the sword of death is on its way to us now, in the shape of pestilence, war (more horrible than has been known for three generations of men), and famine, that shall fall upon the earth, and return upon it at frequent intervals. For the stars accord with such a revolution, and with the written word, " *Visitabo in virgâ ferrea iniquitates eorum, et in verberibus percutiam eos.*" * For the mercy of God, my son, will not be spread abroad for a time, till the major part of my prophecies shall have been accomplished, and have become by accomplishment resolved. Thus oftentimes in the course of these sinister storms the Lord will say, " *Conteram ego, et confringam, et non miserebor.*" † And a thousand other accidents will come by waters and continual rain, as I have more fully and at large set forth in my other Prophecies, which are drawn out at length, *in solutâ oratione ;* ‡ (in these I) designate the localities, times, and terms prefixed, that all men who come after may see, recognizing the circumstances that come about by infallible indications. As we have marked by the others where we speak more clearly, for although

---

* " I will visit their iniquities with a rod of iron, and with blows will strike them." This somewhat resembles a passage in the Psalms (ii. 7), but it is not a quotation.

† " I will trample them and break them, and not show pity." This resembles Isai. lxiii. 3.

‡ In prose, and not in verse, as the quatrains are. These prose forecastings have, I am afraid, been altogether lost.

they are covered with a veil of cloud, they are clear
enough to be comprehended by men of good intelligence : " *Sed quando submoventa erit ignorantia,*" *
the total will stand out with greater clearance still.
Making an end here, my son, take now this gift of
thy father, Michael Nostradamus, hoping to expound
to thee each several prophecy of these quatrains here
given, beseeching the immortal Father that He will
endue thee with a long life of happy and prospering
felicity.

From Salon, this 1st of March, 1555.

* " When the time arrives for the removal of ignorance."

EPISTLE TO HENRY II.

TO the most invincible, very puissant, and most
Christian Henry King of France the Second :
Michael Nostradamus, his most humble, most obedient
servant and subject, wishes victory and happiness.

For that sovereign observation that I had, O most
Christian and very victorious King, since that my face,
long obscured with cloud, presented itself before the
deity of your measureless Majesty, since that in that
I have been perpetually dazzled, never failing to
honour and worthily revere that day, when first
before it, as before a singularly humane majesty, I
presented myself. I searched for some occasion by
which to manifest good heart and frank courage, by
the means of which I might grow into greater knowledge of your serene Majesty. I soon found in effect
it was impossible for me to declare it, considering the
contrast of the solitariness of my long obnubilation
and obscurity, and my being suddenly thrust into
brilliancy, and transported into the presence of the
sovereign eye of the first monarch of the universe.
Likewise I have long hung in doubt as to whom I
ought to dedicate these three Centuries to, the remainder of my Prophecies amounting now to a

thousand. I have long meditated on an act of such audacity. I have at last ventured to address your Majesty, and was not daunted from it as Plutarch, that grave author, relates in the life of Lycurgus, that, seeing the gifts and presents that were made in the way of sacrifice at the temples of the immortal gods in that age, many were staggered at the expense, and dared not approach the temple to present anything.

Notwithstanding this, I saw your royal splendour to be accompanied with an incomparable humanity, and paid my addresses to it, not as to those Kings of Persia whom it was not permissible to approach. But to a very prudent and very wise Prince I have dedicated my nocturnal and prophetic calculations, composed out of a natural instinct, and accompanied by a poetic fervour, rather than according to the strict rules of poetry. Most part, indeed, has been composed and adjusted by astronomical calculation corresponding to the years, months, and weeks, of the regions, countries, and for the most part towns and cities, throughout Europe, Africa, and a part of Asia, which nearest approach [or resemble] each other in all these climates, and this is composed in a natural manner. Possibly some may answer—who, if so, had better blow his nose [that he may see the clearer by it]—that the rhythm is as easy to be understood, as the sense is hard to get at. Therefore, O most gracious King, the bulk of the prophetic quatrains are so rude, that there is no making way through them, nor is there any interpreter of them. Nevertheless, being always anxious to set down the years, towns, and regions cited, where the events are to occur, even from the year 1585, and the year 1606, dating from the present time, which is the 14th of March, 1557.

Then passing far beyond to things which shall happen at the commencement of the seventh millenary, deeply calculated, so far as my astronomic calculus, and other knowledge, has been able to reach, to the time when the adversaries of Jesus Christ and of His Church shall begin to multiply in great force. The whole has been composed and calculated on days and hours of best election and disposition, and with all the accuracy I could attain to. At a moment [blessed] "*Minerva libera et non invita,*" * my calculations looking forward to events through a space of time to come that nearly equals that of the past even up to the present, and by this they will know in the lapse of time and in all regions what is to happen, all written down thus particularly, immingled with nothing superfluous.

Notwithstanding that some say, "*Quod de futuris non est determinata omnino veritas,*" † I will confess, Sire, that I believed myself capable of presage from the natural instinct I inherit of my ancestors, adjusted and regulated by elaborate calculation, and the endeavour to free the soul, mind, and heart from all care, solicitude, and anxiety, by resting and tranquilizing the spirit, which finally has all to be completed and perfected in one respect *tripode æneo* [by the brazen tripod]. With all this there will be

---

* "When Minerva was free and favourable."

† "There can be no truth entirely determined for certain which concerns the future."

many to attribute to me as mine, things no more mine than nothing. The Almighty alone, who strictly searches the human heart, pious, just, and pitiful, is the true Judge; to Him I pray to defend me from the calumny of wicked men. Such persons, with equal calumny, will bring into question how all your ancient progenitors the Kings of France have cured the evil; how those of other nations have cured the bite of serpents; others have had a certain instinct in the art of divination, and other faculties that would be too long to recount here. Notwithstanding such as cannot be restrained from the exercise of the malignancy of the evil spirit, [there is hope that] by the lapse of time, and after my extinction here on earth, my writings will be more valued than during my lifetime.

However, if I err in calculation of ages, or find myself unable to please all the world, may it please your Imperial Majesty to forgive me, for I protest before God and His saints, that I purpose to insert nothing whatever in writing this present Epistle that shall militate against the true Catholic Faith, whilst consulting the astronomical calculations to the very best of my knowledge. For the stretch of time of our forefathers [i.e. the age of the world] which has gone before is such, submitting myself to the direction of the soundest chronologists, that the first man, Adam, was about one thousand two hundred and forty years before Noah, not computing time by Gentile records, such as Varro has committed to writing, but taking simply the Sacred Scriptures for the guide in my astronomic reckonings, to the best

of my feeble understanding. After Noah, from him
and the universal deluge, about one thousand and
fourscore years, came Abraham, who was a sovereign
astrologer according to some; he first invented the
Chaldæan alphabet. Then came Moses, about five
hundred and fifteen or sixteen years later. Between
the time of David and Moses five hundred and
seventy years elapsed. Then after the time of David
and the time of our Saviour and Redeemer, Jesus
Christ, born of a pure Virgin, there elapsed (according
to some chronographers) one thousand three hundred
and fifty years.

Some, indeed, may object to this supputation
as not true, because it varies from that of· Eusebius.
Since the time of the human redemption to the
hateful apostacy of the Saracens, there have been
six hundred and twenty-one years, or thereabouts.
Now, from this it is easy to gather what time has
elapsed if my supputation be not good and avail-
able for all nations, for that all is calculated by the
celestial courses, associated in my case with an
emotion that steals over me at certain subsecival
hours from an emotional tendency handed down to
me from a line of ancestors. But the injuriousness
of our time, O most serene Sovereign, requires that
such secret events should not transpire, except in
enigmatic sentences, having but one sense and one
only meaning, and quite unmingled with calculation
that is of ambiguity or amphibology. Say, rather,
under a veiled obscurity from some natural emotional
effusion, that resembles the sentential delivery of the
thousand and two Prophets, that have been from the

Creation of the world, according to the calculation and Punic Chronicle of Joel: "*Effundum spiritum meum super omnem carnem, et prophetabunt filii vestri, et filiæ vestræ.*" * But this prophecy proceeded from the mouth of the Holy Spirit, which was the sovereign power eternal, in conjunction with the celestial bodies, has caused some of the number to predict great and marvellous events.

As to myself in this place, I set up no claim to such a title—never, please God. I fully confess that all proceeds from God, and for that I return Him thanks, honour, and immortal praise, and have mingled nothing with it of the divination which proceeds *à fato*, but *à Deo, à naturâ*,† and for the the most part accompanied with the movement of the celestial courses. Much as, if looking into a burning mirror [we see], as with darkened vision, the great events, sad or portentous, and calamitous occurrences that are about to fall upon the principal worshippers. First upon the temples of God, secondly upon such as have their support from the earth [*i.e.* by the kings], this decadence draweth nigh, with a thousand other calamitous incidents that in the course of time will be known to happen.

For God will take notice of the long barrenness of the great Dame, who afterwards will conceive two principal children. But, she being in great danger, the girl she will give birth to with risk at her age of death in the eighteenth year, and not possible to outlive the thirty-sixth, will leave three males and

* See Joel ii. 28.
† Which proceeds from fate, but from God, and nature.

one female, and he will have two who never had any of the same father. The three brothers will be so different, though united and agreed, that the three and four parts of Europe will tremble. By the youngest in years will the Christian monarchy be sustained and augmented ; heresies spring up and suddenly cast down, the Arabs driven back, kingdoms united, and new laws promulgated. Of the other children the first shall possess the furious crowned Lions, holding their paws upon the bold escutcheon. The second, accompanied by the Latins, shall penetrate so far that a second trembling and furious descent shall be made, descending Mons Jovis [at Barcelona] to mount the Pyrenees, shall not be translated to the antique monarchy, and a third inundation of human blood shall arise, and March for a long while will not be found in Lent. The daughter shall be given for the preservation of the Christian Church, the dominator falling into the Pagan sect of new infidels, and she will have two children, the one fidelity, the other infidelity, by the confirmation of the Catholic Church. The other, who to his great confusion and tardy repentance wished to ruin her, will have three regions over a wide extent of leagues, that is to say, Roumania, Germany, and Spain, which will entail great intricacy of military handling, stretching from the 50th to the 52nd degree of latitude. And they will have to respect the more distant religions of Europe and the north above the 48th degree of latitude, which at first in a vain timidity will tremble, and then the more western, southern, and eastern will tremble. Their power will become such, that what is brought about by union and concord will prove insuperable by warlike conquest. By nature they will be equal, but exceedingly different in faith.

After this the sterile Dame, of greater power than the second, shall be received by two nations, by the first made obstinate by him who had power over all, by the second, and third, that shall extend his forces towards the circuit of the east of Europe; [arrived] there his standards will stop and succumb, but by sea he will run on to Trinacria and the Adriatic with his mirmidons. The Germans will succumb wholly and the Barbaric sect will be disquieted and driven back by the whole of the Latin race. Then shall begin the grand Empire of Antichrist in the Atila and Xerxes, [who is] to descend with innumerable multitudes, so that the coming of the Holy Spirit, issuing from the 48th degree, shall make a trans-migration, chasing away the abomination of Anti-christ, that made war upon the royal person of the great vicar of Jesus Christ, and against His Church, and reign *per tempus, et in occasione temporis* [for a time, and to the end of time]. This will be preceded by an eclipse of the sun, more obscure and tenebrose than has ever been since the creation of the world, up to the death and passion of Jesus Christ, and from thence till now. There will be in the month of October a grand revolution [translation] made, such that one would think that the librating body of the earth had lost its natural movement in the abyss of perpetual darkness. There will be seen precursive signs in the spring-time, and after extreme changes ensuing, reversal of kingdoms, and great earthquakes [*i.e.* wars]. All this accompanied with the procreations of the Néw Babylon [Paris], a miserable prostitute big with the abomination of the first holocaust [death of Louis XVI.]. It will only continue for seventy-three years seven months.

Then there will issue from the stock so long time barren, proceeding from the 50th degree, [one] who will renovate the whole Christian Church. A great peace, union, and concord will then spring up between some of the children of races [long] opposed to each other and separated by diverse kingdoms. Such a peace shall be set up, that the instigator and promoter of military faction by means of the diversity of religions, shall dwell attached to the bottom of the abyss, and united to the kingdom of the furious, who shall counterfeit the wise. The countries, towns, cities, and provinces that had forsaken their old customs to free themselves, enthralling themselves more deeply, shall become secretly weary of their liberty, and, true religion lost, shall commence by striking off to the left, to return more than ever to the right.

Then replacing holiness, so long desecrated by their former writings [circulating slanders], afterwards the result will be that the great dog will issue as an irresistible mastiff [Napoleon?] who will destroy everything, even to all that may have been prepared in time past, till the churches will be restored as at first, and the clergy reinstated in their pristine condition ; till it lapses again into whoredom and luxury, to commit and perpetrate a thousand crimes. And, drawing near to another desolation, then, when she shall be at her highest and sublimest point of dignity, the kings and generals [*mains militaires*] will come up [against her], and her two swords will be taken from her, and nothing will be left her but the semblance of them. [The following paragraph I can make nothing of, so I give it in the words of Garencières and in inverted commas.] " From which by the means of the crooked- ness that draweth them, the people causing it to go straight, and not willing to submit unto them by the end opposite to the sharp hand that toucheth the ground they shall provoke." Until there shall be born unto the branch a long time sterile, one who shall deliver the French people from the benign slavery that they voluntarily submitted to, putting himself under the protection of Mars, and stripping Jupiter [Napoleon I.] of all his honours and dignities, for the city constituted free and seated in another narrow Mesopotamia. The chief and governor shall be cast from the midst, and set in a place of the air, ignorant of the conspiracy of the conspirators [Fouché, Duc d'Otranto, etc.] with the second Thrasibulus, who for a long time had prepared all this. Then shall the impurities and abominations be with great shame set forth and manifested to the darkness of the veiled light, shall cease towards the end of his reign, and the chiefs of the Church shall evince but little of the love of God, whilst many of them shall apostatize from the true faith.

Of the three sects [Lutheran, Catholic, and Ma- hometan], that which is in the middle, by the action of its own worshippers, will be thrown a little into decadence. The first totally throughout Europe, and the chief part of Africa exterminated by the third, by means of the poor in spirit, who by the madness engendered of libidinous luxury, will commit adultery [*i.e.* apostatize]. The people will pull down the pillar, and chase away the adherents of the legislators, and it shall seem, from the kingdoms weakened by the Orientals, that God the Creator has loosed Satan from the infernal prisons, to make room for the great Dog and Dohan [Gog and Magog], which will make so great and injurious a breach in the Churches, that neither the reds nor the whites, who are without eyes and without hands [meaning the latter Bourbons, " who learn nothing and forget nothing "], cannot judge of the situation, and their power will be taken from them. Then shall commence a persecution of the Church such as never was before. Whilst this is enacting, such a pestilence shall spring up that out of three parts of mankind two shall be removed. To such a length will this proceed that one will neither know nor recognize the fields or houses, and grass will grow in the streets of the cities as high as a man's knees. To the clergy there shall be a total desolation, and the martial men shall usurp what shall come back from the City of the Sun [Rome], and from Malta, and the Islands of Hières [off Marseilles], and the great chain of the port shall be opened that takes its name from the marine ox [Bosphorus].

A new incursion shall be made from the maritime shores, eager to give the leap of liberty since the first taking by the Mahometans. Their assaults shall not be at all in vain, and in the place where the habitation of Abraham was, it shall be assailed by those who hold the Jovialists [followers of Jupiter (Napoleon I. ?)] in reverence. The city of Achem [in the Island of Sumatra] shall be encompassed and assaulted on all sides by a great force of armed men. Their maritime forces shall be weakened by the Westerns. Upon this kingdom a great desolation shall come, and the great cities shall be depopulated, and such as enter in shall come under the vengeance of the wrath of God. The Holy Sepulchre, for so long a period an object of great veneration, shall remain exposed to the blighting dew of evening under the stars of heaven, and of the sun and moon. The holy place shall be converted into a stable for cattle small and large, and applied to other base purposes. Oh, what a calamitous time will that be for women with child! for then the Sultan of the East will be vanquished, driven for the most part by the Northern and Western men, who will kill him, overthrow him, and put the rest to flight, and his children, the off-spring of many women, imprisoned. Then will come to its fulfilment the prophecy of the Royal Prophet, " *Ut audiret gemitus compeditorum, et solveret filios interemptorum.*" *

What great oppression shall then fall upon the princes and rulers of kingdoms, even on those who are maritime and Oriental, their tongues inter-mingled from all nations of the earth! Tongues of the Latin nations, mingled with Arabic and North-African communication. All the Eastern kings will be driven away, overthrown, and exterminated, not at

* " Let the sighing of the prisoner come before thee, to release the children of death " (Ps. lxxviii. 11).

all by means of the kings of the North and the drawing near of our age, but by means of the three secretly
united who seek out death and snares by ambush
sprung upon one another. The renewal of this
Triumvirate shall endure for seven years, while its
renown shall spread all over the world, and the sacrifice of the holy and immaculate wafer shall be upheld.
Then shall two lords of the North conquer the
Orientals, and so great report and tumultuary warfare
shall issue from these that all the East shall tremble
at the noise of these two brothers of the North, who
are yet not brothers. And because, Sire, by this discourse I almost introduce confusion into these predictions as to the time when the event of each shall
fall out; for the detailed account of the time that
follows is very little conformable, if at all, to what
I gave above, that indeed could not err, being by
astronomic rule and consonant with the Holy Scriptures themselves.

Had I wished to give to every quatrain its
detailed date, it could easily have been done, but
it would not have been agreeable to all, and still
less to interpret them, Sire, until your Majesty
should have fully sanctioned me to do this, in
order not to furnish calumniators with an opportunity to injure me. Always reckoning the years
since the creation of the world to the birth of Noah
as being 1506 years, and from that to the completion of the building of the ark at the period of the
universal deluge 600 years elapsed (let them be solar
years, or lunar, or mixed), I hold that the Scripture
takes them to be solar. At the conclusion of this

600 years, Noah entered the ark to escape the deluge. The deluge was universal over the earth, and lasted one year and two months. From the conclusion of the deluge to the birth of Abraham there elapsed 295 years, and 100 years from that to the birth of Isaac. From Isaac to Jacob 60 years. From the time he went into Egypt until his coming out of it was 130 years ; and from the entry of Jacob into Egypt to his exit was 430 years ; and from that to the building of the Temple by Solomon in the fortieth year of his reign, makes 480 years. From the building of the Temple to Jesus Christ, according to the supputation of the Hierographs, there passed 490 years. Thus by this calculation that I have made, collecting it out of the sacred writings, there are about 4173 years and eight months less or more. Now, from Jesus Christ, in that there is such a diversity of opinion, I pass it by, and having calculated the present prophecies in accordance with the order of the chain which contains the revolution, and the whole by astronomical rule, together with my own hereditary instinct. After some time, and including in it the period Saturn takes to turn between the 7th of April up to the 25th of August; Jupiter from the 14th of June to the 7th of October ; Mars from the 17th of April to the 22nd of June ; Venus from the 9th of April to the 22nd of May ; Mercury from the 3rd of February to the 24th of the same ; afterwards from the 1st of June to the 24th of the same ; and from the 25th of September to the 16th of October, Saturn in Capricorn, Jupiter in Aquarius, Mars in Scorpio, Venus in Pisces, Mercury within a

month in Capricorn, Aquarius, and Pisces ; the moon in Aquarius, the Dragon's head in Libra, the tail in her sign opposite. Following the conjunction of Jupiter to Mercury, with a quadrin aspect of Mars to Mercury, and the head of the Dragon shall be with a conjunction of Sol with Jupiter, the year shall be peaceful without eclipse.

Then will be the commencement [of a period] that will comprehend in itself what will long endure [*i.e.* the vulgar advent of the French Revolution], and in its first year there shall be a great persecution of the Christian Church, fiercer than that in Africa [by the Vandals from 1439 to 1534], and this will burst out [*durera*] the year one thousand seven hundred and ninety-two ; they will think it to be a renovation of time. After this. the people of Rome will begin to reconstitute themselves [in 1804, when Napoleon is emperor], and to chase away the obscurity of darkness, recovering some share of their ancient brightness, but not without much division and continual changes. Venice after that, in great force and power, shall raise her wings very high, not much short of the force of ancient Rome. At that time great Byzantine sails, associated with the Piedmontese by the help and power of the North, will so restrain them that the two Cretans will not be able to maintain their faith. The arks built by the ancient warriors will accompany them to the waves of Neptune. In the Adriatic there will be such permutations, that what was united will be separated, and that will be reduced to a house which before was a great city, including the Pampotan and Mesopotamia of Europe, to 45, and others to 41, 42, and 47. And in that time and those countries the infernal power will set the power of the adversaries of its law against the Church of Jesus Christ. This will constitute the second Antichrist, which will persecute that Church and its true vicar, by means of the power of the temporal kings, who in their ignorance will be reduced by tongues that will cut more than any sword in the hands of a madman.

The said reign of Antichrist will only last to the death of him who was born near the [commencement] of the century, and of the other in the city of Plancus [Lyons], accompanied by him the elect of Modena, Fulcy by Ferara, upheld by the Adriatic Piedmontese, and the proximity of the great Trinacria [Sicily]. Afterwards the Gallic Ogmion shall pass the Mount Jovis [Barcelona], accompanied by so great a number that from afar the Empire shall be presented with its grand law, and then and for some time after shall be profusely shed the blood of the innocent by the guilty recently elevated to power. Then by great deluges the memory of things contained in such instruments shall suffer incalculable loss, even to the Alphabet itself. This will happen among the Northerns. By the Divine Will once again Satan will be bound, and universal peace established amongst mankind, and the Church of Jesus Christ delivered from all tribulation, although the Azostains [debauched voluptuaries] would desire to mix with the honey the gall of their pestilent seduction. This will be near the seventh millenary, when the sanctuary of Jesus Christ will no longer be trodden down by the infidels

who come from the North ; the world [will be then]
approaching its great conflagration, although by my
supputation in my prophecies, the course of time runs
much farther on.

In the epistle that some years since I dedicated
to my son Cæsar Nostradamus, I have openly
enough declared some points without presage. But
here, Sire, are comprised many great and marvellous
events to come, which those who follow after us
shall see. And during the said astrological supputation, harmonized with the sacred Scriptures, the
persecution of the Ecclesiastics shall take its rise in
the power of the kings of the North, united with the
Easterns. And this persecution shall last eleven
years, or somewhat less, by which time the chief
Northern king shall pass away, which years being
run, a united Southern king shall succeed, which shall
still more fiercely persecute the clergy of the Church
for the space of three years by the Apostolical seduction of one who will take away all the absolute power
from the Church Militant, and holy people of God
who observe its ritual, and the whole order of religion
shall be greatly persecuted and so afflicted that the
blood of true ecclesiastics shall float everywhere. To
one of those horrible temporal kings such praise shall
be given by his adherents that he will have shed
more human blood of innocent ecclesiastics, than any
could do of wine. This king will commit crimes
against the Church that are incredible. Human blood
will flow in the public streets and churches, like water
after impetuous rain, and will crimson with blood the
neighbouring rivers, and by another naval war redden

the sea to such a degree that one king shall say to
another, " *Bellis rubuit navalibus æquor.*" * Then in
the same year and those following there will ensue the
most horrible pestilence and the most astonishing
on account of the famine · that will precede, and
such tribulation that nothing approaching it ever
happened since the first foundation of the Christian
Church ; this also throughout all the Latin regions,
leaving traces in all the countries under the rule of
Spain.

Then the third King of the North [Russia ?], hearing
the complaint of the people from [whom he derives]
his principal title, will raise up a mighty army, and
pass through the limits [*destroits*] of his last progenitors and great-grandfathers, to him who will [*qui*
for *lui qui*] replace almost everything in its old condition.   The great Vicar of the Cope shall be put
back to his pristine state ; but, desolated and abandoned by all, will return to the sanctuary [that was]
destroyed by Paganism, when the Old and New
Testament will be thrust out and burnt.   After that
Antichrist will be the infernal prince.   Then at this
last epoch, all the kingdoms of Christianity, as well as
of the infidel world, will be shaken during the space
of twenty-five years, and the wars and battles will be
more grievous, and the towns, cities, castles, and all
other edifices will be burnt, desolated, and destroyed
with much effusion of vestal blood, married women
and widows violated, sucking children dashed and
broken against the walls of towns ; and so many evils
will be committed by means of Satan, the prince

* " The sea blushed red with the blood of naval fights."

infernal, that nearly all the world will become undone and desolated. Before the events occur certain
strange birds [imperial eagles] will cry in the air,
" *To-day! to-day!*" and after a given time will disappear [June, 1815]. After this has endured for a
certain length of time [twenty-five years he has said
before, 1790 to 1815], there will be almost renewed
another reign of Saturn, the age of gold [this might
be the discovery of California, but for what follows].
God the Creator shall say, hearing the affliction of His
people, Satan shall be precipitated and bound in the
bottomless abyss, and then shall commence between
God and men a universal peace. There he shall
abide for the space of a thousand years, and shall turn
his greatest force against the power of the Church,
and shall then be bound again.

How justly are all these figures adapted by the
divine letters to visible celestial things, that is to say,
by Saturn, Jupiter, and Mars, and others in conjunction with them, as may be seen more at large by
some of the quatrains! I would have calculated it
more deeply, and adapted the one to the other ; but,
seeing, O most serene King, that some who are given
to censure will raise a difficulty, I shall take the
opportunity to retire my pen and seek my nocturnal
repose. " *Multa etiam, O Rex potentissime præclara, et
sane in brevi ventura, sed omnia in hâc tuâ Epistola,
innectere non possumus, nec volumus, sed ad intellegenda
quædam facta, horrida fata pauca libanda sunt, quamvis
tanta sit in omnes tua amplitudo et humanitas homines,
deosque pietas, ut solos amplissimo et Christianissimo
Regis nomine, et ad quem summa totius religionis*

auctoritas deferatur dignus esse videare." * But I shall only beseech you, O most clement King, by this your singular and most prudent goodness, to understand rather the desire of my heart, and the sovereign wish I have to obey your most excellent Majesty, ever since my eyes approached so nearly to your solar splendour, than the grandeur of my work can attain to or acquire.

Faciebat MICHAEL NOSTRADAMUS.

Solonœ Petræ Provincœ.

From Salon this 27th June, 1558.

---

* "Many things, O most potent king of all, of the most re-markable kind are shortly to happen, that I neither could nor would interweave them all into this epistle ; but in order to comprehend certain facts, a few horrible destinies must be set down in extract, although your amplitude and humanity towards all men is so great, and your piety to the gods, and that you alone seem worthy of the grand title of the most Christian King, and to whom the highest authority in all religion should be deferred."

MAGIC.

BEFORE we enter upon the historical application of those quatrains which admit of interpretation, it will be well to devote a little attention to the views of magic entertained by Nostradamus, to learn from his own mouth what class of readers he proposed to address, and to gather, as far as we may be able, in what manner he proceeded to cultivate the spirit of prophecy and the divine gift with which he thought himself to be endowed. Were he even as certainly an impostor as Cagliostro, this inquiry would have an interest of its own attaching to it ; but if we can for a moment suppose that he genuinely believed himself to be endowed with a faculty of divination, the investigation of that assumption on his part would present a considerable psychological interest merely as a human phenomenon. On the other hand, if he were a man truly gifted with forecast, I do not know that, in this age of scepticism as to things spiritual, anything more wholesome could be proposed to our contemplation than a prophetic record fulfilling itself before the eyes of disbelievers and gainsayers ; who, wishing to scoff and desiring to suppress such things, find themselves utterly powerless to annul the harmony between the vision recorded three hundred years ago and the event of yesterday. Whether such things are or not, it will be for the reader, when he has gone through the book, to say. At present we will only busy ourselves with what Nostradamus says of himself. He is a notability and worthy of criticism, be the final verdict for or against him.

At the end of Century VI. occur four Latin lines headed—

Legis cantio Contra ineptos Criticos. [1. 51.]

Qui legent hosce versus maturè censunto,
Profanum vulgus et inscium ne attrectato,
Omnesque Astrologi, Blenni, Barbari procul sunto.
Qui aliter facit, is ritè sacer esto.

The sense of these lines is much clearer than the prosody, but that matters little.

Translation.

An Incantation in Arrest of Inept Critics.

Let those who read these verses meditate them seriously! Let the profane and ignorant vulgar not handle them! Let astrologers, fools, and savages stand off! Who acts contrary to this, let him be cursed according to the rites of magic.

We now come to the magic formula.

Century I.—Quatrain 1. [1. 52.]

Estant assis de nuict secret estude,
Seul, reposé sur la sele * d'airain,
Flambe exigue sortant de solitude,
Fait prospèrer † qui ‡ n'est à croire vain.

* Romance tongue, *sele* for *selle*, tripod seat, *tripode æneo*, such as the priestess of Apollo or Pythia sat on to deliver oracles.
† Latin, *prosperare*, to succeed, or realize an experience.
‡ *Qui* for *ce qui*.

Translation.

Gathered at night in study deep I sate,
Alone, upon the tripod stool of brass,
Exiguous flame came out of solitude,
Promise of magic that may be believed.

Being seated at night and wrapt in secret study, entirely alone, I placed myself on the brazen tripod of prophecy. A still small flame came forth of solitude, helping me to realize successfully what it will not prove vain to have believed.

The reader will here refer to the "Préface à mon fils," p. 48.

"L'entendement cree intellectuellement ne peut voir occulte-ment, sinon par la voix faicte au lymbe moyennant la exigue flame, en laquelle partie les causes futures se viendront à incliner."

This passage conveys in prose what the last and the following quatrain conveys in verse.

THE MAGICAL CALL BY WATER. [I. 53.]

Century I.—Quatrain I.

La verge * en main mise au milieu de BRANCHES,
De l'Once il mouille et le limbe,† et le pied :
Un peur et voix fremissent par ‡ les manches ;
Splendeur divine, Le Divin près s' assied.

Translation.

The rod in hand set in the midst of the Branches,
He moistens with water both the fringe and foot ;
Fear and a voice make me quake in my sleeves ;
Splendour divine, the God is seated near.

To make this entirely clear is almost impossible.

* Latin, *virga*, branch or wand.
† Latin, *limbus*, hem, border, fringe.
‡ Latin, *per*, in, or through.

But what we *can* get at is very curious, showing as it does, if nothing else, that the borderland of the unseen world was actually contiguous with that of the world of Nostradamus. They even overlapped, in his estimation, so as to form an intermediate neutral territory like the marches in the North, where the inhabitants of each district could meet and communicate. We are positive that this is all illusive, superstitious, demoniacal. It may be so. But one effect it undeniably produces. It unites man more to the universe, and less to the world ; it makes death less strange and less cold, and furnishes to the soul, and the things of the soul, more nutriment than it can extract from modern life and culture.

The general meaning seems to be that he sat with a wand, branch, or divining-rod of laurel, probably forked like the winchel rod of the water-finders, one fork being held in each hand. This in some way had power to evoke his Genius (or *génie familier*, as Le Pelletier styles it). When he appeared, he moistened in the brazier that held water, himself, the fringe of his robe (*limbe*), and his foot. The rod, held as I have suggested, then becoming electrical, caused fear with the sound of a voice and a shuddering up to the elbows. Then shone forth the fatidical splendour of a divine light, and the Deity is present, seated near to him.

M. le Pelletier tells us that there was a pagan rite of the god Branchus that corresponded with this fatidical ceremony practised by Nostradamus. He even suggests that this very Branchus might have been the familiar spirit of our prophet. It must be admitted that in the *texte-type*, in the words "*au milieu de* BRANCHES," *Branches* is printed in capital letters, so that the probable reason for that peculiarity is that the God *Branchus*, as well as the *branches d'un laurier*, is shadowed forth. But to suppose that a pagan deity could ever be either the familiar or the guardian angel of a son of the Church of Rome makes such a Renaissance-jumble of the two religions that I think we had better not meddle with it.

As to the assertion that there was a pagan rite of Branchus, I doubt it much; and, if there were, certain it is that Nostradamus speaks here far too covertly for us to assume from his writing that he was discharging any rite special to Branchus. He seems to be following out the usual magical forms employed for establishing vaticinatory connection with the other world, or setting up the counter analogy between mind and spirit, according to that beautiful esoteric verse in Ecclesiasticus (xlvii. 24), "All things are double, one against another; He hath made nothing imperfect." Were such things never to interlink, men might well say, as they do now in the wisdom of science, that spirit and intellect are not doubles, and that no knowledge can be reached save by physical experiment. In this case there will be a particular link missing if science be right. The sage, *Estant assis de nuict secret estude*, will earnestly desire such assumption may prove to be erroneous. He will readily formulate with St. Paul that the invisible things from creation may be known from the visible; but also that the visible things can never be understood but by the invisible. Recollect that the visible is not visible to the visible, but to the invisible alone. The eye is the machine of sight, but not sight ; and who has seen the eye of the eye ?

The Greek myth about Branchus, so far as I can see, is this, with sundry forms and variations. He was a youth of Miletus. The reputed son of Smicrus (*Lempriere*), or Macareus Varro says, but begotten by Apollo. The mother dreamed that the sun entered her mouth, and, passing through her, the child at birth was named *Branchus*, or βρόγχος, the throat. Afterwards he kissed Apollo in the woods, and became endowed with the gift of prophecy. He had a temple at Didyma, which Pausanias calls the Temple of Apollo ; but Varro goes on to say that after the kiss of the god he prophesied, but quickly after disappeared, when a grand temple was jointly dedicated to him and to Apollo,—*Philesius*, from φιλεῖν, to kiss. His oracles at Didyma were inferior to none but Delphi. The name Didymean, *double* or *twain*, was from the double light of the sun and its reflection in the moonlight. Sun-touched and moon-struck madness and inspiration may in Branchus be said to meet, as out of one throat come things good and evil. The name Didymean was changed to Branchidæ. Strabo (Book xiv.) relates that the priests of this grand temple betrayed its treasures to Xerxes, and accompanied him in his retreat to escape the punishment of their sacrilege. They had settled near to Sogdiana, when Alexander arrived there (Strabo, Book xi.) ; he destroyed them and their city. This Byronical madman, who could see no iniquity in the slaughter of thousands to gratify the lust of a crack-brained ambition, thought to promote morals by slaughtering the descendants of traitors, they, the descendants, being innocent of everything except being born. The Milesians had long ago rebuilt the temple of Branchus on such a scale that in magnitude it surpassed all others in Greece. It was, in fact, too big to be roofed in, being four or five stadia in compass. Those who wish to see more can consult Suidas, s. v., βραγχίδαι.

The gloss of M. le Pelletier on the quatrain is as follows : that Nostradamus, wand in hand, touches the branches of the tripod, like the priests of Branchus (this I have tried to expunge), and invokes his familiar spirit, which appears to him in the vapour floating above a basin of water, which he had consecrated beforehand according to prescribed magical rites, and in which he dips the fringe of his garment, and his feet. An involuntary shivering (*peur*) agitates his hand when about to write from the dictation (*voix*) of the spirit. The fatidical light shines, and the angel is seated at his side Le Pelletier takes occasion here to remark that mediums at this day write under a spirit of dictation, to which they simply lend their arm as an instrument.

Garencières' interpretation is that of most of the old commentators, even down to the time of M. Bareste, 1840. The rod is a pen, in the middle of the branches means his fingers, the water is the ink, and wetting limb and foot is covering the paper all but the four margins. It is hardly unfair to say that this is both nonsensical and ignorant, although not devoid of ingenuity. I think it will fit the circum-

stances far better to take it, as I have done, that the
wand was a forked laurel branch that dipped forcibly,
like the winchel rod, when Nostradamus held it over
the water, that it strained, as the hazel-rod does,
almost to breaking ; and that at this invitation it is to
be supposed that the spirit appears.   The incantation
being completed and successful, the operator must be
supposed to set aside the winchel, and assume the pen,
quaking with a solemn sense of the spiritual presence.
This fear was, Garencières says, to prevent the puffing
up of pride, as we read in Daniel, John, and the 4th
of Esdras.

Readers who take no interest in this, and are consequently weary by this time of the length we have
run into in the investigation, will leap over what
follows to get to the next quatrain.

M. le Pelletier refers to Ficinus' translation of
Jamblicus' " De Mysteriis Ægyptiorum," 1607.   He
gives the Latin and French.   I will merely introduce
here the English translation, as the book is of easy
reference to those who wish to examine further for
themselves the sources which Nostradamus had consulted, and from which he drew his summary exposition.

" The sibyl at Delphi received the god in two forms,—either
by a subtle and fiery spirit, which burst forth upon any one
through the crevice of some cavern, or else sitting on a brazen
seat of four or three feet in the inner shrine, dedicated to the god,
and where she was exposed on two sides to the divine influx,
whence she was irradiate with a divine light " (p. 66).

" Now, the prophetess of Branchus either sits upon a pillar,
or holds in her hand a rod bestowed by some deity, or moistens
her feet or the hem of her garment with water, or inhales the
vapour of water, and by these means is filled with divine illumi-

nation, and, having obtained the deity, she prophesies. By these practices she adapts herself to the god, whom she receives from without " (p. 67).

" Porphyrius says that the art [or magic] is not to be despised which, out of certain vapours due to fire under favourable stellar influences, forms the images of gods spontaneously appearing in the air, in a certain degree like the gods themselves, and possessing a very similar efficacy " (p. 91).

" For amongst the demons there is one who is chief, and who exercises influence at the moment of birth, and apportions to each his demon (or familiar). After this there is present to each one his own guardian, that develops a *cultus* congruous to his nature, and teaches him both his name and the most suitable form of invocation (to bring him when required), and this method is most congenial to the demons " (p. 171).

These forms of Jamblicus are analogous to those employed by Nostradamus ; but there the person prophesying wets the feet and fingers, whilst according to our version of the quatrains it is the demon or spirit applies them to himself : *Le Divin près s'assied.* In Jamblicus the one who prophesies becomes possessed by entry of the spirit. Nostradamus describes an external and visible presence which corresponds to Porphyrius' account of *deorum idola in aere.*

CORPOREAL DEMONS. [1. 59.]

Century I.—Quatrain 42.

La dix Calendes d'Avril de faict gotique
Resuscité encor par gens malins :
Le feu estainct, assemblée diabolique
Cherchant les os du Damant et Pselin.*

Translation.

The 10th of the Calends of April Gothic computation have been again put in practice by sorcerers (*gens malins*). The

* Ex Michaele Psello, *de Dæmonibus.* Works of Marsilius Ficinus, ii. 884, ed. 1641, folio.

lights put out, the diabolic assembly searching for the Demon [*Damant* for *Démon*] treated of by Michael Psellus.

The *texte-type* is most corrupt in this quatrain ; for *Damant et Pselin* read *Démon e or ex Pselin*, the demon as treated of by Psellus.

The scholium of M. le Pelletier on this is— The magical incantations, which were successful formerly when wrought on the night of Good Friday, were reintroduced into practice by sorcerers of skill on the 10th Calend of April according to the ancient computation (*de faict gotique*). In a note added he professes that the 10th Calend Old Style would be the last day of March by the Gregorian, and he thinks it probable, that Nostradamus here designates some particular year, when Good Friday fell on the 31st of March. Garencières upon this notes that it falls on the 23rd of March, called Gothic, because adhered to by the northern nations long after the Gregorian had been adopted at Rome. I do not see how the 10th Calend could ever fall on the 31st, nor indeed what the 31st has to do with the matter. Those who are more familiar with such calculations may perhaps explain. Like the witches' sabbath, these diabolic meetings were accompanied by the lewdest rites, as will at once be seen by the following passage from Psellus, which I leave untranslated. It is from the Latin translation of Psellus by Marsilius Ficinus, and will be found in his collected works (ii. 884) in folio ed. 1641.

"Euchetæ et gnosci, ut dæmonia toto concipiant pectore, nefanda sacrificia perpetrant. Conveniunt die quo passus est

Salvator,* vespere, statutum in locum, unà cum puellis sibi notis, et post quædam sacra extinctis luminibus,† mistim coëunt, sive cum sorore, sive cum filiâ, sive cum quâlibet " (*Psellus* as above, p. 884).

" There is a further kind of vaticination by a basin, by means of which rustics frequently predict. Just as there is a mode of predicting by means of the air and the leaves of trees, so there is a kind of predictive power in the basin, known and practised by the Assyrians, which has a great similarity to this incarnation or coupling of demons with matter. Thus those about to prophesy take a basin full of water, which attracts the spirits moving stealthily in the depths (*dæmonibus congruentem in profunda repentibus.*) Le Pelletier translates this, *approprié à l'usage des démons cachés au fond des eaux*). The basin then, full of water, seems in sort to breathe (or move) as with sounds (*s'il allait émettre des sons*) ; it seems to me that the water was agitated with circular ripples, as from some sound emitted below. Now, this water diffused through the basin differs but little in kind from water out of the basin, but yet it much excels it from a virtue imparted to it by the charms [that have been droned over it], and which have rendered it more apt to receive the spirit of prophecy. For this description of spirit is tetchy and terrene, and much under the influence of composite spells. When the water begins to lend itself as the vehicle of sound, he [the spirit] also presently gives out a thin reedy note [of satisfaction], but devoid of meaning ; and close upon that, whilst the water is undulating, certain weak and peeping sounds whisper forth predictions of the future. A spirit of this kind is vagrant everywhere, for he is endowed with the solar pass [so that our terrestrial atmosphere lies everywhere open to him], and that order of spirits, in the work appointed to it, speaks at all times with a subdued voice, that by its indistinct obscurity it may be less easy to seize the falsehoods that it utters " (Psellus as above, p. 885).

* This refers to some Good Friday evening on the 10th Calend of April Old Style, as set forth in the first line of this quatrain.

† This is exhibited in the third line of the quatrain : *Le feu estainct, assemblée diabolique.*

From the mode in which Psellus describes the matter in hand, it is very perceptible that he was no great conjuror, and was merely speaking upon hearsay and report. If lies were the business of the spirit, he would be no prophet. Again, if he wished to circulate lies, he must still make things clear enough to his votaries for them to circulate them and work mischief thereby. Are we to suppose that, like an abandoned human being, he had some sense of shame left still, and, like Lord John Russell, would only tell as few lies as possible? Psellus's demon is so foolish that he would soon have been without any one to consult his shrine. He could not have given a reason for his own conduct, in the past or present, and was the last being that any one would resort to to anticipate intelligence of the future. Still the procedure might have been somewhat as Psellus describes it, although the reasons could not.

An historian of the fourth century, and a man of veracity, Marcellinus has given us curious details of how prophetical tripods were considered by the Romans in his day. It comes out quite naturally in the judicial proofs investigating a conspiracy against the life of Valens the Emperor; what we should call a state trial. The conspirators were put to the torture, and as an item in the indictment the figure of a little table becomes prominent, as to which the accused were questioned by the judges. At last one of them, Hillarius, broken by pain, revealed the secret in these words:

"Honoured judges, we constructed this unfortunate little table that you see here after the fashion of the tripod [or, more strictly, the cauldron *] at Delphi, with dark incantations, out of branches of laurel ; and with imprecations of secret song, and numerous ceremonies repeated over daily, we consecrated it by magic rites, till at last we put it in motion. When it reached this capacity of movement, as often as we wished to interrogate it by secret inquiry, we proceeded thus.

" It was placed in the middle of a room (*in medio domûs*) purified throughout by Arabian perfumes ; a round dish was simply laid upon it, formed of a composite material of many metals. On the phlange of its outer round were skilfully engraved the scriptile forms of the alphabet separated into as many exactly measured spaces. Over this basin (or dish) a man stood clothed in linen garments and shod with linen socks, his head bound round with a turban-like tuft of hair, and bearing a rod of vervain, the prospering plant. After we had favourably conciliated the deity, who is the giver of all presage, with duly formulated charms and ceremonial knowledge, he communicated a gentle movement to a ring that hung suspended over the basin. . . . This was tied up by an exceedingly fine Carpathian thread, which had been initiated with mystical observances. This ring, moving by little leaps or jumps, so as to alight upon the distinct intervals with the separate letters inscribed, each in its compartment to itself, gives out in heroic verse answers suitable to the inquiries made, comprehended perfectly in number and measure ; such as are called Pythic, or those delivered by the oracles of the Branchidæ.

" To us inquiring who should succeed to the present empire, because it had been already mentioned that it would be one entirely suitable [to our aim and purpose], the leaping ring had glanced upon the two syllables THEO. With the last addition of a letter [that is, D], a man present exclaimed, ' THEODORUM,' the fatal necessity of the portent indicating as much. Nothing further was sought upon this head ; for it was agreed amongst us that this was the individual we wanted " (*Ammianus Marcellinus*, Rerum Gestarum, xxix. 1).

In this case the ambiguity of the oracle is due to the precipitance of the inquirers. The oracle was

---

* Æneid, iii. 92 and vi. 347.

true as far as they allowed it to proceed, but had they waited to spell it out they would have learned that the name was not THEOD*orus*, but THEOD*osius* the Great, who was to be the successor to Valens.

This is an authentic passage of high interest. It shows considerable analogy with the table-turning of the moderns ; it also gives insight into singular and elaborate processes of divination by magic as being frequently practised at Rome in the fourth century. Clearly the Pagans had no notion in that century that oracles had at all finally ceased on a Good Friday in the first century, or that Pan, the god of rumour, was dead. The sun still shone to them as the Apollo of prophecy, and they still sought presage of a spirit who was made free of the solar order (*qui solarem ordinem est sortitus*).

HISTORICAL FRAGMENTS.

I SHALL now give a few detached historical fragments that relate to France, commencing with the
Peace of Cateau-Cambresis, 1559, and running down
to the death of Louis XV., 1774, in chronological order,
just as M. le Pelletier has found the counterpart to
lie embedded in the quatrains of Nostradamus, in a
fashion seemingly interpretable to him. This, for
any but French readers, will probably be sufficient to
indicate the style and value of the presages enveloped
in the strange and fatidical diction of the quatrains.
I doubt not but that, by original research instituted
and by careful re-reading of the text throughout, a
good many more of the mysterious stanzas might be
unravelled and elucidated ; also by collation of all that
has been written by commentators on our author, a
good deal of light might be thrown upon what they
have done, even where their own interpretation has
fallen short of clearness. All that my book purposes
to accomplish is,—at least for England,—to establish,
without doubt, and at once, for all future time, that
Nostradamus is no impostor, but, when rightly understood and unlocked, a very wonderful anticipator of
events to happen hereafter ; and, farther than this,
that his works are, to all intents and purposes, the

most startling oracles ever put on paper by mortal man not professing divine inspiration. From immemorial time instances of human prescience have occasionally been manifested. The whole human race has an ardent and ingrain desire to search into and anticipate futurity. Very few individuals, however, have from time to time been able to gratify and keep alive their passion in this respect. But no one has done so in a degree that at all sets him on a par with Nostradamus in the felicitous and reiterated coruscations whereby he has anticipated the more prominent points and epochs of time Future ; and sometimes in minuteness he even mentions by name some individual who emerges though it be but for an instant from the general obscurity of his life.

THE PEACE OF CATEAU-CAMBRESIS (APRIL 3, 1559). [I. 71.]

Century IX.—Quatrain 52.

La paix s'approche d'un costé, et la guerre
Oncques * ne fut la poursuitte si grande :
Plaindre hômes, femmes, sang innocent par terre,
Et ce sera de France a † toute bande.

Translation.

Peace approaches on one side, and [as to] war
Never was the pursuit of it so great :
Men and women [have cause] to weep innocent blood on earth ;
All through France it shall be from end to end.

The peace was that concluded with Spain at Cateau-Cambresis, whilst the war, carried on with such hot pursuit, was the civil conflict that raged

---

* Old word for *jamais*, never.   † Latin, *a*, by.

between Romanist and Calvinist. This it was made men and women lament the blood spilt upon the earth in all parts of France, from north to south.

DEATH OF HENRI II. (JULY 10, 1559). [1. 72.]

Century I.—Quatrain 35.

Le lyon jeune le vieux surmontera
En champ bellique par singulier duelle :
Dans cage d'or * les yeux lui crevera,
Deux classes † une,‡ puis mourir, mort cruelle.

Translation.

The young lion shall overcome the old
On the field of war in single combat [duelle] ;
He will pierce his eyes in a cage of gold.
This is the first of two loppings, then he dies a cruel death.

Montgomery, who at the moment of the narrative bore the name of Captain Coryes (Garencières, p. 25), afterwards became Earl of Montgomery, overthrew Henri II. (*le vieux lion*) in the tournay-lists or duel, and pierced him above the eye through the gilt visor of his helmet. This is the first of the two blows that will destroy the dynastic tree of the house of Valois. Henri II., wounded mortally, shall be the first to die a violent death ; whilst his son, Henri III., will be the second, who fell by the hand of Jacques Clément.

* Bouys [*Oracles*, p. 103] says that the King alone had the right to a visor of pure gold. I believe this to be pure nonsense. It would be little stronger than lead. It merely means a gilt casque, and I think some of the accounts say so in as many words. If Bouys were right, the King courted death.

† Greek, κλάσις, breaking or lopping.

‡ Latin, *una*, the one or first.

August 1. 1589.

This is a very celebrated quatrain. It is found in the earliest edition of the quatrains published at Lyons in 1555, containing merely 300 quatrains. It lifted Nostradamus into celebrity at once. He had applied it to Henri II. several years before it happened, and had even announced it as a prediction to the King himself. He was well known to Henri II., to whom he dedicated the last three Centuries, in a long and curious epistle, which we have already given in full. The King seems to have had infinite confidence in Nostradamus, for he let him draw the royal horoscope, as well as that of his two children, in 1556.

The story of this is curious, as given by Guynaud in his "Concordance des Prophéties de Nostradamus," 1712,* pp. 86–91. Henri II., it would seem, proclaimed a tournament in the Rue St. Antoine, the site of the Bastille, then in the country, for July 1, 1559, in honour of the marriage of his daughter Elizabeth of France with Philip II. of Spain. He listed himself as one against all comers. The joust being nearly over and the sun setting, the Duc de Savoie begged him to quit the running, as his side was already victorious ; but the King wanted to break another lance over it, and commanded the young Comte de Montgommeri, captain of his Scotch Guard, to run a tilt in conclusion. He excused himself, but the King insisted and grew angry. Of course the young man then obeyed, put spurs to his horse, and struck the King upon the throat, below the vizor. His lance shivered, and the butt raising

---

* See also Brantôme, *Vie des hommes illustres de son temps.*

the vizor, a splinter wounded the King above the right eye, cutting several of the veins of the *pia mater.* The King swooned. He lived on, however, for ten days in terrible agony, as foretold in the prophecy, *Deux classes une, puis mourir, mort cruelle.* Nostradamus styles both of them lions, as they both fought under that device. The King wore a gilt helmet, so that the *cage d'or* was literally fulfilled.

The strange part is that another astrologer, named Luc Gauric, had once been visited by the King in company with two other gentlemen, to whom he feigned to give precedence ; but the astrologer, perhaps knowing him, insisted on addressing him first, and told him he would die in a duel. He also prophesied a violent death to the King's companions, and managed to displease the whole trio. The King said of this, "We are making peace now with the King of Spain, so it is not very likely that I shall challenge him, and as a king I could in no other way be challenged, whatever may be the fate of the other gentlemen." Guynaud quotes this story from the Princesse de Clèves, who, in the second volume of her writings, represents the Court as discussing the credibility of astrologers, the prevalent opinion apparently being rather strong against them. Still, we know that Henri II. greatly honoured Nostradamus. Prophetic warning is evidently futile, for the King had two separate warnings and heeded neither.

PRINCESSE DE CLÈVES. [II. 145.]

Quelques jours après, le Roy étoit chez la Reine à l'heur du Cercle ; l'on parla des Horoscopes et des prédictions. Les opinions étaient partagées sur la croyance que l'on y devoit donner. La Reine y ajoûtait beaucoup de foi ; elle soûtint qu'après tant de choses qui avaient été prédites, et que l'on avait vu arriver, on ne pouvait douter qu'il n'eut quelque certitude dans cette science. D'autres soûtenaient, que parmi ce nombre infini de prédictions, le peu qui se trouvaient veritables, faisait bien voir que se n'etait qu'un effet du hazard.

" J'ai eu autrefois beaucoup de curiosité pour l'avenir," dit le Roy ; " mais on m'a dit tant de choses fausses et si peu vraissemblables que je suis demuré convaincu que l'on ne peut rien savoir de véritable. Il y a quelques années qu'il devint ici un homme d'une grande reputation dans l'Astrologie. Tout le monde l'alla voir, j'y allai comme les autres, mais sans lui dire qui j'étais, et je menai Monsieur de Guise et Descars, je les fit passer le premier. L'Astrologue neanmoins s'addressa d'abord à moi, comme s'il m'eut jugé le maitre des autres : Peut-être qu'il me connaissait ; cependant il me dit une chose qui ne me convenait pas, s'il m'eut connu. Il me predit que je serai tué en duel. Il dit ensuite à Monsieur de Guise, qu'il serait tué par derrière, et à Descars, qu'il aurait la tête cassée d'un coup de pied de cheval. Monsieur de Guise s'offensa quasi de cette prédiction, comme si l'on eut accusé de devoir fuir. Descars ne fut guerre satisfait de trouver qu'il devait finir par un accident si malheureux. Enfin nous sortimes tous très malcontents de l'astrologue. Je ne scais ce qui arrivera à Monsieur de Guise et à Descars, mais il n'y a guerre d'apparence que je sois tué en duel. Nous venons de faire la paix le Roy d'Espagne et moi, quand nous ne l'aurions pas faite, je doute que nous nous battions, et que je le fisse appeller comme le Roy mon père fit rappeller Charles Quint."

The story, as told by the Princesse de Clèves, is fuller than I have given it, but does not correspond at all with the version given to Lord Bacon when in France, as told to him by Dr. Penn, who said (Bacon's " Essay on Prophecies ") that the queen-mother, Catherine de Medici, was given to curious arts, and caused the King's nativity to be cast under a false name. The astrologer adjudged that he should be killed in a duel. The queen laughed, supposing her husband to be above challenges to duel ; " but he was slain upon a course at tilt, the splinters of the staff of Montgomery going in at his beaver." History, in events large or small, hath so many variants that any man, whose view of things is a little sinister, may well be allowed to say all history is a variant of truth, and all that is sure in it is that it cannot be relied upon at all. In this case the astrologers were right, spite of the odds against them.

ARREST OF MONTGOMERY (MAY 27, 1574). [I. 73.]

Century III.—Quatrain 30.

Celuy qu'en * luitte † et fer au faict bellique
Aura porté ‡ plus grand qui luy le prix,
De nuict au lict six luy feront la pique,
Nud, sans harnois, subit § sera surprins.||

Translation.

To him who in strife and armour in the warlike field
Shall have carried away the prize from one greater than himself,
By night in bed six men will stab him ;
Unprotected he will be surprised naked and unarmed.

This means that Montgomery, who in joust (*au faict bellique,—bellique*, we are told, means an engagement on horseback) with lance in hand will have carried away the prize from Henri II. (*plus grand que luy*) will be suddenly surprised in bed at night, naked and unarmed, by six men, who will deliver him into the vengeful hands of Catherine de Medici.

---

* *Qu'en*, for *qui en*.   † Romance, for *lutte*.
‡ *Porté*, pour *remporté*.   § Latin, *subito*, suddenly.
|| Romance, *surprins* for surpris.

Some say the dying King gave him free pardon ; others report that he fled to England to save himself : but at any rate he came to England, and there embraced Protestantism. When he returned to France, he placed himself at the head of the revolted Huguenots in Normandy, and was besieged in Domfront by the Marshal de Matignon and a large force, to which he was obliged to surrender. The terms of the surrender guaranteed his life, but by express command of Catherine he was arrested in his own castle of Domfront on the night of May 27, 1574, by six gentlemen of the royal army, and carried to the Château of Caen, thence to the Conciergerie at Paris, and there immured, where the great tower still goes by his name.

THE REGENCY OF CATHERINE DE MEDICI (1559–1574). [1. 74.]

Century VI.—Quatrain 63.

La Dame seule au regne demeurée,
D'unic esteint premier au lict d'honneur ;
Sept ans sera de douleur esplorée,
Puis longue vie au regne par grand heur.

Translation.

The lady shall remain to rule alone,
Her unique spouse dead, who was first in the field of honour.
She will weep for grief through seven long years,
And gifted with long life will reign long.

Catherine de Medici did not put off her weeds till August 1, 1566, seven years and a few days from the death of the King in July, 1559, on her return from a progress with her son Charles IX., in the course of which she had visited all the mutinous cities throughout

the kingdom, with a view to satisfy them. She survived till the year 1589, and practically retained the
whole power during the reigns of her two eldest sons,
François II. and Charles IX., but she entirely lost it
on the succession of Henri III.

The quatrain applies to no one so well as to
Catherine de Medici ; and, if it be allowed to be
realized as to her person, there is no denying the
singular exactitude of the prophecy. We have no
evidence that the Queen applied the quatrain to
herself, or that her contemporaries bore it in mind ;
but the second line is remarkable as assuming with
reposeful confidence the previous death of the King
as predicted. The third line is a startling example
of the precision with which our prophet can mark
out the duration of a period : seven years the Queen
is to wear mourning, and she does so all the time she
is travelling. The sceptical will say she did it to
fulfil the prophecy ; but it looks rather as if that
had fallen quite out of remembrance, and as if it was
due much more to policy, and for the purpose of
creating sympathy, during her state tour, than to
motives either of superstition or any singular attach-
ment to her deceased husband. The quatrain is most
unobtrusively worded, and yet so confidently assured
and searching, that it seems to me, as if perfectly
unbiassed and disinterested observers might take it
as a kind of moral voucher for the simple integrity
of its author. I merely draw attention to it so far,
and every reader will form his own judgment upon
the point. I hold myself aloof from theory ; but this
is how the particular fact we are upon impresses my

mind, and probably it may affect many others in the same way.

EXTINCTION DES VALOIS (1559–1589). [I. 77]

Presage 40.

De maison sept par mort mortelle suite ;
Gresle, tempeste, pestilent mal, fureurs :
Roi d'Orient, d'Occident tous en fuite,
Subjuguera ses jadis conquereurs.

Translation.

The death of the house of seven by a suite of deaths,
Hail, tempest, pestilent evil, fury.
A king of the East will put all the West to flight,
And will subdue his at-one-time conquerors.

The house of Valois consisted of the seven children of Henri II. By the death of the fourth son, Henri III., in 1589, the whole of the seven were dead except Marguerite, who married Henri IV., so that the family may well be said to have died out by a suite of deaths (*mortelle suite*). Heresy was rampant (*pestilent mal*) and civil war. Soliman II., called the Magnificent, threatened all Christendom, and recovered all the Holy Places that the Crusaders had wrested from his predecessors.

CIVIL WAR (1575, 1576). [I. 78.]

Century VI.—Quatrain 11.

Des septs rameaux à trois seront reduicts,
Les plus aisnés seront surprins * par mort,
Fratricider les deux seront seduicts,
Les conjurés en dormans seront morts.

* Romance, *surprins = surpris.*

Translation.

The seven branches when they shall be reduced to three,
And the four eldest shall have been surprised by death,
The two (males) shall entertain fratricidal aims,
And the conspirators sleeping shall be reduced to death.

This means that, when the seven are become but three (*i.e.* the three youngest), Henri III. and the Duc d'Alençon will enter upon a fratricidal war. In 1575 Alençon escaped from the Court, where he was under surveillance, and put himself at the head of the Malcontents, who were in alliance with the Huguenots. He was successful, and forced the edict of pacification, May 14, 1576, upon his brother the King. Daniel, in his "History of France" under Henri III., shows that they mutually sought each other's death by dagger and poison. The Guise (*les conjurés*) and the Leaguers will come by their deaths from indulging in a false security.

THE MURDER OF HENRI III. (1589). [I. 79.]

Century V.—Quatrain 67.

Quand chef Perouse n'osera sa tunique,
Sans au couvert tout nud s'expolier.*
Seront prins † sept, faict aristocratique !
Le père et fils morts par poincte au colier.

Translation.

When the chief of Perouse dare not risk casting off his tunic
Without stripping himself entirely naked,
The last of the seven taken, what an event in the upper circles !
Father and son killed by a stab in the throat.

When Sixtus V. (*chef de Perouse*) will not dare

---

* Latin, *exspoliare*, totally despoiled. † Romance, for *pris*.

to excommunicate Henri III., having already lost England in 1534, and feeling he must not be entirely stripped by a further Gallican schism, will be rid of the posterity of Henri II. (*seront prins sept*) by a tremendous event in aristocratic circles. Father and son will both perish by a thrust in the throat.

DEATH OF THE GUISE (DECEMBER 23, 24, 1588). [I. 80.]

Century IV.—Quatrain 60.

Les sept enfans en hostaine * laissés ;
Le tiers † viendra son enfant trucider ‡ ;
Deux par son fils seront d'estoc percés ;
Gennes Florence les viendra enconder. §

Translation.

Seven children will be left in his house ;
The *tiers état* will come to murder his child ;
Two will have been pierced by the sword of his son ;
Genoa and Florence will come to disorder them.

This is, Henri II. at his death will leave seven children in his house. The *Conseil des Seize* (*le tiers*) will incite Jacques Clément to go to St. Cloud to assassinate Henri III., because he has caused Henri de Guise and the Cardinal to be slain by sword thrusts. Then Charles Emmanuel I., Duke of Savoy (*le Génois*), and Alexander Farnese, Duke of Parma (*le Florentin*), General of Philip II., will come to make war on Henri IV., who will be compelled by Farnese to raise the siege of Paris (1590) and Rouen (1592) with precipitation.

* Romance, *hostaige*, maison, house, palace.
† Romance, *tiers*, third.
‡ Latin, *trucidare*, cut the throat.
§ Latin, *inconditus*, dispersed.

Parma was, originally, of Etruscan foundation (Bouillet, " Dictionnaire d'Histoire " *s.v.* Parme), and in this respect rises above Florence, the capital of Modern Tuscany. This justifies Nostradamus in designating the Duke of Parma as *Florence.* Genoa, by synecdoche, may stand for Savoy, as being its more commercial emporium.

BURIAL AT ST. DENIS OF THE LAST OF THE VALOIS (1589-1610). [I. 82.]

Century I.—Quatrain 20.

Serpens * transmis en la cage de fer
Où les enfans septains du Roy sont pris,
Les vieux et peres sortiront bas † de l'enfer, ‡
Ains mourii voii de fiulet mort et crls.

Translation.

The coffin being lowered behind the grille of iron,
Where the seven children of the King are buried,
The ancestors of the Valois will rise from the depths of the tomb,
And cry out to see their withered fruit thus die.

Henri III. was deposited, provisionally, in 1589, at Compiègne, in the Abbey of St. Corneille ; and it was only in 1610 that his body was conveyed to the vaults of St. Denis, at the same time with the bodies of Henri IV. and Catherine de Medici. This quatrain is not very remarkable, but the interpretation hangs pretty well together. It has perhaps this value, that it shows us one incident in a vast procession of historical dissolving views that seem to have passed before the eye of Nostradamus, and one would say in

---

* Greek, σάρπος, wooden case, coffin.
† *Sortiront bas*, for *d'en bas.*
‡ Latin, *infernus*, subterranean.

chronological sequence, which he must himself have broken up purposely afterwards, fearing that the chronological clue would often render the prophecy too open to interpretation to be good for either his own safety or the public advantage.

MARRIAGE OF FRANÇOIS II. AND MARY STUART (APRIL 24, 1558). [I. 84.]

Century X.—Quatrain 39.

Premier fils vefve * malheureux mariage
Sans nuls enfants, deux Isles en discord,
Avant dix-huict incompetant âge. †
De l'autre près ‡ plus bas sera l'accord.

Translation.

The eldest son leaves, with his wretched marriage,
Widow, no children, and two isles in strife,
And dies before eighteen, incompetent of age.
The younger son will marry earlier still.‖

The matter seems to stand thus. François II., eldest son of Henri II., shall die and leave his wife, Mary Stuart, a widow without children, after an unhappy marriage that extends over less than two years, before he is eighteen, or of competent age. The particularity of this detail is wonderful, and far more like history than prophecy, except as to the brevity with which it is expressed. His enunciations

---

* Romance, *vefve*, veuve. The word is made here to apply to the wife, Mary Stuart, whom he leaves a widow without children. The grammatical effort is somewhat violent ; but *vef* or *veuf* is the masculine form, so there is very little choice given.

† In the quatrain this ought to be written *eage*, as it stands in the *texte-type*, or the line will not scan.

‡ *Près*, for après.

‖ This is how M. le Pelletier renders the last line.

amount to hints only, but they are so pregnant that, when you fill in the indispensably connected particulars, the statement reads like history. So here the instant you recognize that François II. is the subject of the lines, you refer to history for his birth and death, January 19, 1543, December 15, 1560—that is, 17 years, 10 months, and 15 days, or a month and 15 days short of 18 years. *Avant dix-huict* is Nostradamus's phrase. Again, his death establishes discord between Elizabeth of England and Mary of Scotland (*deux Isles en discord*). Charles IX., his younger brother, was affianced to Elizabeth of Austria when still younger, at eleven years of age, though he did not marry till twenty. This is how M. le Pelletier harmonizes the line. But, as affiancing is not marriage, this cannot have any affinity at all with marrying at an incompetent age. I should propose to read the line thus. Of the younger one afterwards, and lower down, will the concordance, account, or accord be given ; and accordingly we shall have now to enter upon several stanzas that relate to Charles IX.

CHARLES IX. (*Le roi farouche*). (1560–1574). [1. 86.]'

Century III.—Quatrain 66.

Le grand Baillif d'Orleans mis à mort
Sera par un de sang vindicatif :
De mort mérité ne mourra ni par sort ;
Des pieds et mains mal le faisoit captif.

Translation.

The great Bailiff of Orleans shall be put to death
By one of vindictive blood :
Not undeserved death shall he die, nor by fate ;
For they will insecurely make him captive by feet and hands

Jérôme Groslot shall be arrested November 9, 1561, and condemned by the Inquisition to beheadal for delivering the city to the Calvinists.   But he will not suffer the death merited, nor undergo his fate ; his keepers being bribed, he shall escape.

DEFECTION OF ADMIRAL COLIGNY (1559–1567).   [I. 87.]

Century VI.—Quatrain 75.

Le grand pillot * par Roy sera mandé, †
Laisser la classe ‡ pour plus haut lieu atteindre :
Sept ans après sera contrebandé, §
Barbare armée viendra Venise craindre. ||

Translation.

He who shall have been appointed admiral by the king,
Shall leave the fleet to take a higher post ;
Seven years later, shall take the opposite side to the king ;
Venice shall dread an army of barbarians coming.

Gaspard de Coligny, made grand-admiral by Henri II., in 1552, shall quit the fleet in 1559, on the death of the King, and place himself at the head of the Calvinist party.   In 1562 he will be general of their forces, and in 1567—that is, seven years after withdrawal from the fleet, he will head the rebellion in the civil war.   At the same moment Venice will dread the armies of Selim II., that will wrest Cyprus from her in 1570.   The peace between the Catholics and Protestants was signed at St. Germain in this very year.   The Venetians, however, in this year

* Italian, *piloto*, pilot.
† Latin, *mandatus*, appointed to a charge.
‡ Latin, *classis*, fleet.
§ Romance, *contrebandé*, marching in a contrary band.
|| *Ordo* is, *Venise craindra une armée de barbares qui viendra.*

gained the naval victory of Lepanto over the Turks in 1570.

MURDER OF LOUIS DE BOURBON, PRINCE OF CONDE (MARCH 13, 1569). [I. 88.]

Century III.—Quatrain 41.

Bossu sera esleu par le conseil :
Plus hideux monstre en terre n'apperceu.
Le coup voulant crevera l'œil *
Le traistre au Roy pour fidelle receu.

Translation.

Crookback shall be elected by the council :
A more hideous monster never seen on earth.
An intentional shot pierces the eye of the traitor
Who had sworn to be faithful to the king.

Prince Louis of Condé, the Humpback, shall be elected general-in-chief by the council of notables of the Calvinists. Such a monster of wickedness was never seen on earth. Montesquiou killed him with a pistol-shot in the eye, who had twice escaped from his treasonous practices against the King. Here Nostradamus' forecast is miraculously clear, although it has baffled Guynaud to find its concordance with events. He here also exhibits his religious partisan-ship. A hunchback is always considered to be morally as well as physically deformed ; and, as Louis de Bourbon took the side of the Calvinists, he became at once to our prophet *le plus hideux monstre en terre.* Evidently, however, he was a grand fighting fellow, and spent his life in camps, if we go no further than Moreri for his history. He was condemned for a con-

---

* This line is a foot short. Garencières reads :
  Le coup volant luy crevera un œil.

spirator in 1560 to lose his head. But the sentence was never carried out, as King François II. died at the moment, and none was bold enough to see to it. When Charles IX. set him at liberty, the *Cour des Pairs* found out that he was innocent, and declared him so. He perished at the battle of Jarnac. He had his leg broken by the kick of a horse, and was seated at the foot of a bush when Montesquiou, captain of the Duke of Anjou's guards, saw him, and, for some old pique, coolly, but like the veriest coward, shot the wounded Condé in the eye with his pistol. The body was conveyed for burial to St. George of Vendôme, either by chance or insult, on the back of a she ass, at Jarnac; which led to one of those impromptu epitaphial epigrams that the French turn so prettily:

> L'an mil cinq cens soixante neuf,
> Entre Jarnac et Chateauneuf,
> Fut porté mort sur une ânesse
> Le grand ennemi de la Messe.
>
> (*v.* MORERI, *s.v. Louis de Bourbon.*)

ST. BARTHOLOMEW'S DAY (AUGUST 24, 1572). [I. 89.]

Century IV.—Quatrain 47.

> Le Noir * farouche, quand aura essayé
> Sa main sanguine par feu, fer, arcs tendus, †
> Trestous le peuple sera tant ‡ effrayé
> · Voir les plus grans par col et pieds pendus.

Translation.

> The savage king, when he shall have tried
> His blood-stained hand with fire, sword, and bows,
> All the people shall be terrified
> To see the great hung by the neck and feet.

---

* *Noir*, anagram of roi, cutting off *n*.
† *Arcs tendus*, arquebus.   ‡ Latin, *tantum*, much.

When Charles IX. shall exercise his sanguinary hand with fire, the sword, and the arquebus, the people will be horrified to see the great Calvinist lords strung up by the neck and feet. One of the savage amusements of Charles, in hunting, was to cut off at a single blow the heads of any asses or pigs he came across on the way. During the very massacre he placed himself at a window of the Louvre and took several shots with a long arquebus at the Huguenots who fled from the other side of the Seine in the Faubourg St. Germain. The body of Coligny was dragged by the populace, at the end of a rope, through all the mud of the kennels, and then hung up by one foot to the gibbet at Montfaucon. This 24th of August fell on a Sunday. The King himself died two years after, with some suspicion of poisoning. He is said to have been a man of high courage and of a lively, quick wit, possessing a good share of eloquence ; was given much to dissimulation ; and full of oaths, unreasonably violent, and without self-control. He turned a verse well, and loved hunting. His poems still remain, but I do not know they can ever command a single reader. In speaking of poets, he used to say they ought to be well fed, like good horses, but not satisfied, or they become lazy. The world in general prefers to starve them if they are first-rate, and enrich them if they are second-rate. We cannot expect people to reward what they cannot understand : though inevitable, we cannot but deplore the arrangement. With good abilities, Charles had so little judgment that his actions would always have been mischievous ; the best thing that could have happened was his death at twenty-four. He is said to have remarked, when dying, that he was glad to die young and have no children, for he had sadly learnt, in his own case, how miserable is the conduct of a prince who mounts the throne a child, and so governs through the ministry of others. This only shows a little recovery to sober reason, but none of the remorse that is attributed to him on his death-bed, as being the ostensible author of the blackest act that has ever disfigured Christianity or stained Europe. In perfidy and crime it cannot be surpassed, nor as the outcome of religious perversion. The crimes of an atheistic democracy, perpetrated two hundred years later on the same theatre precisely, have only been able to surpass it, in the carnal lusts exhibited, in the inhuman degradation of the body of man, and in the ubiquity of iniquity, when the whole people are thirsting to satiate their debased passions in sin. Nostradamus has elsewhere called Paris the City of the Sword. It is the wine-press of the earth, fat with the blood of man : Lutetia of mud and blood. Haussmann rebuilt it, but nothing can cleanse it. Their very guillotine is an instrument contrived to publicly gratify the populace in its tiger-taste for the reek of blood in the streets of the City of Blood. If you wish to see the disgrace of religion, read Sully's description of the endeavour of the ferocious priests on that day to have *his* blood. Look also on the medal of Gregory XIII.,* struck rejoicingly to commemorate

---

* The family name of Pope Gregory XIII. was Hugo Buon-Compagni. On May 13, 1572, he was made Pope. He assumed the name of Gregory out of respect to St. Gregory Nazianzen.

that awful crime. Bonanni shows it ; and, as a work of medallic art, the head of the Pope is of the very highest order of beauty and Italian grace. But, then, it commemorates the blood of sixty thousand victims, he says. Ranke (ii. 69) puts it at fifty thousand. Take this number, if you like ; it is enough to satisfy the successor to St. Peter, to whom the special mandate was addressed, " Feed my sheep,"—as other shepherds do for the butcher, is the Gregorian gloss. Tradesmen, however, have the decency to shut the shambles on the Sunday morning ; but the *servus servorum* is at home in *his* ministrations on the Dominical day. That Sunday in August is indeed

He caused the Church to encourage the murder of refractory kings ; he promoted the massacre of St. Bartholomew's Day, which Sir Paul Rycaut, the historian of the Popes, does not so much as mention in the life of Gregory. He only says towards the end that " he may be numbered amongst the good Popes." As Buon-Compagni was a good lawyer before he became a good Pope, he was pre-qualified for a virtuous career in any line of life. He re-confirmed the excommunication of Queen Elizabeth ; he rectified the Calendar which goes by his name,—the Gregorian. The Jesuits' College was finished by him at Rome, dedicated so oddly—

Religioni et bonis Artibus.

In his day Japan was, by Jesuit missionary effort, brought within the pale of the Church : on which a wit remarked that Japan varnish was introduced into Europe, and Christian varnish into Japan. He died at eighty-three, and to the last could almost mount on horseback without the help of his servants. His place of retirement, Rycaut says, was Frescati, about ten miles distant from Rome, where the Borghese Palace now is, and was then called *Monte Dragone*—a most fit name for the residence of the *Old Worm* of St. Bartholomew's massacre.— *V.* Paul Rycaut, " Lives of the Popes," ed. 1688, vol. ii. p. 163.

a Saints' rubric! For that day there is no need of a calendar. Time, till the world ruptures, can never forget it,—nor forgive.

Le noir farouche of this quatrain is, by Guynaud, p. 113, said to stand for Admiral Coligny, who is designated, according to him, very variously in the quatrains. The *noir farouche* alludes to his rough and forbidding exterior. *Le grand Pillot* (VI. 75) is another epithet; *le tiran* (Présage III.) another. The conclusion of the quatrain is admitted, both by Le Pelletier and Guynaud, to stand for Coligny. In the earlier portion, most will, I think, prefer to take *noir* as the anagram of *Roi*.

Guynaud gives a surprising account from the historians of Provence and France, of what happened to Coligny when he was at Angoulême in 1568. He set up a gibbet there, and on his own authority hanged upon it Michel Grêlet, Guardian of the Cordéliers, and a most zealous preacher against the heretics. In his dying speech on the scaffold, the latter said, "Admiral, you put me to death very unjustly. I am going to God now to give account to Him of my actions; but remember, you and all the people present here to-day, I predict that in a short time you will yourself be thrown from an upper window, and your body will be cut to pieces." The histories go on to say that an Italian cut off Coligny's head to send it to Cardinal de Lorraine at Rome, whilst other men cut off his hands and other parts of his body; also that at about six in the morning the mob found his body on a dunghill in a stable, dragged it to the Seine, and threw it in. It was again fished out, and hung by the foot to the gibbet of Montfaucon, where it became blackened in the smoke of the fires that were lighted below it. (Guynaud, "Concord. Nostra.," p. 113.)

Sixain 52. [I. 90.]

La grand' Cité qui n'a pain à demy
Encor un coup la Sainct Barthelemy
Engravera au profond de son ame:
Nismes, Rochelle, Geneve et Montpellier,
Castres, Lyon, Mars entrant au Belier,
S'entrebattront ; le tout pour une Dame.

Translation.

The great city that has bread at only half rations
Will have the further blow of Saint Bartholomew
Cut deep into its soul :
Nismes, Rochelle, Geneva, and Montpellier,
Castres, Lyons, with Mars entering the Ram,
Will fight one another ; and all for the Queen mother.

The great city is, of course, Paris, and *une Dame* is the Queen, Catherine de Medici. It has to be borne in mind that these sixains were not published till thirty-three years after the massacre of St. Bartholomew's. Naturally, the prediction loses all special authority in this case. It raises, however, a singular question : Why, if it was written after the event, it was not rendered more explicit, if those who published it had an interest in augmenting the fame of the prophet? It looks very much as if the testamentary duties were performed in perfect good faith, mechanically, and without even understanding the purport or meaning of the words.

Another passage relating to St. Bartholomew's massacre occurs in the text of 1605, and its authority is no greater than that of the sixain just quoted, as it was not published till after the event. It goes, however, to strengthen the remark I above made. Those who caused the work to be printed seem to have been perfectly unconscious of the meaning of the stanzas; they regarded the whole procedure as a mere form of respect to the memory of a celebrated relative. Their duty was clear to them, and they performed it; but the writings were to them perfectly unintelligible.

Presage III. (ii. 252) is dated as if written January, 1555, and for anything that I can see there is nothing whatever to make one doubt but that it was so. Having made this point as clear as I can, the reader will take it or reject it as he pleases.

> Le gros airain qui les heures ordonne,
> Sur le trespas du Tyran cassera : *
> Pleurs, plaintes et cris, eaux, glace pain ne dône
> V. S. C. † paix l'arme passera.

Translation.

> The brazen bell that rings the daily hours
> Will play full volley at the tyrant's death :
> Tears, cries, and groans ; the waters freeze up bread,
> With son of Charles the Fifth a peace is made.

The tyrant here is interpreted by Guynaud (p. 107) as Coligny, and he appends some interesting remarks from Favin's "Histoire de Navarre," touching St. Bartholomew's Day in Paris. He says they marked

---

* Will sound in full volley.

† These letters are interpreted by the old commentators and Guynaud (p. 107) as meaning the peace concluded with Philip II. of Spain : V., cinq, S., sucesseur, C., Charles—*i.e.*, Successor to Charles Quint.

the lodgings of the Huguenots that they might
know where to find them in the hurry, and it was
arranged that at the tocsin of the great bell at
the palace, as well as that of the church of St. Germain de l'Auxerrois, they were to lay violent hands
(*main-baisse*) on all the heretics. Two p.m. was
the hour appointed. The Catholics who went into
the street were to distinguish themselves by a white
cross upon their hats. The bodies of the slain were
for the most part thrown into the river. Mezerai
records that the queen-mother hastened the signal by
a full hour, and that it was, contrary to arrangement,
started by the bell of St. Germain de l'Auxerrois,
although that was immediately followed up by the
big bell of the palace.

Coligny was slain in bed, and flung out of window
in his shirt only. His face, being covered with blood,
the Duc de Guise coolly wiped it with his hand-
kerchief, to assure himself that it actually was Coligny.
We shall shortly see this bloodthirsty villain himself
murdered at Blois.

The massacre continued the whole week through,
for seven days that is, but the chief fury had spent
itself by Tuesday night. The Janus Gallicus professes,
though how Aimé could have any certainty of it I
cannot tell, that Nostradamus, by *tyran*, alludes to
Coligny, and says that the bell tolled so long that it
broke. The quatrain does not necessitate the sup-
posal of any such thing, and I believe the fact is not
elsewhere recorded. Of course, if it be, it would be
so literal a fulfilment that all the sceptical world
would immediately take advantage of what I have

pointed out, that this is a prophecy *après coup*. If so doing should rejoice anybody, I can only say that he has my consent. My business is to put the facts, without a shred of disguise, before the reader ; he can weave them into theories for himself. If I at any time manifest what I think, he will be pleased to accept it merely as a contribution towards the same end.

In January, 1572, the river Seine was frozen over for a long time, and the roads became almost impassable. This *may* perhaps be thought to interpret *eaux glace pain ne dône*, with such hieroglyphic symbolism of scarcity as oracular utterance delights in. It is pretty certain that provisions did not enter Paris that winter with their usual flow. In allusion to the army mentioned, Guynaud says that the Duc d'Anjou marched with fifty thousand men to the siege of Rochelle, where, after firing thirteen thousand shots, they at last effected a breach. What they battered down, oddly enough, was the Boulevard of the Gospel (*Boulevard de l'Évangile*), but they could not storm it, and lost twenty thousand men without taking the place.

In that eulogium on Catherine de Medici which de Brantôme ("Panthéon Littéraire," ii. 116) calls her Life, he relates that she died of a broken heart, from grief at having consented to the massacre on this ill-starred day, and that without intending it she (p. 133) had invited the nobles and lords of the land to gather to it. The Cardinal de Bourbon said to her, " Madam, you have brought us all to the butchery without intending it." This touched her to the quick ; she took to her bed and never left it again. One can only say this does not quite accord with Mezerai and her sounding the tocsin an hour earlier by anticipation. Further, as the massacre took place in 1572, and the queen-mother did not die at Blois till 1589, seventeen years after, her heart resisted grief much as granite does vinegar. The lady must originally have possessed a very good heart. De Brantôme says poison was talked of ; but he considers the broken heart more likely.

CIVIL WAR UNDER HENRI III. (1559-1589).   [I. 93.]

Century III.—Quatrain 55.

En l'an qu'un œil en France regnera
La Cour sera en un bien fascheux trouble :
Le Grand de Blois son amy tuera ;
Le regne mis en mal et doute double.

Translation.

In the year when a one-eyed man shall reign in France
The Court shall be in very vexatious trouble :
The great one of Blois shall kill his friend ;
The Kingdom, plunged into evil and doubt, shall divide in two.

M. le Pelletier's version here seems to be a little forced. The one-eyed man he makes to be Henri II., whose eye was destroyed by Montgomery's lance. The Court is to be in great embarrassment. Henri III. (*le Grand de Blois*) will convoke at that place the States-General, and will there assassinate the Duc de Guise, first taking with him, in Italian fashion, the Holy Communion, as a sign of entire reconciliation. Then the desolated kingdom will divide into two camps—the Royalists on one side, and the Leaguers on the other.

Regency of Catherine de Medici (1537–1574).   [I. 94.]

Century VI.—Quatrain 29.

La vefve * saincte entendent les nouvelles
De ses rameaux mis en perplex et trouble :
Qui † sera duict ‡ appaiser § les querelles
Par son pourchas ‖ des razes ¶ fera comble.

Translation.

The holy widow shall receive news
Of the difficulties that perplex and trouble her children ;
He whom she calls home to quiet disturbances
Shall bring them to a crisis by his pursuit of shaven heads.

There is a little difficulty in applying the epithet *saincte* to the queen-mother, and Garencières supposes it to signify *Roma la Santa;* but, if so, the rest will have no meaning. Nostradamus is so entirely for Henri II., his wife, and the Romish Church, that in spite of his designating her son *le roi farouche,* he might think the term *saincte* not inappropriate to her. She sent a private despatch to her son, Henri III., to hurry back from Poland, as we shall see him doing in the next quatrain cited, that he may take the direction of the French Government. He enters into an alliance with Henri IV. and the Huguenots to counterbalance the Catholic League. Thence follows the murder of the Cardinal, brother of the Duc de Guise, who was murdered by the King's order on December 24, 1588, one day after his brother. This is the prosecution of the Church (*pourchas des razes*), coupled

---

* Romance, *vefve* = veuve, widow.
† Latin, *qui*, celui qui.   ‡ Latin, *ductus*, led.
§ *Appaiser*, for pour apaiser.
‖ *Pourchas*, old word, pursuit, active intrigue (*proquassatio*).
¶ *Razes*, tonsured priests and monks (*têtes rasées*).

with the repression of the League, which culminates the crisis. The only jarring word in this concordance, when once it is comprehended, lies in the word *saincte,* to which I have already drawn attention, and which may be explained by the devotion felt by Nostradamus to the crown of France and to Rome. It is evident that Brantôme was able to regard her as a most admirable and lovable lady. The tocsin and the blood spoil our appreciation.

HENRI III. RENOUNCES POLAND (JUNE 26, 1574). [I. 96.]
Century VII.—Quatrain 35.

La grande Pesche * viendra plaindre,† plorer
D'avoir esleu : trompés seront en l'âge :
Guiere † avec eux ne voudra demourer .
Deceu § sera par ceux de son langage.

Translation.

The great gambler‖ shall complain and weep
To have elected him : deceived in his age :
The duke had no desire to stay with them :
He will be slain by men of his own tongue.

* Greek, πεσσικός, draught-playing, or gambling. The word was applied to gaming by the Greeks, as we find a story in Plutarch [Liddell and Scott, Lex.], exhibiting Hermes as playing draughts (on the πεσσευτήριον) with Selene, and winning five days, which he adds to the year. Guynaud (p. 119) reads *poche,* which I take to be an abscess, wolf, or devouring ulcer ; both he and Le Pelletier interpret it as meaning Poland.

† *Plaindre,* for se plaindre.

‡ *Guiere.* Nobody explains this word, and yet it seems to stand much in need of it. It is given by Roquefort, as from *gubernator,* a general. Leader, or we may say *dux,* for the Duc d'Alençon. It is really *guides* or guide. *Guber, govern, guide,* being all three cognate.

§ Latin, *decisus,* cut off, severed.

‖ This term is applied to Poland by Nostradamus in allusion to its elective throne, which became purely venal—a thing at

Poland, then, will deplore having elected the Duc d'Anjou in 1573, for he stayed only one year with them, and absconded on the 26th of June at night, at his mother's summons, to France. The Comte de Fanchin, the Grand Chamberlain, was sent after him, and overtook him at Piesna, a frontier town in Austria, but the duke was deaf to all intercession (Guynaud, p. 119). He never took the Polish throne because he wished it, but because he was pressed by the Court of France; and now French affairs called him back. Guynaud thinks that the last line means that his friends deceived him into taking it; but this is because he did not discover the Latin meaning in *deceu*. For certainly Nostradamus meant that he would go home to die by Clement's hand, as he shows in as many words a little later on. Guynaud says that Poland had been deceived as to the prince's age, and that he was represented to be much older than he really was.

EDICT OF POITIERS (OCTOBER 3, 1577). [I. 97.]

Century V.—Quatrain 72.

Pour le plaisir d'edict voluptueux,
On mestera le poison dans la foy :
Venus sera en cours si vertueux,*
Qu'obfusquera du soleil tout aloy.†

___

last coming to be played for as a hazard at dice. But, curiously enough, the less authentic reading *poche* is almost equally descriptive—a burning ulcer eating into the body politic till it destroys it.

* Latin, *virtuosus* ; according to M. le Pelletier "vigorous." Classical Latin has no such word, and the lower Latin means *probus, bonis moribus et virtute præditus*. Nostradamus probably meant *vertueux*, in old French, to be equivalent to *robuste*.

† *Aloi*, the quality of the substance of a metal. The battle

Translation.

To pass an edict of a sugared sort,
They'll mingle poison with our holy faith :
And Venus darken, in her course robust,
All law and light from out the sacred Sun.

The Sun, in Nostradamus, often stands for the Church or Christianity, by him believed to be within the palisade of Popery. It might also mean France, whose King's name was *Rex Christianissimus.* Louis XIV. assumed the device of the sun, with the motto *nec pluribus impar.* Venus stands for sensual pleasure—the world triumphant over the Church. The edict of Poitiers, October 8, 1577, so far favoured the Protestants that they were authorized to hold public services on the reformed footing. Calvinist ministers might marry, and auricular confession was suppressed. Thus did Henri III. mingle the poison of unchastity, etc., with the Catholic faith. The licence of morals (*Vénus*) became unbridled and tarnished the law of Christendom (*Soleil*).

Guynaud interprets with Le Pelletier in this, and considers the poison to consist particularly in freeing the Huguenots from the Sacrifice of Penance ; in condemning the monastic orders ; in encouraging unchastity, by allowing the Calvinist ministers to marry ; in abandon-

of French etymologists is very instructive over this word, as may be seen in Littré. Of course, however, it comes from *à loi*, conformable to law. But I think there is a misprint, and that we ought to read *toute loi* = *toute la loi.* Guynaud (p. 122) reads *loi* in the second line for *foy.* We might suppose that that variant had been introduced to correct the fourth line, and was only by a " devil " carried to the second instead, by which that imp of mischief contrived to leave two errors in place of one. In confirmation somewhat of this, the *texte-type* reads *tout à loy.*

ing confession. *Vénus sera* is a line showing that many monks will quit the cloisters to indulge in marriage and *other* debauchery. The last line may be understood, that the glory of the King will be tarnished, and make him to be ill thought of by the Catholics ; or that it will obscure faith in the Church (p. 122).

Journée des Barricades (May 12, 1588). [I. 98.]

Century III.—Quatrain 50.

La republique de la grande cité
A grand rigueur ne voudra consentir :
Roy sortir hors par trompette cité,
L'eschelle au mur la cité repentir.

Translation.

The Republic of the great city (Paris)
Would not submit itself to the very rigorous treatment ;
The King summoned by trumpet to quit the city,
Which is called to repent by the ladder at the wall.

This quatrain and the event it prefigures are alike wonderful. Garencières is much puzzled over it. What city has a commonwealth ? Is it Venice, Genoa, Geneva, Luca ? He cannot tell. However, the "great city" in Nostradamus almost always stands for Paris. The League, mistress in Paris, would not submit to the coercive measures of Henri III., and by a call to arms—perhaps the old tocsin of St. Germain de l'Auxerrois sounding the while—told him, as *par trompette*, he had better quit the city with all speed. Trial and sentence in one word, "Take yourself off,"—for the first time uttered to a king of the race Capetian, in some eight hundred years of history. Later on, the drumming and trumpeting

crack-brained citizens, with nothing about them to be
called sane but their river, will feel themselves called
to repentance when the escalading ladders are laid
by Henri III. to the wall.

Let it be noted now that this *Day of the Barricades*
is very remarkable, and, as such, is not to be found at
all in Bohn's "Index of Dates." It was, however,
repeated in the civil war of the Fronde, August 26,
1648 ; in the three days' war, July 27, 28, 29, 1830, that
set Philippe Citoyen on his rickety perch ; and again
in June 23, 1848. But close on two hundred years
after, in 1789, when the philosophic Republic was at
hand and the Bastille was taken ; when another Capet
was to be handled by the mob ; offering *cul pour tête* to
the admiration of a wise world, then was to be best
discerned the result of this first reaction from St.
Bartholomew's Day ; pretty well that tocsin of treason
has rung alarum to a world on fire. A further curious
analogy demands attention here. The Popes of Rome
were the earliest patrons of the principle of regicide,
and Clément the monk, whom we shall soon introduce,
was the first to practise it ; here we see the Catholic
League to be the first organized body to repudiate
kingship, to set up a republican form, and consecrate
a day to revolt and insurrection, which has become
memorable in history for ever, though forgotten by
Bohn, as *la Journée des Barricades.* But what shall
we say of this forecast by Nostradamus, fifty-three
years before the event happened ? He is, I think, the
first who ever put in type the word *Republic*, as
representative of rebellion and revolt, throughout the

modern world. But here we have it,—the dough of prophecy made out of the ground wheat-seed of time, and baked by the oven of events into the bread of history ; not Walpole's lies, nor the principles, mostly false, that philosopher Hume finds so cleverly for us, but the facts divested of motive,—like a petrified coral reef of insect humanities concreted into permanence and solidity by the death of myriads. For those who can see, it lies all contained in that linear rune, *La république de la grande cité.*

MURDER OF THE DUC DE GUISE (DECEMBER 23, 1588).
[I. 99.]
Century III.—Quatrain 51.

Paris conjure un grand meutre commetre,
Blois le fera sortir en plein effect :
Ceux d'Orleans voudront leur chef remettre ;
Angers, Troye, Langres leur feront un meffait.

Translation.

Paris conspires to commit a great murder ;
Blois will carry it into full effect :
The Orléanois will try to place a Leaguer at their head ;
Angers, Troye, Langres will try and undo this.

Henri III. at Paris contrived the murder of the Duc de Guise, who had incited and led the Parisians on the day of the Barricades, when Henri was compelled to fly to Chartres. Henri de Lorraine, Duc de Guise, was murdered the day after the Cardinal, his brother, had been, at the Convention of the Estates at Blois. The murder took place at the Château de Blois. The Orléanois, on learning this, rose against Balzac d'Entragues, the governor of the town, and set Charles de Lorraine, Chevalier d'Aumale, at their

head,—he was one of the chiefs of the League,—whilst
Angers, Troyes, and Langres took the side of
Henri III.   It is not very easy, says Le Pelletier, to
distinctly prove the exact position taken up by these
three towns, but Nostradamus habitually puts a part
to stand for the whole.   In the divided interests
various cities took differing sides.   At the time he
wrote there was nothing to show that such internecine
separations would take place.   He clearly anticipated
them, and, so far, is absolutely right.   We cannot, it
seems, prove him to be right in all the details; but
equally, there is nothing to show him wrong.

Le Duc de Mayenne (1589-1593).   [i. 100.]

Century I.—Quatrain 85.

Par la response de dame Roy troublé,
Ambassadeurs mespriseront leur vie :
Le Grand ses freres contrefera doublé
Par deux mourront ire,* haine, et envie.†

Translation.

The King shall be troubled by the Queen-mother,
The deputies at risk of life remonstrate :
The Guise will act for both his brothers dead,
The two whom envy, hatred, malice slew.

Henri III. will be troubled by the response of
Catherine de Medici, who disapproves of the murder
of the Guise ; the deputies (*ambassadeurs*) from both
Paris and Blois make lively remonstrance at the peril
of their lives.   The Duc de Mayenne (*le Grand*),
when proclaimed chief of the League, will take the

* Latin, *ira*, anger.
† Ordo, deux mourront par ire, etc.

title of Lieutenant-General of the Kingdom, and, as if doubled in authority, will represent his two brothers, Henri de Guise and the Cardinal de Lorraine, whom the envy, hatred, and malice of Henri III. and his Court had assassinated. We seem to have here a republic tempered by daggers, in place of what followed, a tyranny tempered with epigrams. This active forging of daggers, knives, and sword-cutlery in France, to carve out an idol of a republic, with its bloodstained heathen Phrygian cap ; taken together with its repetition sixty years later, in the Barricades of the Fronde, August, 1648, was clearly generating the poison and concentrating its venom for the most startling act of death known to mankind, but one, in all history,—at Whitehall, on that wintry 30th of January, 1649,—the venom, that by the subtle inoculation of a Raleigh could, for a time, strike silly such a soul as Milton's—" Psalmist of Paradise,"—who, but for this damned virus in the world, might have taught men how to realize a paradise on earth.

CRIME OF JACQUES CLÉMENT (AUGUST 1, 1589).   [I. 102.]

Century IX.—Quatrain 36.

Un grand Roy prins * entre les mains d'un Joyne †
Non loin de Pasque, confusion, coup cultre.‡
Perpet,§ captifs temps que foudre en la husne,||
Lors que trois freres se blesseront et murtre.¶

---

* Romance, *prins*, pris.
† Romance, *joyne*, jeune homme.
‡ Romance, *cultre*, couteau.
§ Latin, *perpetratio*.
|| *Husne*, a small tower, or belvidere.
¶ Romance, *murtre*, meurtre.

Translation.

A great King taken by a young man's hand
Close upon Easter, confusion, and a knife :
There's powder on the tower for captives then,
Three brothers perish ; this death takes the last.

Henri III., in his camp at St. Cloud, will be struck by the hand of a young monk,—*Joyne* might easily be a misprint for *Moyne.* Jacques Clément was twenty-five. He came straight from receiving the Communion (*non loin de Pasque*). He thought he did God service (*confusion*) ; he struck him in the lower bowel with a knife. The crime will be committed when the Parisians are cut off (*captifs*) by the King beleaguering, and his vengeance is ready to fall upon their ramparts. This murder completes the violent deaths of the three sons, the issue of Henri II. and Catherine de Medici.

There is no occasion to call attention to the remarkable lucidity of this forecast, when once the linguistic difficulties of its conveyance have been studiously solved. The demilune towers projecting at intervals from the wall, as at the Haute Ville, Boulogne, well enough represent the *husne*, or tower of vantage, in the quatrain, they need but a shield or belvidere added.

DEATH OF HENRI III. (AUGUST 2, 1589). [I. 103.]

Présage 58.

Le Roy-Roy n'estre, du Doux la pernicie,*
L'an pestilent, les esmues † nubileux.

---

* Latin, *pernicies*, destruction.
† Romance, *esmues*, émus, seditious.

Tien * qui tiendra, les grands non letitie,†
Et passera terme de cavilleux.‡

Translation.

The twice King dies, by Clement hand is slain ;
War and revolt make the year pestilent.
Hold who hold can, the great oppose not well,
Live laughter down and teach the cavillers.

This is a most singular prophecy. Henri III., King, first of Poland then of France is quaintly called *Roy-Roy*. *Le Doux* is an excellent synonym for *Clément*, all must admit. The year was harassed by civil and religious war, and the Leaguers (*les esmues*) begin to grow anxious about the consequences. Let Henri IV. hold hard his own, the lilied sceptre : "Let Curzon holde what Curzon helde" be his motto. The time is passed for the Catholic grandees (*les grands*) to woo Lætitia. The King can laugh now at the laughers of the Guise ; he laughs best who laughs last.

The murder by Clément of the anti-papal king, Henri III., followed very close upon the setting up of Jesuit Clubs in Paris under papal sanction (Elliot's *Horæ Apoc*, iii. 321). The pulpits also had been filled by clerical preachers of sedition and bloodshed. Precisely two hundred years later the Bastille was taken, and in the Jacobin Clubs of that day were hung, says Alison, the pictures of Clément and Ravaillac, in the gloomy rooms of the old convent, in which they met like night-birds of ill-omen, and within little

---

* *Tien*, for *tienne*.
† Latin, *Lætitia*, joy, pleasure, and play on *Lutetia*, Paris.
‡ Romance, *cavilleux*, cavillers.

wreaths beneath each picture might be seen inscribed the words, "He was fortunate ; he killed a king." This is so sentimental, petty, and petulant, that it would move to laughter any large good-natured mind, were it not for the slaver of malignity that accompanies everything that drops from the tongues of that sack of reptiles gathered out of the Jacobin dunghill, as they crawled forth one by one poisoning and to poison.

HENRI QUATRE.

THE COMING OF HENRI IV. (AUGUST 2, 1589). [I. 105.]

Century IX.—Quatrain 50.

Mendosus * tost viendra à son haut regne,
Mettant arriere un peu les Norlaris : †
Le rouge blesme, la masle à l'interregne,
Le jeune crainte, et frayeur Barbaris.

Translation.

Mendosus shall soon come to his high dominion,
Setting back those of Lorraine a little.
The old cardinal pale, the male of the interregnum,
The young man timid, and the barbarian alarmed.

HENRI IV. the heretic Vendôme, changed his religion thrice. Jeanne d'Albert, his mother, brought him up a Protestant. To escape St. Bartholomew's Day, he professed Catholicism, in 1572. In 1576, he turned to Protestantism, to head the Calvinist party. He declared himself Catholic to take the throne of France. Through the Salic law

* *Mendosus*, anagram of *Vendosme* (the *u* standing for *v* of course). The *texte-type* reads *Mandosus ;* but as *Mendosus* is the perfect anagram of Vendosme, and makes also the Latin word's meaning *full of faults*, it is best to read *Mendosus*.

† *Norlaris*, anagram for Lorrains the patronymic of the Guise family.

he ascended, to the exclusion of the Lorraine princes (*Nolaris*). In this way, he shut out the old Cardinal de Bourbon, pale (*blesme,*) with age, the Duc de Mayenne, Lieutenant General of the kingdom during the interregnum, the young Duc de Guise, and the barbarously savage Philip II. of Spain, who had pretensions to the crown through Elizabeth his wife, the daughter of Henri II.

The Cardinal is *rouge* because of the dress of all cardinals. Philip allied himself with the Guises, and supported the Catholic League.

THE DEPRESSION OF THE DE GUISE FAMILY (1589-1593).
[I. 107.]

Century X.—Quatrain 18.

Le rang Lorrain fera place à Vendosme,
Le haut mis bas, et le bas mis en haut,
Le fils de Mamon sera esleu * en Rome,
Et les deux Grands seront mis en defant.

Translation.
The house of Lorraine yields to the Vendôme,
The high put low, the low put high instead,
The son of Mamon they elect at Rome,
And the Pretenders both are in default.

The house of Lorraine is now eclipsed by that of Vendôme. Mayenne, the chief, is put down, *and le petit Béarnais*, Henri IV., rises to respect and power. This heretic son of mammon is accepted by choice at Rome for King of France, and neither of the Pretenders will ever be king.

The Cardinal de Bourbon had been actually proclaimed King by the League, as Charles X., but he was

---

* Romance, *esleu, élu,* chosen.

K

dead in 1590. Isabella, the daughter of Philip II., was incapable by the Salic law. So that the only two remaining were the Duc de Mayenne and the young Duc de Guise. They were shut out by Henri IV. and never reached the throne.

HENRI IV. ABJURES PROTESTANTISM (JULY 21, 1593).
[I. 108.]

Presage 76.

Par le legat du terrestre et marin,
Le Grande Cape * à tout s'accommoder ;
Estre à l'escoute tacite † Norlarin, ‡
Qu'à § son advis ne voudra accorder.

Translation.

Before the legate of the earth and sea,
Henry the Great will yield to all required :
Mayenne to all will listen and not speak a word,
And will grant nothing of his own free will.

Sixtus V. had boldly fulminated an excommunication against Henri Quatre, the Great Capet, but the latter subscribes to all required by the legate of him who can bind and loose all on the earth and sea. He abjures Protestantism at St. Denis, on July 25, 1593, the Archbishop of Bourges officiating. The Duc de Mayenne (the *Lorraine*), Lieutenant-General of France and Master of Paris for the League, will look on in silence, and as far as he can will prevent Paris from receiving the King. The city did not open its gates to him till March 22, 1594, eight months after the abjuration.

* *Cape*, for *Capet*, a descendant of Hugh Capet.
† Latin, *tacite*, silently.
‡ *Norlarin*, anagram for *Lorrain* ; here it represents the Duc de Mayenne.   § *Qu'a* for *qui à*.

Marseilles taken by the Spaniards (February 17, 1696).
[I. 109.]

Century III. —Quatrain 88.

De Barselonne par mer si * grand' armée,
Toute Marseille de frayeur tremblera :
Isles saisies, de mer ayde fermée,
Ton traditeur † en terre nagera. ‡

Translation.

From Barcelona a great fleet shall come,
And terror strike into the town Marseilles:
The isles are seized, and help by sea cut off,
But the betrayer is made swim on land.

A Spanish fleet of a dozen galleys, commanded by Charles Doria, was sent by Philip II. to help the Leaguers. He took possession of the islands Château d'If and Ratonneau, and thus cut off all help to seaward. Charles de Casau (*le traditeur*) was consul, and proposed to place the city in the hands of the Spaniards ; Pierre Libertat, however, ran him through with a sword, and the populace dragged the dead body through the muddy channels of the streets.

Guynaud refers to the same event as fulfilling this quatrain in the time of Henri IV., but by a misprint gives 1536 instead of 1596. The islands he mentions are those of St. Honnorat and of St. Marguerite. Black's pretentious *Imperial Gazetteer* professes to give a plan of the town, and you see a number of nameless vermicelli streets running all about, but not

* Romance, *si* for *très*, very.
† Latin, *traditor*, traitor.
‡ His body shall be dragged through the streets in the mud of the gutters.

a single island off the coast is visible. One may suppose, however, that the islands are there, and that all the four were occupied by the Spaniards.

BIRON'S PUNISHMENT (DECEMBER 2, 1602). [I. 110.]

Sixain 6.

Quand de Robin * la traisteruse enterprise,
Mettra Seigneurs et en peine un grand Prince,
Sceu † par la Fin ‡ chef on lui tranchera.
La plume au vent, amye dans Espagne, §
Poste ‖ attrappé estant dans la campagne,
Et l'escrivain dans l'eaüe se jettera.

Translation.

When Biron's treason and disastrous act,
Shall put King Henry and his Lords in fear,
Lafin betrays him, and the King beheads.
Treason dispatched to Spain in amity, ¶
The carrier caught when he has entered France,**
And the scriv'ner will throw himself into the water.

* *Robin*, anagram for *Biron*.

† Romance, *sceu* for *su*, known.

‡ *Lafin* was the name of the secretary, the accomplice of Biron.

§ The ordo here is *dans l'Espagne amye* which means, then at peace with Henri IV.

‖ Romance, *poste*, messenger, postillion.

¶ *La plume au vent* is supposed by le Pelletier to stand for *currente calamo*. I should rather think it means the feather (wing) to the wind. It was written with a quill, and started on its way as a bird flies ; but *irrevocabile semel emissum*. We are to understand this line to relate to l'Oste's treasonable complicity with Spain, of which an account will be given further on. Also, *l'escrivain*, in the closing line stands for the same individual.

** We shall see that the two Spanish couriers were arrested at the post office in Paris. Le Pelletier confuses all this from

One thing has carefully to be borne in mind in relation to the Sixains, that they were presented to Henri Quatre, and printed for the first time in 1605. That is to say, they first appeared three years after this had happened. To the sceptically disposed they can furnish no authority, but to ordinary men, who only look for ordinary evidence, it will appear that there is very little as to style that would not appropriately spring from the pen of Nostradamus; and further, that if they are forgeries, the forgers have not taken advantage of their knowledge of the events to make the prophecies any clearer or more striking. These are quite as enigmatical as if our author had written them, and I think that common sense will generally be content to take them for what they are worth, and will regard them as probably genuine "chips of the old block" and as such very curious.

Guynaud in his *Concordance*, p. 137, gives a full and interesting account of Biron ; chiefly extracted from Davila, Montluc, De Thou, Mezeray, Le Père Anselm, and so forth, where the reader can refer for further details, if interested. I may just note that I have copied the date of December 2, 1602, from Le Pelletier, but that Moreri gives the date of Biron's decapitation as July 31, 1602, in the Court of the

not happening to know that l'Oste is the scrivener, so he applies it to the affair of Lafin, whose messenger, when carrying Spanish despatches, had thrown them into the river when he found himself pursued. Unfortunately, when he finds himself in the difficulty which this involves him in, he glozes till he has forced the words to fit his erroneous view. He had far better have stated the difficulty, and said that he could not harmonize the text. But he very rarely trips thus.

Bastille. The name of the messenger (*poste*) was Picoté, a native of Orleans, sold, as they say, to the King of Spain (Guynaud, p. 140).

Garencières has (p. 464) a very elaborate annotation upon this stanza, giving the whole history of Biron and Lafin in twenty-eight folio pages. Biron appears to have been a vain, a violent, and foolish man, though of great courage and audacity in war, which made him highly valued by Henri IV. After Amiens he refused to go to quiet the towns of Picardy, unless his statue were erected in brass before the Louvre. His sudden prosperity had turned his head. The treasonous proposals with Spain were, that he was to have a daughter of the Duke of Savoy in marriage, 500,000 crowns, and sovereign rights in Burgundy. These were negotiated through Lafin ; and Lafin told the King. The whole trial is given, with Biron's defence in reply, which is audacious and eloquent, but much of it is highly contradictory. He was condemned and executed in the court of the Bastille, on July 31, 1602, which coincides with Moreri. The superstitious, igno-rant, violent, but able soldier comes out most charac-teristically. He shows in emergency great rapidity of thought, decision, and presence of mind ; but a deficient judgment, very little principle, and an over-whelming conceit, that, encouraged by success, almost merged into madness. A man of this sort is always a compound of inconsistencies ; accordingly he said to the Chancellor, in speaking of death, "I have not been afraid of it these twenty years." And that was true, when in war, a duel, or hot blood ; but in the court of the Bastille he was thought to show great fear of dying. In earlier life he had wondered at himself for fearing nothing from the thrust of a sword, though very nervous over the prick of a lancet, when he had occasion to "be let blood," as they used to phrase it. The fear of death is most in apprehension ; but the apprehension is most, perhaps it may be said, of the wicked in cold blood, and of the good in violence, and when the blood is hot, if but the least pause give time for reflection to enter. Garencières notes that the greatest courage and stoutness of a man is nothing in comparison of the weakness of human nature.

Two of Biron's adventures with astrologers are so characteristic of the manners of the time, as recounted by Guynaud [p. 137, etc.], that I think the reader should not be deprived of them. Whatever is strange and rivets the attention must have something of humanity in it, and repay the record, though a few superior people may look down upon such trifling. I shall give them at the risk of running this annotation to too great length.

When at Court with his father, at the age of eighteen or twenty, he had a duel, and killed his man. He had to hide for this, till his father could sue out his pardon, through the Duc d' Espernon, to whom fortunately the father was known. He took the disguise of a letter-carrier, and in this garb consulted an astrologer called La Brosse, who lived in a garret at the top of a house near the Luxembourg. He told the man that it was his master's horoscope he had need of. La Brosse told him that one day he would be a very great man, in fact, might almost be king, but for a *caput algol* that stood in the way. What this was the man would not explain. Biron, however, continuing to press very hard, got him to say at last that he would be beheaded on a scaffold. Upon this, he burst out with the want of judgment he showed all through his life (forty years in all) and beat the old man mercilessly, leaving him nearly dead. He locked him maliciously into his room, took away the key with him, and kicked down the little ladder that gave access to the loft. But still he believed what had been communicated.

On another occasion he consulted César, who was thought at the time to be the most able astrologer in France. This man also affirmed that he would have good fortune in almost everything. Except for a blow from a Burgundian from behind, he might even be king. But he could not get from him a word more.

When he was confined in the Bastille, a friend called on him, and Biron asked him to ascertain for him from what part of the country the executioner of Paris was ; and when he came back and told him that he was a Burgundian, Biron changed colour and said—"There will be no reprieve then ; I am as good as dead."

Now as to the fulfilment of the last two lines. It will appear that my rendering is right, and that the scrivener will throw himself into the water. The scrivener turns out to be a man named Nicholas l'Oste, born at Orleans, secretary to Lord Villeroy, Chief Secretary of State, who, finding him a most capable person, confided much in him, and the more so that Oste's father had spent the greater part of his life in his service. When Lord Rochepot was starting as ambassador for Spain, Oste begged to accompany him as secretary. Villeroy immediately recommended him, and he was engaged. In a few months' time he mastered the language to such perfection, and so thoroughly accommodated himself to Spanish manners, that he might well pass for a true-born Spaniard. When Rochepot had got the treaty at Vervins ratified, the King of Spain gave him rich presents—a chain of jewels, and six gold chains valued at a hundred and fifty crowns apiece—to distribute amongst his suite, as he thought fit. Oste was so full of himself that he thought he ought to have one of them, but his master thought otherwise; on which, says Garencières, "the Devil crept into his soul," and, as he wanted money to supply his debaucheries, he determined to betray the State secrets which passed through his hands.

With this in view, he applied to Don Fanchese, a Secretary of State, and made his proposals, but the dignified Spaniard, for some reason or other, received him coolly. "The Catholic King was in good amity with the most Christian one, and required to know no more than the French Ambassador should communicate to him." Nothing discouraged, our traitor hurries off to Don Ydiaques, another secretary, and there meets with excellent reception. He was presented to the Duke of Lerma, to whom he betrayed the Alphabet of Ciphers. He received twelve hundred crowns upon the spot, and was promised the like amount as a yearly pension. By his means the

Spanish Council knew the contents of all French in-
structions as soon as the ambassador himself. When
La Rochepot's mission ended, Oste got back into
Villeroy's service, and so was able to maintain corre-
spondence with Spain. Tuxis was ambassador from
Spain in Paris, and after him Don Baltazar de Caniga.
With these men he established a close intimacy, so
that finally the Council in Spain got his letters before
Des Barreaux at Madrid could receive those from
Henri IV.

Des Barreaux told the King that he was always
now forestalled. Oste had let a certain reprobate
Raffis into his secret, and this fellow, who had been
banished, in order to obtain a reprieve of sentence,
betrayed Oste to Des Barreaux. When he got
his pardon, he gave up the name of Oste. Raffis
came to Paris to communicate with Villeroy, and
orders were given to detain the two Spanish couriers
that had reached the post-office. They then kept a
watch upon Oste, who was "doing his devotions at
the Charter-house of Paris,"—excellent Catholic,
plotter as he was. On reaching the post-office, he
soon found he was betrayed ; and Descardes, who was
to watch him, did not let him out of his sight
until he brought him to Villeroy's. When there,
he thought his man was safe, and went to announce
his capture to Villeroy. Oste instantly ran down to
the stable, where his horse stood, still saddled, and
galloped away. A hue and cry was soon raised.
Oste got a Spanish disguise at De Cuniga's, and made
off post-haste for Luxembourg. Postmasters were
forbidden to let out horses to any one ; but at Meaux

the postmaster had received the order too late, for Oste was already on horseback, but no sooner did he begin to gallop than his horse fell under him. His look of dismay impressed the postillion who accompanied him, and he told his master on his return. The postmaster told the sheriff, who came up with him at the second ferry of *la Ferte sous Jouare;* but he was already on the boat, and threatening the ferryman's life, the man put him ashore, in spite of the sheriff's commands, shouted to him from the bank. He rushed into the bushes and brambles near the Marne, hoping to escape in the darkness of the night, the sheriff scattered his men everywhere, raised the whole country side, and caused bonfires to be lighted in all directions. Oste crept from bush to bush, but, either accidentally or with intention, fell into the river Marne and was drowned. His hat was found next day, stopped between two posts, and his body two days later. So befitting a close to the career of a gifted dastard is a wholesome exemplar of retributive justice, and should not easily be suffered to fall out of men's recollection. Horace thinks that lame-foot Justice always trips the sinner. No doubt, if we could see both worlds; but, as we cannot, I wish that here the lame foot were considerably less lame. In England law and the lawyers, her two crutches, seem to reduce Justice to a gouty incapable. With our new Palace of Justice the morals of a Court seem to have dawned upon us.

POPULARITY OF HENRI IV. (AFTER HIS DEATH). [I. 112.]

Century VI.—Quatrain 70.

Au chef du monde le grand Chyren * sera,
Plus outre après aymé, craint, redouté ;
Son bruit et los † les cieux surpassera,
Et du seul titre victeur ‡ fort contenté.

Translation.

Chief of the world *Henri le Grand* shall be,
More loved in death than life, more honoured he :
His name and praise shall rise above the skies,
And men will call him victor when he dies.

French self-esteem has always appropriated to France a throne of pre-eminence beyond all other thrones. If it were possible, they would set theirs above that of Jupiter. They pretend a most manly contempt for kings. But the throne, you are to remember, is the work of *sans cullottes,* French cabinet-makers,

* *Le Grand Chyren* is the anagram of *Henri le Grand.* Before mounting the throne, he bore the name of Vendosme, from his father Antoine de Bourbon, Duke of Vendôme and King of Navarre. In the first Quatrain of the series, *Henri Quatre, Vendosme* was anagrammatically given as Mendosus ; as to *Chiren* it is the precise anagram of *Henri,* as spelt in the old language *Henric,* from the Latin *Henricus.* Numerous etymologies have been assigned to Henry. Camden derived it from *honore,* Verstegan from the Teutonic *Han,* a haven, and *Rice,* Saxon for rich. Killian writes it *Heynrick,* or *Heymrick,* rich home. This is very nearly right, but now it is generally considered that *rick* stands for powerful ; so chief of a house or district.

† *Los,* old word for glory. Latin, *laus.*
  "A la sainte divinité,
  Soit *los,* honeur, et potesté."
          Le Mystère des Actes des Apôtres.
‡ Latin, *victor,* conqueror.

and therefore the best thing of its kind in the universe, and so *chef du monde.* If Nostradamus is no prophet for you, you shall at least admit that he was a Frenchman. The Frenchman whips the old world, and the American whips creation. The rest of us may look forward to an eternity of corporal punishment in spite of the nominal abolition of slavery. Condillac will furnish the logical distinction, that establishes the honour of the throne, when a manly contempt has been duly engendered for the sanctity of the king's majesty. Honest Democrat! Do you read Condillac?

One of Voltaire's rhetorical squibs in the *Henriade*, which the French are so indulgent as to call not only verse, but poetry, runs—

> " Il fut de ses sujets le vainqueur et le père."
> " He was the papa and conquestor of his people."

When our Charles II. was addressed as "the father of his people," he said he thought that he might be of a good many of them. But Henri Quatre is too noble a creature for any good and wise man to wish to dwell long upon his foibles. What a contrast between him and the Napoleons!

LOUIS XIII.

(1610–1643.)

PUNISHMENT OF THE GREAT MONTMORENCY
(OCTOBER, 30 1632.)   [I. 113.]

Century IX.—Quatrain 18.

Le lys Dauffois * portera † dans Nanci
Jusques en Flandres electeur de l'Empire ;
Neufve obturée ‡ au grand Montmorency,
Hors lieux prouvés § delivré‖ á clere peyne. ¶

Translation.

The Dauphin shall carry his lily standards into Nancy, just as in Flanders the Elector of Trèves shall be carried prisoner of the Spaniards into Brussels. A new prison will be given to the great Montmorency, who will be delivered for execution into the hands of Clerepeyne. This man will behead him in a spot not devoted to executions.

I HAVE given this in prose, as it could only yield ingenious doggerel in verse.

Louis XIII., of whom it may be remarked that he was the first who bore the title of Dauphin de France

---

* *Dauffois,* for *Dauphinois* synonym, for *Dauphin.*

† *Portera,* for supportera, says Le Pelletier. For my part, it seems best to leave it to its natural rendering, that he wil. carry his colours into Nancy.

‡ Latin, *obturare,* to shut up in.

§ *Prouvés* is for approuvés.   ‖ *Delivré,* is for livré.

¶ This is a play upon words, unrecognized by Garencières, as he did not know that *Clerepeyne* was the name of the man who since the publication of Century IX., in 1566, entered Nancy on September 25, 1633, a day after his army. In 1635 he enters Flanders on behalf of the Elector, whom the Spaniards had, on the 26th of March of that year, carried prisoner to Brussels. Nostradamus then reverts to October 30, 1632, when the great Montmorency was executed for rebellion, being first confined in the newly built (*neufve obturée*) Hotel de Ville at Toulouse. In the courtyard of this building Clerepeyne, a soldier, shall cut off his head, and not, as ought to have been the case, at the place appointed for public executions, such as was *La Grève* at Paris.

It so happens that Clerepeyne's name is fully attested by Étienne Joubert and by the Chevalier de Jant, both contemporary with the event. Further than this, M. Motret has brought to light, after minute historic research, that the family, by solicitation of the King, could obtain only two concessions of mere formality—that the execution should be with closed doors, and by a soldier in lieu of the common headsman. The *place publique* or *marché* would be the place mentioned in the official order.

cut off Montmorency's head, although, of course, Garencières is quite alive to the fact that the quatrain refers to Louis XIII. and the great Montmorency. In Latin *clara pœna* means celebrated punishment. Here is another instance of the mention of a name of an obscure individual that history for a moment flashes light upon, and then drops him back into the mud of oblivious ooze for ever,—emblem apt of Fame! This was written, if not printed, a good eighty years before Clerepeyne became the midge-mote of a sunbeam upon that late autumnal day in history, when the night struck chilly on high roofs in Dauphiny.

If the reader will carefully give his attention to the full drift of this quatrain, when the mere difficulty of verbal contortion has been resolved, he must feel that the prognostication has to be reckoned as one of the most astounding of oracles ever set forth in history. A French King takes Nancy. The Elector of Trèves is bandied about between France and Spain, like a shuttlecock of State ; and then, by name, comes the execution of the great Montmorency, detailed with, it is true, the brevity of Tacitus, but, when understood, with a singular felicity of detail implied in the pregnant words *neufve obturée*, of the newly built town hall. Not in the market-place is he executed, but in the central courtyard. Let *clere peyne* (*clara pœna*) stand merely for celebrated attainder, the thing is still prodigious beyond all precedent. But when you know, in addition, that a part of Nostradamus's prophetic method consists in using every possible play of words, including paronomasia and anagram, and you find that the soldier who acted as headsman—a man called upon by chance to gratify the almost absurd sensibilities of the family—was *Clerepeyne*, a name that corresponds to a tittle with the two words employed by the prophet, then, indeed, the marvel mounts into the stupendous. It cannot be paralleled out of the works of the individual we are busy with. It is incredible, and yet you must believe it. It is not to be understood, but it must be accepted. Joubert, de Jant, the Curé de Louvicamp, and Motret, have all contributed to its historical confirmation on independent lines. It was in print, beyond possibility of gainsaying, more than fifty years before any of the events occurred. Clerepeyne could not have been even born at the time his name was being put through the printing press at Lyons. The mind that can realize all these details, and then be content to fall back upon chance to explain them, or upon the verbal fact that visions must be visionary— an axiom quite as philosophic, by-the-bye, as Hume's " Essay on Miracles " is built upon—is a mind not at all to be envied. Such incredulity is more astounding than the prophecy itself. It is easier to believe the prophecy than the philosopher who says he does not believe it. The Tower is below London Bridge. Has anybody ever asked "why?" This 18th quatrain of Century IX, of Nostradamus is just as much a fact as the Tower of London is, and vastly more impregnable. Intelligent people will be amused by an explanation ; but the substantive fact can stand without any, till the day of Doom if necessary. It is only some human popinjay, Plato Pry, the philosopher, who would like to gossip to us the *How*, and so sport another borrowed feather in his feather-brain,— or hum us with another bee from his bonnet ; that hive of mad insects.

THE CONSPIRACY OF CINQ MARS (MARCH 13, 1642.)

[1. 115.]

Century VIII.—Quatrain 68.

Vieux Cardinal par la jeusne deceu,*
Hors de sa charge sa verra desarmé,

---

* Latin, *decisus*, suppressed cut off.

L

Arles ne monstres * double †soit apperceu ;
Et Liqueduct ‡ et le Prince embausmé.

Translation.

The old cardinal is supplanted by a young man, and will
see himself deprived of his charge, and disarmed. [Le Pelletier
renders] : If Arles you do not show, in a manner that shall be
visible, a counterpart of the treaty, then the man who will
cause himself to be conveyed by water will be embalmed, and
the Prince also.

The above is the contortion to which Le Pelletier
resorts to force out of it the sense it undoubtedly
contains. My proposed reading reduces the difficulty.

The old Cardinal Richelieu shall find himself supplanted by the young Cinq Mars. He was but
twenty-two when he achieved this bit of dexterous
Court intrigue against Richelieu,§ the most *rusé* fox
in Europe, as rumour ran.

* *Ne monstres.* I think there is a printer's error here in the
texte-type, and that we should read *le monstre.*
† *Double,* diploma, or duplicate of a treaty.
‡ Latin, *ille aquâ ductus,* he that is taken by water.
§ Richelieu, if you examine him by Philippe de Champagne's
splendid triple portrait of him, hanging in our Gallery, may be
read as if in life by any physiognomist who pleases to devote
the time to it. I have gazed many a time, through long years,
with gifted friends and others, and oftener still alone, into those
heartless eyes, attracted irresistibly (I only now see why) by the
vast discrepancy between the world-wide renown of this French
Minister, and his cynically petty face—sly, vulpine, unfeeling,
unprincipled, spiteful, a coxcomb of feminine manners, of an
egotism and paltry vanity inordinate, but of a refinement,
showing the highest social culture, a tongue that could gloze
with ladies ; he might, by *lettre de cachet,* have shut up a French
Walsingham in the Bastille to prevent his own overthrow ; but as
to coping with him or a Burleigh as a statesman, as an equal in any
powerful cabinet in Europe, by force of character, he could not

Cinq Mars was his own *protégé*, and no doubt threw him with a trick learned from his master. A sprightly youngster of the apt breed can learn such things quickly. But when the cardinal was at Arles he learnt that a certain treasonable treaty was negotiated with Spain by his rival in the name of the King's brother, and this made known brought Richelieu back to power straight. Now, if we read the line

> Arles, le monstre double soit apperceu :
> At Arles, let the monster diploma (treacherous treaty) be discovered,—

or Cinq Mars himself might be the double monster, —it would be but a gentle emendation in a classic line, and it makes the sense run well. Richelieu returned by water (*Liqueduct*) from Tarascon to Lyons, by the Rhone, with his bed upon the boat, but sick unto death, carrying Cinq Mars and De Thou prisoners along with him. In the same style he descended the Seine from Fontainbleau to Paris, where he died, two months later, on December 4, 1642. Louis XIII. died on the 14th of the following May. Both were embalmed, which was the practice then customary. The King when dead becomes a Prince again, when the breath was out of the body that 4th of December. Le roi est mort, vive le Roy Louis XIV.

have done it. Artifice, backed by the force of France, then rising into unity of action, or helped by circumstances that tied the hands of his antagonist, he might even throw a giant unawares. Richelieu was an artificial contriver, not a born ruler, if a mature face of fifty be any index to the volume or memoir of a man's life.

IMPROVEMENT IN FIREARMS (1630–1671.) [I. 116.]

Century III.—Quatrain 44.

Quand l'animal à l'homme domestique,*
Après grands peines et sauts viendra parler,
Le foudre à vierge † sera si ‡ malefique,
De terre prinse ‖ et suspendue en l'air.

Translation.

When the dog,‖ after many trials, shall begin to leap and speak, the powder loaded by ram-rod shall spread destruction round (*sera très malefique.*) Powder taken from the earth and exploded in the air.

When the firelock shall have been invented after many trials, and shall speak through the mouth of the gun, with recoil [*sauts*, or kick], after the powder-charge is well driven home with the ramrod, it will be most murderous by explosion in the air. The invention of the musket dates 1630. Troops, Le Pelletier says, were first armed with it in 1671. Nostradamus, it is to be observed, anticipates by an ingenious amplification and periphrasis the very name *chien*, by which the French designate this portion of the lock. It would not have served its purpose for the name of the same thing in English. This anticipation of the slang term of manufacture, a hundred years before the thing itself was used or named, seems to show an intimacy with what would be called matters of chance, that is inconceivable and beyond all comprehensibilty.

* Arrange these words, *l'animal domestique à l'homme*, i.e. *the dog.*

† Latinism, *fulmen à virgâ*, saltpetre ; that is, the powder and ram-rod.

‡ Romance, *si*, synonym of *très*, very.

§ Romance, *prinse*, *prise*, taken, brought.

‖ The *chien* is the cock or hammer of the lock.

I cannot but append here a translation of Guynaud's remarks upon this quatrain. They are, I think, the funniest that occur in the whole book. He says :

" Nostradamus warns us here that two prodigious things are to occur at last : one, that the industry and care of man will arrive at such a point that a domestic animal, such as dogs are, will be got to speak. For to imagine that this can be intended of birds is out of the question quite, as they are excluded from the list of domestic animals created by God for the service of man, as quadrupeds are. The words of the two first lines of the prophecy are *Quand après grande peine l'animal domestique viendra parler à l'homme et qu'il sautera,*—just as dogs do in approaching their master. A further thing is to happen that is no less astonishing : a demon is to mingle himself with powder, and suddenly transport a girl into the air, when she will remain suspended for possibly a whole day long, according to these words : ' *La foudre à vierge sera si malefique ; de terre prinse et surpendue en l'air.*' The critics may suppose that to mean that the girl will be hanged ; but this is not so, in my opinion, because the word *malefique* is derived from the Latin *maleficus,* which in itself indicates a maleficent spirit delighting to work evil, as the devil always is."—GUYNAUD, " Concordances," p 271

LOUIS XIV.

(1643–1715.)

Commencement of his Personal Reign (March 10, 1661). [I. 118.]

Quatrain added to the Xth Century. *

Quand le fourchu sera soustenu de deux paux,†
Avec six demy-corps ‡ et six sizeaux ouverts,
Le très puissant Seigneur, heritier des crapaux,
Alors subjugera sous soy tout l'univers.

Translation.

When a fork sustained by two stakes (*i.e.* V, *fourchu*, sustained by two stakes upright, II. = M, a thousand,) and six half horns and six scissors open (CCCCC, XXXXX). (Half horn is the *cor de chasse*, or French horn cut in half, like a C, making altogether 1600).

The very mighty King, inheritor of the toads, shall subjugate to his power the whole universe.

THESE two first lines are clumsily employed in giving the date, but still were in print fifty-five years before the date named.

Mazarin died on March 9, 1661. The following day Louis XIV. became full inheritor of the lilies,

* Added to the text in the edition of 1605.
† *Paux*, plural of *pal, pieu*, a term of blazonry, stake.
‡ Read *cors*, horns.

took the reins of government, and subjected everything to his will.

Upon this Le Pelletier remarks that the toads, as emblematic of France, were standards borne under the early kings of the Merovingian race. The *fleurs-de-lys* were of later introduction, under Clovis, son of Childeric I., the founder of the Christian monarchy of the Franks.

TREATY OF WESTPHALIA, ETC. (1648–1661). [I. 119.]

Century X.—Quatrain 7.

Le grand conflit qu'on appreste à Nancy ;
L'Æmathien * dira, tout je soubmets ;
L'isle Britanne par † vin sel en soucy ;
Hem-mi † deux Phi § longtemps ne tiendra Metz.

* Æmathien, or Emathion, Le Pelletier says, son of Cephalus and Aurora, who opened the gates of the morning to the sun. I do not find this account of him anywhere. Cephalus is the chaste Joseph of mythology, tempted by Aurora. But Hesiod makes him father of Phaeton by her. Possibly M. le Pelletier has mistaken Æmathion for Phaeton. Generally, Emathion is reckoned as son of Titan and Aurora, and a King of Macedonia. His connection in some way however with the sun is certain, and this suffices for the use made of his name by Nostradamus. 'Ημαθίων is given by Suidas as a proper name. Now, 'Ημάθιος is *daily*, with but the change of one letter. Further than this 'Ημάθιος is Macedonian, and Alexander is called *Emathius dux*, as in Milton, "the Emathian conqueror bid spare ;" implying that Louis le Grand should be a counterpart to Alexander the Great, an impostor who also pretended birth from Apollo. By which flight of ambition he bastardized himself by choice, dishonoured his mother, and put his father outside the door. Shakespeare says, "By this sin fell the angels ;" but a too prosperous fool seems equally ready to annihilate himself by it, and all belonging to him, of his own act.

† Latin, *per*, through.

‡ Romance, *emmy*, entre, between.　　§ *Phi*, for Philip.

A great conflict will approach Nancy ;
The Æmathion will say, I submit all to me ;
The isle of Britain will be agitated for lack of force and wisdom ;
Metz will not hold out long against the two Philips.

Nancy was taken in 1660 by the French, when they razed the fortifications and united it with France. It appears to me that the first two lines of this quatrain should have formed the last two, but how any such error as that could have crept in is quite inexplicable. The reader will discern that a difference of about twelve years exists between the dates involved in the two distichs, that, as they are given, they are contrary to chronology, and that for such disarrangement no reason is assignable. If this is the way in which visions presented themselves to our seer, there is no reason to suppose, as I do, that he shook up the separate quatrains purposely to destroy a sequence that would have rendered them too easy of interpretation. It might have been a printer's error.

We have already seen what is the classical meaning to be attributed to Æmathion—that it relates to the sun and to Alexander the Great. In Nostradamus it refers to Louis XIV. (*Louis le Grand*). Of him it is to be remembered that he assumed as his emblem and that of France, the sun, with the motto *Nec pluribus impar.* Now, the sun, in the language of alchemists, stands for gold, and, in the metaphorical language of the Church, for Christianity. Gold is all the Christianity that many Christians possess. *Les Solaires*, in Nostradamus, is used for Christians. It is especially connected with France, inasmuch as her King is held at Rome, that centre of titles and of prelatical humility, to be *Christianissimus.* But this stout Capetian glorious King meant it of sovereignty. It was to signify, as Nostradamus has it, *tout je soubmets.* What is this man's own choice of a posy, to be cut around his signet ? *Nec pluribus impar.* What is the axiom his blind self-pride invents when the death of Mazarin emancipates him from tutelage, and he grips the reins of France in his sole left hand (in 1661)? *L'État, c'est Moi.* Can insolence rise higher ? Wait an odd century or so and see a scaffold spring before your Tuilleries windows, see an Æmathion, but twice removed in blood, roll his head, red, gushing, spurting, and bounding on the sawdust-sprinkled planks there ; its motto, could it speak, would be your axiom recast fatally, *L'État du Capet! (Caput!)*

We have not quite concluded yet. When the treaty of Westphalia shall be agreed to between France and Philip IV. of Spain in 1648, and before the war of Succession to seat Philip V., grandson of Louis XIV., on the throne, Metz shall be ceded to France, and lose for ever its title of Imperial City, between the two Philips—Philip IV. and Philip V., *protégé* of France.

England about the same time, in revolution kindled by that imp of malevolence, Richelieu, shall behead its king, 1649, and be in anxiety because of the want of force and wisdom (*vin et sel*). This symbol Le Pelletier interprets thus : Wine is the symbol of force, because of its *heat;* and salt, because of its incorruptibility, is the symbol of *wisdom.* I think it clear that this is not to be the interpretation here. He does not allude to *want* of force and wisdom ; but anxiety (*soucy*) is caused by force and wisdom (*à l'envers*, as he puts again in reference to England, Century IX. 49 ; vol. i. 141) applied in the wrong direction.

This, though a highly unsatisfactory quatrain, as I have shown above, is, nevertheless, one of the most remarkable of the whole series.   The time of the Westphalian treaty synchronises with the revolt in England—a revolt which we have seen to be fostered out of mere pique by the vulpine Richelieu ; a Churchman plotting royal murder, taught by Rome's consent that regicide was God's service, when a king (Henri III.) stood in her way ; and when the Church once corrupted herself, baptizing her St. Bartholomew whose emblem was a knife, in blood, she absolved Paris, [*cité au glaive*, i. 182] who in midsummer madness stained her kennels red. The example of Whitehall—in re-enactment before the Tuilleries (*vin et sel à l'envers*), with force and wisdom converted into violence and democratic sensibility,—next turned Paris *rouge*, and the blood carnation burst into bloom at every street corner.

> " When nations are to perish in their sins,
>   'Tis in the Church the leprosy begins ; "

says the wise, mild, thoughtful, but much underrated bard, Cowper, who has done Gilpin inimitably, and Homer better than anybody else, by a long way.

Loss of de la Ferrière's Squadron (1655). [I. 121.]

Century III.—Quatrain 87.

Classe * Gauloise n'approche de Corsegue, †
Moins de Sardaigne, tu t'en repentiras :
Trestous mourrez frustrés de l'aide grogne ;
Sang nagera, captif ne me croiras.

Translation.

Approach not Corsica, thou fleet of France,
Nor yet Sardinia, lest thou rue the chance :
For ye no headland aids, ye all shall die,
The captive drown, for unbelieved am I.

M. le Pelletier tells us of a French squadron, commanded by the Chevalier de la Ferrière in 1655, that foundered in the Gulf of Lyons in coasting Corsica and Sardinia. All hands perished : they did not, he says, pass Cape Pourceau. He points out that *Grogne* is the synonym of Pourceau, which is a cape with a little port in the Mediterranean. This may have more to support it than appears at first sight, but I think it much simpler to take it for what it says. *Grogne* is the same as *Groin*, cape, or headland which runs out into the sea. In other words : nothing will put off to you from the headland where you founder ; there will you all be drowned ; for what the better will your master pilot be for this advertisement of mine ? Jean de Rian was this master pilot, and *Le Captif* was his nickname, as he had been a slave.

Though perfectly useless for interpretation, Garencières makes annotations on this quatrain, that have an interest of their own. He takes the fulfilment to

---

* Latin, *classis*, fleet.
† *Corseque*, Romance for Corsica.

have been in 1555, just about the time when the quatrains were copied out for presentation to Henri II. But he remarks that *Greigne*, which is the word in his reading, signifies *galley* in the Provençal language, which was that of Nostradamus by his mother's side ; and this makes very good sense: "they shall all founder without a galley putting out to them from the shore."

Of course Garencières knows nothing about Jean de Rian, or the curious precision with which Nostradamus gives us his nickname *Captif ;* but he appends to his " Poor prisoner, thou shalt not believe me " the following comment that is worth recording, as it may furnish a link to some inquiry in the future :

" We find in this work many examples of those who went to consult with the author concerning the success of their under-takings, as did the Earl of *Sommerive,* before the besieging of Bagnole ; to whom he answered, that he should leave the trees loaded with a new kind of fruit, that is to say, the rebels, whom he caused to be hanged on the trees."

Fortifications of Vauban and the Canal of Languedoc (1659-1666). [I. 122.]

Century IX.—*Quatrain* 93.

Les ennemies du fort bien esloignés,
Par chariots conduict le bastion,
Par sur les murs de Bourges esgrongnés,*
Quand Hercules bastira l'Hæmathion. †

Translation.

When the enemy are driven from French soil,
And earthworks or bastions are brought by carts ;
When the walls of Bourges have crumbled by time,
Then will Æmathion undertake a work of Hercules.

* Romance, *esgrongné,* or *esgruné,* pulverised.
† Turn this ; when Æmathion shall build Hercules.

When the peace of the Pyrenees, concluded with Spain in 1659, had removed the enemy from the French frontiers, and Vauban had invented earthworks: at least so says Le Pelletier; Nostradamus only says he used them. Moreri tells us that the castle of Grosse Tour at Bourges was not repaired by Louis XIV., and was already partly ruined in 1651. This line seems to be a whimsical, but special announcement of the fact. Then Æmathion, or Louis XIV., will undertake the Herculean labour of constructing the Canal of Languedoc, which opened the Mediterranean to the ocean. It was begun by Paul Riquet in 1666, and terminated in 1681. It cost thirty-four million francs. It is said that when Vauban visited it he gave some useful hints that were acted upon with advantage. Vauban, like Turenne, was a glory, not to France, but to mankind. He was truly great, for he despised riches, and loved truth to indiscretion; yet his life shows that in judgment he much excelled those who loved truth less.

PEACE OF THE PYRENEES (NOVEMBER 7, 1659). [I. 123.]

Century X.—Quatrain 58.

Au temps du dueil que le felin * monarque,
Guerroyera le jeune Æmathien :
Gaule bransler, perecliter la barque, †
Tenter ‡ Phossen, § au Ponant ‖ entretien.

* Latin, *felinus*, like a cat.
† *La barque* of St. Peter, the Holy Seat, Rome.
‡ Latin, *tentare*, to assail.
§ *Phocen* is another reading. Marseilles, founded by the Phocians, A.C. 660.
‖ Old word for west, or sundown.

Translation.

When the court of France shall be in mourning, the cat-like monarch shall make war against the young Æmathien. France will stagger ; the bark of St. Peter be in danger. Marseilles will be taken. Two great personages will meet in the West of France.

More at large this may be read, that at the death of Louis XIII., when the French Court is in mourning, shrewd Philip IV. of Spain will make war on the boy King. France will be greatly shaken (1648-1653) by the civil war of the Fronde, whilst Rome will be endangered by the growth of Jansenism. This is Le Pelletier's version. Garencières says that Paris is signified, as she carries a ship represented in her arms. The 2nd of March, 1660, Louis XIV. enters Phocea or Marseilles by a breach, after which it submits to him. He then hurries to the west of the Isle of Conference on the Bidassoa, and there concludes the peace of the Pyrenees with Philip IV., and marries his daughter, the infanta Maria Theresa, of Austria.

THE EXPEDITION TO IRELAND IN SUPPORT OF
JAMES II. (1689-1691). [I. 125].

Century II.—Quatrain 68.

De l'Aquilon les efforts seront grands,
Sur l'Ocean sera la porte ouverte,
Le regne en l'Isle sera reintegrand,
Tremblera Londres par * voilles † descouverte.

Translation.

Ireland, on the north of England, shall make great efforts. The door of the ocean shall be opened to the fleets of France ; the kingdom in the island of Ireland shall be set up again ; London shall tremble at the discovery of sails.

* Latin, *per*, because of.   † *Voiles*, for vessels.

When William III., in 1688, shall have established
himself on the throne, when James II. absconded ;
Ireland will still be a stronghold, and the French
fleets, commanded by Château Renaud and Tourville,
will convoy the King to Ireland, in spite of the combined fleets of England and Holland, in 1689–1690.
They will become masters of the sea, and London will
for a moment tremble before the fleets of Louis XIV.
This is Le Pelletier's statement. After the fight off
Beachy Head on June 30, 1690, it seems to have been
pretty much as he relates ; for Smollett's account (ed.
1822, i. 93) is that ;

"Torrington retreated without further interruption into the
mouth of the Thames ; and, having taken precautions against
any attempts of the enemy in that quarter, returned to London,
the inhabitants of which were overwhelmed with consterna-
tion."

There is a most remarkable passage in the work of
M. Bouys on this quatrain. He professes to apply
it to the coming victory that was to confer on
Napoleon the coveted command of the seas, saying
that you need not always wait until after the event
to interpret Nostradamus. His own conduct, however, in this very instance does but enforce the rule.
He pretends not to know anything of the fulfilment
in 1689–1690. In furtherance of the same view he
cites Century VIII., Quatrain 37 :

La forteresse auprès de la Thamise
Cherra pour lors le roi dedans serré,
Auprès du pont sera vu en chemise,
Un devant mort, puis dans le fort barré.

The word *cherra* presents the only difficulty here

as to the mere words. It is the future of the verb *choir*, tomber, to fall. Of the prophecy I know of no interpretation. Garencières significantly quotes Dan. iv. 10: "The dream be to them that hate thee, and the interpretation thereof to thine enemies."

WAR OF THE CAMISARDS (1702-1704). [L. 126.]

Century IX.—Quatrain 38.

L'entrée de Blaye par Rochelle et l'Anglois,
Passera outre le grand Æmathien :
Non loin d'Agen attendra le Gaulois,
Secours Narbonne deceu par entretien.

Translation.

The great Æmathion shall pass out of the Garonne at Blaye, the seaport of Bordeaux, no longer impeded by Rochelle and the English; the Camisards shall look for aid from their co-religionists on the side of Agen and Narbonne, but will be disappointed by an arrangement.

Louis XIV. shall pass out by the *Pâté* de Blaye, a fort of that name, built by him in 1689 to command the entrance of the Gironde against the English and the Protestants of Rochelle. The Camisards in revolt in the Cévennes (*les Gaulois*) will wait at Agens and Narbonne for promised help, but quite in vain, after the submission of Jean Cavalier (1704) to Marshal Villars, at a Conference held at Nîmes. Louis XIV. was so beset by the enemies of France that he sent the Marshal into Languedoc to pacify the districts he despaired of subduing by force.

In this quatrain, Garencières shows that there is some analogy between *Æmathien*, which we are quite sure is Louis XIV. from the frequency of the application to him, and the country of Macedon, so-called, where Cæsar and Pompey fought their last battle in the field of Pharsalia ; and he quotes Lucan's line—

> Bella per Æmathios plus quam civilia campos.

It is very probable that line was in the mind of Nostradamus at the moment.

WAR OF THE SPANISH SUCCESSION (1701–1713). [I. 127.]

Century IV.—Quatrain 2.

Par mort la France prendra voyage à faire,
Classe * par mer, marcher monts Pyrenées,
Espaigne en trouble, marcher gent militaire ;
Des plus grands Dames en France emmenées.

Translation.

By reason of a death, France shall undertake a foreign expedition. The fleet will go by sea, the troops will cross the Pyrenees. Spain in trouble will march her military forces, because great ladies have migrated to France.

Philip V., grandson of Louis le Grand, by will of Charles II., will ascend the Spanish throne. But Austria, England, Holland, Prussia, Portugal, and Savoy will coalesce to support the pretensions of the Archduke Charles. The fleets of France will put to sea, her armies will cross the Pyrenees. Spain, in two camps, will be trampled by troops in every direction : all springing out of Bourbon marriages with the two Infantas ; one, daughter of Philip III. married to Louis XIII., the other, a daughter of Philip IV., married to Louis XIV. This war lasted twelve years, and was disastrous to France. Philip V. found himself chased from Spain by the Austrians. By the

---

* Latin, *classis*, fleet.

Peace of Utrecht, 1713, the Spanish monarchy was dismembered, and some of his earlier conquests were snatched from Louis XIV.

OVERTHROW OF PHILIP V., *grandson of Louis XIV.* (1706). [I. 129.]

Century IX.—Quatrain. 64.

L'Æmathion passer monts Pyrenées,
En Mars Narbon * ne fera resistance,
Par mer terre fera si † grand menée,
Cap ‡ n'ayant terre seure pour demeurance.

Translation.

The Æmathion is to pass the Pyrenean Mount ;
In Narbo Martius no resistance shows ;
By sea and land are greatest efforts made ;
The Capet holds no foot of land is safe.

Louis XIV. will leap the Pyrenees, and will treat (as we have before seen) with the Camisards of Narbonne. He will make desperate efforts by sea and land. But the Capetian, his grandson, Philip V., will be driven out of Spain by the Imperial forces, and not retain a foot of soil on which to live.

In all these passages of history, quite detached as they seem to be, we find analogies springing up at all points : Æmathion the Macedonian, and Louis le Grand ; the Spanish succession which came up again in Louis Philippe's time, even to uniting the very two names of Louis XIV. and his grandson Philip V.

* Latin, *Narbo Martius*, Narbonne, in the department de l'Aude, said to be so called from its founder *Martius*. [See p. 160, IX. 38.]
† Romance, *si*, very.
‡ *Cap*, for Capet.

in his own baptismal one. Louis wished to expel a Charles, and Louis Philippe actually expelled Charles X. Leibnitz made an express journey to Paris to persuade Louis XIV. to undertake a grand expedition against Egypt. Napoleon, the next Æmathion or Apollon leading France to mischief, was thrust into an Egyptian expedition, and entered into a desperate Spanish war to follow, that crippled France again. History repeats itself, they say. It seems at every turn to be perpetually engaged in a process of replaiting its old lines and once-discarded threads.

LOUIS XV.

MINORITY OF LOUIS XV. (SEPTEMBER 1, 1715). [I. 131.]

Century III.—Quatrain 15.

Coeur, vigueur, gloire, le regne changera.
De tous points contre ayant son adversaire :
Lors France enfance par mort subjuguera ;
Un grand Regent sera lors plus contraire.

Translation.

Heart, vigour, glory, change with change of reign,—
At every point opposed by something cross :
An infant is set up in France by death ;
And a great Regent helps the contrary.

WITH the death of Louis XIV., the splendour of his reign will pass away, and every point show contrary in his successor. By failure of direct inheritors of the throne, Louis XV., a child of five will rule, under Philippe d'Orléans (*un grand Regent*), whose vices will show him more contrary to Louis XIV. than even to Louis XV.

DECADENCE OF MONARCHY (1715-1774). [I. 132.]

Century V.—Quatrain 38.

Ce grand monarque qu'au mort succedera,*
Donnera vie illicite lubrique,

---

* Ordo. He who shall succeed to the great monarch dead.

Par nonchalance à tous concedera,
Qu'à la parfin faudra * la loy Salique.

Translation.

He who succeeds to the great monarch dead, will lead an evil
and illicit life. By his neglectful habit he will entrust business
to the management of others, so that at last (*à la parfin, per
finem*) the Salic law will fail.

In other words, this is a plain announcement that
the reign of Louis XV. will serve as a simple prelude
or introduction to the establishment of a Republic ;
the annihilation of the Salic law ; and of the French
throne.

* *Faudra,* future tense of *faillir,* fail, or disappear.

ENGLAND.

Changes of Government in England (1501-1791).
[I. 135.]

Century VI.—Quatrain 57.

Sept fois changer verrez gent * Britannique.
Teints en sang en deux cens nonante an ;
Franche † non point, par ‡ appuy Germanique ;
Aries § doubte son pole Bastarnan.‖

Translation.

You will see the British nation change seven times, stained with blood, in two hundred and ninety years ; but not so France, thanks to the strength of its Germanic Kings [of the Capetian race]. The sign of the Ram will not know (*double*) the northern district (*son pole Bastarnan*), so changed will it be.

ENGLAND will change its governnment seven times in a period of 290 years, inundated with blood, says Le Pelletier,—making this long run of years commence at what he calls the Renaissance (1501–1791). Not so in France ; thanks to the firmness of the Germanic kings, she will hold out till 1792.

* Latin, *gens*, nation.
† *Franche*, for *gent Franche*, French nation.
‡ Latin, *per*, by reason of.
§ Latin : *Aries* sign of the Ram.
‖ *Bastarnie*, corresponding to ancient Poland.

I take this to be, in effect, a French endeavour to chalk out a grand epoch in French annals. Poland (*la Bastarnie*) will be dismembered. The first partition took place in 1772. There will arise in the north of Europe,—Peter the Great ascending the Russian throne, 1682, and Lutheranism triumphing in Germany, 1517,—so that Aries cannot identify the regions adjacent to its northern pole (*son pole Bastarnan*).

M. le Pelletier gives an elaborate statement of what he conceives to be the seven Revolutions in England (1501–1791). But starting from the Renaissance, at the fancy date 1501, he vitiates the whole of the interpretation as it relates to England ; but for the last half of the quatrain he is excellent. His interpretation of the fourth line is masterly. Garencières gives a lengthy annotation, to me in the main unintelligible, but he makes the period to run out about the year 1845 ; in which year I can see nothing to chronicle but the Maynooth Grant of £26,000 per annum. He says the two first lines refer to England, and he leaves the English nation to interpret them We shall shortly try to do so.

(1) The Revolution Le Pelletier dates 1532, when Henry VIII. is proclaimed by Parliament the head of the Church ; 1534 this should be. (2) Re-establishment of Popery under Queen Mary. (3) Elizabeth comes back to Protestantism. (4) Commonwealth follows upon death of Charles I. (5) Restoration under Charles II. (6) William III. takes the throne of James II. (7) The House of Hanover succeeds.

This is exceedingly faulty. It omits as one Revolution the most important of all, if consequences are to be regarded, that is, the lapse of the Tudor race in Elizabeth and the succession of the Stuarts. Another very weak point is the commencing of the 290 years prior to the first issue of the quatrains. According to this, two of the Revolutions were already elapsed. A man does not prophesy of what is past. Nostradamus was writing in the reign of Queen Mary, so that the first Revolution would naturally count from 1558, when Elizabeth re-introduced Protestantism.

Now that we have contrived a firmer basis, let us see what this leads to.

No. 1. Elizabeth comes to the throne, November 17, 1558.

No. 2. James I. (Stuart succession), March 24, 1603. Queen Elizabeth dies exactly one hundred years after her namesake, Queen of Henry VII.

No. 3. Commonwealth on death of Charles I., January 30, 1649; Protectorate, Cromwell, December 16, 1653.

No. 4. Restoration, Charles II., May 29, 1660 (on his 30th birthday).

No. 5. William III. and Mary, November 5, 1668; Revolution (Gunpowder Day),

No. 6. Hanoverian succession, George I., May 21, 1714.

No. 7. Reform Bill, June 17, 1832. (Dulling the lustre of the Crown, as we shall see the French King *mitré*.)

Those who wish to prophesy pleasant things can do away with the disagreeable date of the Reform Bill, in part, because the No. 3 Revolution can fairly be interpreted as two Revolutions. Cromwell's usurpation belied the pretended principles of his whole life and conduct prior to that assumption, and can be called a new order of things. This arrangement will obviate the necessity of classifying the Reform Bill as the 7th Revolution. But the 290 years must end where they do, though you can regard the matter in what light you please. But I look upon Cromwell's treason, not to the King, but to himself as a man, as being practically part and parcel of the Commonwealth, or a horn growing out of the head of that rhinoceros or unicorn : nothing more. Given a popular revolt, a self-seeking horn always grows out of the forehead of the beast, till, with a ring in its nostril, it is driven whither its sublime libertios shall dictate.

Take it either way, it seems to me quite beyond the reach of the ordinary human mind, simply left to its own resources, to strike out four lines so pregnant as these, and await silently, for three hundred years, an interpretation, so little forced or driven as this is. I may say that to even pack into the space of four lines a mass of assertions so pregnant with hints, is a feat in condensation that no poet has ever equalled. Tacitus, the tersest of historians, has never approached it. No précis writer of the most accomplished skill has ever reduced the facts furnished to him in a well-drawn manuscript to such a compass. He could not, and remain intelligible. To those who will merely look at it in this light it may afford endless matter of reflection and curious study. As a forecast, its appearance to me is purely miraculous. Let any one explain it otherwise who thinks he can ; we shall all be ready to learn.

Stuart Dynasty (1603-1649).   [i. 138]

Century X.—Quatrain 40.

La jeunne * nay au regne Britannique,
Qu'aura le pere mourant recommandé
Iceluy mort, Lonole † donra ‡ topique, §
Et à son fils le regne, demandé.

Translation.

The young Prince of the Kingdom of Britain,
Whose dying father will have recommended him ;
This one being dead, Lonole will perorate,
And snatch the kingdom from his very son.

James I. of England and VI. of Scotland was born
June 19, 1566 : the son of Mary Stuart and Henry
Lord Darnley ; who, before his assassination by Both-
well, had commended the young prince to the fidelity
of the Scotch lords.   He ascended the throne of
England in 1603, and under him England and Scot-
land were first denominated Great Britain (*au regne
Britannique*). ‖   When King James I. dies (*Iceluy*

* Romance, *nay, né,* born.

† *Lonole,* anagram for 'Ολλύων, destroying, from the verb
ὀλλύειν, to destroy.   Destroyer.

‡ *Donra,* for donnera, will give.

§ *Topique,* flowers of rhetoric, oratory.

‖ When hempe is sponne,
England's done.

When Elizabeth was in the flower of her age, Bacon remembered well to have heard the above ; hempe standing for
Henry, Edward, Mary and Philip, and Elizabeth.   "Which,"
says he, " thanks be to God, is verified only in the change of
name ; for that the King's style is now no more of England but
of Britain."   Observe the wonderful propriety of the words used
by Nostradamus.   He noted at the right spot and instant a
national change of name ; a point of precision that nine out
of ten lettered Englishmen would fail to reply to correctly,

mort), *Lonole* will seduce England with artificial rhetoric, and demand the kingdom and the life of his son Charles I.

Lonole is the right reading, according to the *Texte-type;* others read *Doudlé,* and Garencières reads *Londre.* He also fancies that the prophecy concerns Charles II., because Charles I. commended him to the people of England. It is rather curious that *Lonole* should give the anagram of Olleon, or 'Ολλύων, as Napoleon does that of Ναπολλύων and Apollyon. Cromwell and he have many analogies and points of contact, whether in history, character, or prophecy. But a further anagram, still more wonderful, springs here into view, which, I believe, has hitherto escaped all the commentators. *Ole Nol,* or *Old Noll,* has always been the Protector's nickname, and in the first form is letter for letter *Lonole.* It may stand for Apollyon also, and as such for "Old Nick" too.

I ought not to pass away from this mass and congeries of singular hints and disclosures without pointing out the remarkable fact or link connecting James I. with Nostradamus, and the particular quatrain we are now dealing with. James I. was born June 19, 1566, and thirteen days after, July 2, 1566, Nostradamus breathed his last. This quatrain, once understood, is one of the clearest and most extraordinary of the forecasts of Nostradamus. The

in answer to the sudden question, When was England first called Great Britain? It would be interesting to know the history of this "trivial prophecy" as his lordship calls it, for it has a good deal of the true spirit of forecast in it. It certainly was genuine, as it evidently was known to the narrator as being in circulation before it was accomplished.

commencing event, the birth of James I., just touches his own death ; and the last event, the death of Charles I., 1649, stretches to nearly a hundred years later.

Anagram seems to have been once a passion with the people. We find the white cloth of Lincoln in the thirteenth century alluded to as " Drap blanc de *Nicole*," that standing for *Lincoln*. [Le Roux de Lincy " Livre des Prov. Franc." i. 195.]

Fall of Charles I. (March 31, 1646). [i.139].

Century III.—Quatrain 80.

Du regne Anglais le digne dechassé,*
Le conseiller par † ire ‡ mis à feu,
Ses adherans iront si bas tracer, §
Que le bastard sera demy receu.

Translation.

He who had the right to reign in England, shall be driven from the throne, his counsellor abandoned (*mis a feu*) to the fury of the populace (*par ire*). His adherents will follow so low a track that the usurper (*le bastard*) will come to be Protector (*demy receu*, or half King).

Garencières fancies this to relate to Charles II., and, that it is very clear. But evidently *le digne dechassé* is Charles I. Strafford was surrendered weakly to the unreasoning rage of the people (*par ire*). The Scotch, his countrymen (*ses adherents*), will sell him for £400,000 (Hume, vii. 76) to the Independents with unexampled baseness (*si bas tracer*). After this Crom-

---

* Romance, *dechassé*, simply *chassé*.
† Latin, *per*, by reason of.
‡ Latin, *ira*, anger.
§ Romance, *tracer*, follow a road, track.

well (*le bastard*) will become Protector, or half king
(*sera demy receu*).

This could scarcely be made more remarkable than
it is, had it been written historically after the event,
as history, than it is now before it, as prophecy.
Look, again, at the overwhelming insight and terseness : the King defeated, Strafford sacrificed, the
Covenanters' money bargain, and the Protectorate
chalked out in decisive outline nearly a century before
the realization : and each event is contained in one
metrical phrase.

EXECUTION OF CHARLES I. (JANUARY 30, 1649). [I. 141].

Century IX.—Quatrain 49.

Gand et Bruceles marcheront contre* Anvers,
Senat de Londres mettront à mort leur Roy :
Le sel et vin luy seront à l'envers,
Pour eux avoir le regne en desarroy.

Translation.

Gand and Brussels will march past Antwerp,
The Senate at London will put their King to death ;
Salt and wine will be applied contrariwise,
So that they will set the whole kingdom in disarray.

Philip IV. in the Netherlands, being at war, will
move Gand and Brussels towards Antwerp against
Holland in revolt. Holland had, in 1579, detached
itself from the Low Countries. Thus Antwerp became
the border town of the Spanish possessions. Philip
claimed rights over her till the treaty of Westphalia,
or Munster, of which we have Terburg's curious
portraiture in the National Gallery, concluded on

* *Contre*, à côté de, opposite, or near to.

October 14, 1648 ; three months only before the death of Charles I., so that the conjunction of the two events is extraordinarily definite and remarkable.

The second line is as definite and marvellous as anything that occurs in Nostradamus. By the treaty of Munster it fixes the date to within three months. Garencières says : "It is the most remarkable of all those [prophecies] that ever Nostradamus was author of." He notifies also, what I think nobody else has, that the number of this quatrain, 49, gives the very year of the occurrence in the seventeenth century. For though we in England then called it 1648–49, Nostradamus, by the Gregorian Calendar used in France, would reckon it as 1649. We need lay no stress whatever upon this, for the quatrain wants nothing to strengthen it. Yet, be it the offspring of chance or intention, it is most singular. I have before said how much value lies in mere curiosities, and it is part of my business to point one out whenever I am able.

We have already handled the phrase *vin sel* at p. 151 and 153 [I. 119], but from a French, and not English point of view ; yet even there the line is

L'Isle Britanne par vin sel en souci.

—showing the consistency with which the visions must have shaped themselves in the mind of Nostradamus. The one we are treating of now appears in the ninth century of the prophet's quatrains, but the above line occurs in a quatrain of the tenth century. Still, what is said in the one is consistent with what is said in the other. If we call this chance, we shall have to admit an axiom far from self-evident ; namely, that method is discernible in chance as well as in madness. Here, as at disgraceful Old Pancras grave-yard, there is clearly a slight derangement of epitaphs.

Bouys and nearly all the commentators treat the figure of *le vin et sel*, as representing force and wisdom, which were wanting to the King of England. I think we are not at all necessitated to adopt this interpretation. Supposing *salt* and *wine* in a good sense to symbolize wisdom and power, before we settle that to be their application here, we shall have to understand what *à l'envers* means. In the first place, it is not the preposition *envers*, meaning *for*, or *in regard to*. It is a noun substantive, masculine, and stands for the wrong side of a fabric, as contrasted with, or opposed to, the right side, called *l'endroit*. It means that wisdom and power will present their wrong aspect at this juncture, and become intrigue and violence, and will so stand to him (*lui seront à l'envers*), as that they will convert into their opposites, intrigue and violence. It has the old sense of *inversus*, as in the *Roman de la Rose*. A person is there told that on going to bed no sleep will come, but tossing from one side to the other :

> Une heure *envers* et l'autre adens
> Come cil qui a mal aus dens.

Here it reads one hour on the *back*, another on the teeth. Molière says of a character (*l'Et*. ii. 14) :

> Vous serez toujours. . . .
> Un envers du bon sens, un jugement à gauche.

Nothing can better describe the mockery in West-minster Hall of the trial of the King than *un juge-ment à gauche*. The third line of the quatrain is the precise equivalent. *Vin* so nearly resembles *vis* that it is sure to mean force, the two extremes of which are power and violence, law and lawlessness. We see this very distinctly in the old French word *vimaire*, force majeure (*vis major*) and the word further signified storm, tempest, famine, and pestilence (*vide* Roquefort, *s.v.*). That wine does not at all definitely stand for power well directed, is plain enough from "the wine of fornication" (Rev. xvii. 2) ; and that salt is not to be taken as wisdom personified with fixity may be gathered, if from nothing else, from the sanctification of the sacramental elements in the Church of Rome ; where before salt is used, it is first exorcised, to purify it from the stain of original sin, that passed upon all creation at the fall (Auber's "Symbolisme," iii. 394). Whatever wisdom Godwin, Carlyle, and other modern revolutionists may suppose themselves to have discovered in the character of Cromwell, Nostradamus certainly had formed no such notion of him, as we shall immediately feel assured by the next quatrain. Nostradamus's opinion of Cromwell may determine nothing at all as to the final estimate of that man. I adduce it only to help to settle what he meant by the words we are studying, *le sel et vin*. The next line is plain enough. The Independents set the whole kingdom by the ears.

I think we have reached a point at which every line of this quatrain has become tolerably clear. A wiseacre, writing about it in the *Quarterly Review* (vol. xxvi. p. 189) says : "Œdipus himself could not give the sense of the whole verse." This is the way in which people treat a difficult, abstruse, and intricate subject. It is so easy to say we have made up our mind about a man ; that he is unintelligible, a charlatan, an impostor ; that his forecasts are oracular nonsense, meaning nothing, or that if at times they do light on something, chance has more to do with it than seership or vision. You would certainly think that a sane man, finding in a book,—that indubitably was in print,—in 1558 a line prophesying the death of the King of England nearly a hundred years after, " Senat de Londres mettront à mort leur Roy," would be struck with astonishment at the clearness of that, rather than with the difficulty of making sense of the other three lines. But this is what prejudice can do with us all.

CROMWELL'S PROTECTORATE (1653-1658). [I. 142].
Century VIII.—Quatrain 76.

Plus Macelin * que Roy en Angleterre,
Lieu obscur nay † par force aura l'empire,
Lasche sans foy sans loy saignera terre :
Son temps approche si près que je souspire.

Translation.

A Butcher more than king rules England. A man of no birth will seize the government by violence. Of loose morals, without faith or law he will bleed the earth. The hour approaches me so near that I breathe with difficulty.

Here we have a most remarkable forecast. It puts in a clear light what view Nostradamus had formed of Cromwell. There appears to have been visually present to him the butcher-like face of Cromwell,

---

* Italian, *macellaio*, butcher, from Latin *macellum*.

† Romance, *nay*, né, born.

N

with its fleshly conch and hideous warts. This seems to have struck him with such a sense of vividness and horror, that he is willing to imagine that the time is very near at hand. A full century had, however, to elapse; but he sighs as with a present shudder, and the blood creeps:

Son temps s' approche si près que je souspire.

One of the most remarkable features throughout the work of Nostradamus, is the general absence of any sense of time, apart from the mere enumeration of years as an algebraic or arithmetical formula; further than this, he so regulates and controls his feelings as to appear almost impassible ; but this announcement is of such unparalleled and terrific import that he departs from his usual practice and stands horror-stricken as in the presence of a fearful vision.

It was intended to treat here of the portraiture of Cromwell. To complete, however, my observations, I had to go to Chequers Court, the Print Room, and the National Portrait Gallery. These and other necessary steps occupied so much time that the printers had to commence paging ; then, as the enlarged matter could not find room here, there was no alternative but an Appendix, which will be found at p. 351. My remarks, which make so little show now that they are done, cost me far more trouble than ten times the mere amount of writing would. The final settlement depends on the cast at Florence, if still in existence. I have cleared the road for a decisive conclusion; which, though it is not much, is yet something.

Bouys specially comments (p. 109) upon the word

Lasche in this quatrain, and takes it to mean cowardly, the same as *lâche* does in modern French. Both forms of the word are alike deduced from the Latin, *laxare, laxatus,* and then it might well mean of *loose morals,* as I have rendered it. That the Latin may mean this Bailey's " Facciolati " shows, *s.v. Laxitas:* " Liber membris cum mollibus fingitur, et liquoris feminei dissolutissimus laxitate "; and Cromwell's dissolute life in early youth has been insisted on by many, though, of course, contradicted by others. Frederic Harrison is the last of these, and passes over the charge of vice with a very light hand, saying that " Such testimony as theirs we cannot trust ; but we cannot now refute it." Suffice it to say, I do not think cowardice was what Nostradamus meant to impute to Cromwell.

The obscure birth requires a moment's consideration, as none of the French commentators allude in any way to it. The household of Robert Cromwell, Oliver's father, in Huntingdon, was of the industrious, jog-trot, somewhat over-professingly pious, middle-class order, common enough then in the Eastern counties. What is most remarkable, perhaps, is that the homestead, in which he was born, had been built upon the ruins of a convent of Augustine Friars, and that the two estates which came to him, one from his father and the other from his mother's brother, consisted of old church-lands. Oliver's branch of the family had rather fallen away from the county position which such inheritance infers. But it was always the more prominent families that stole, or possessed themselves of, the church-lands at the spoliation, and thus the Cromwells were married in and in with gentry. This scion of the robbers of the Church was soon to develop, on his own account, into a robber of the State; a man of violence and passion quite after the heart of Thomas Carlyle. Carlyle's notion of a hero, is a strong devil in a tantrum, mollifying, now and again, to the drone of a Psalm tune. Cromwell's branch seems to have drifted from the more courtly side to Calvinistic burghers and narrow-souled Independents; whilst Milton, who was born a London citizen, far away from gentry, was floated by his tastes and nature to the Court side of things, to the Bridgewaters, Ludlow Castle (see his deathless Masque of Comus), until a lofty idea of principle, — taken up by an unripe judgment, and dazzled by that false illusion, Liberty,—dashed him headlong into polemics, and irretrievably damaged the greatest poet ever born to England. They were exact opposites—these two. Milton sacrificed himself to his principles, Cromwell his principles to his person. Still, an old brewing concern at Huntingdon may well be designated by Nostradamus *lieu obscur*, as contrasted with Whitehall, and a burial, if you please, in Westminster Abbey, so wastefully extravagant as that it might well break a nation's treasury to meet it. Such prodigious pageantry belies the professions of the life, and can in no way be harmonized with "Take that bauble hence." Such empty, worthless show has less, for me, of the saint and hero in it, than of the froth of beer, and of the littleness and vanity of man. If this is to be great, prythee, tell us, what is it to be little?

British Ascendancy of the Sea (over three Centuries). [I. 143.]

Century X.—Quatrain 100.

Le grand empire sera par Angleterre,
Le pempotam * des ans plus de trois cens :
Grandes copies † passer par mer et terre,
Les Lusitains ‡ n'en seront pas contens.

Translation.

England the Pempotam (πᾶν *potens*) will rule the great empire (of the waters) for more than three hundred years. Great armies will pass by sea and land ; the Portuguese will not be satisfied.

The French render this as meaning the destruction of England by large forces coming to overwhelm her by sea and land, but the reader will see that it does not at all necessarily show this. If we altered the colon, and put it at the end of the third line, it would simply mean that, whilst she was "all powerful" at sea, she moved large bodies of troops by both elements. I do not think it is very clear what the last line intends. But the three hundred years' dominion of the sea is a very palpable and most important object. That it is now drawing to a close is a somewhat melancholy subject for the contemplation of Englishmen, when we consider the searching revolution introduced by steam. If it really forebodes evil to England, it would involve dissatisfaction to the Lusitanians, as, if England fell, Portugal would be overwhelmed simultaneously by Spain.

* *Pempotam*, a shocking word made out of Greek and Latin πᾶν—*potens*, all powerful.
† Latin, *Copia*, military forces.
‡ Latin, *Lusitani*, Portuguese.

The Invincible Armada of Philip II. was destroyed in 1588 by storms first, and the residue by Drake in Cadiz Bay. From that epoch we naturally date the maritime supremacy of our country, which, according to Nostradamus, is to last for more more than three centuries, but not four. Nelson's death at Trafalgar in 1805 was the culminating event of our naval history. Its salt-sea tale still stirs young hearts in far-off seaboard cottages on stormy nights in winter with a flush of heroism, and that yet more sacred thing, a solemn sense of duty. But the old sobriety and obedient spirit of reverence, that was common in English homes last century is greatly decadent under the rotten knowledge dropping widely from the Upas Board Schools,—with reverence banished and obedience lost. The bare three hundred years ended in 1888. What the *plus* may count for, with Revolt thus bred at every hearth, a wise Englishman might ask with some emotion now.

It is said, in James's "Naval History," that from 1793 to 1815—I have not referred to verify—two hundred ships of the line, and three to four hundred frigates were taken or destroyed of the fleets opposed to England ; and of the sea as at the pouring out of the second vial, ἐγένετο αἷμα ὡς νεκροῦ, it became as the blood of a dead man (Rev. xvi. 3). This completely crushed out all chance of Napoleon's descent upon England ; but, with the lying spirit that distinguished his administration at all times, he managed to disguise the fact from Frenchmen at the time ; so that we find Bouys, at p. 92, promising him—out of two misinterpreted quatrains—in 1806, when his fleet was annihilated, the empire of the sea and a conquest of England as complete as that of William the Conqueror. It only proves once more how far from truth is the wish that is father to the thought. Let him stand aloof who would read the future by the light of the lantern of his prejudices.

We are now at the end of the guidance of Le Pelletier. Nevertheless, I will adduce several other quatrains to bring the English sequence down to the succession of the House of Hanover. They will perhaps not be devoid of instruction, though they will not be so remarkable as those already adduced. Several quatrains, more or less intelligibly wrought out, are enumerated in a pamphlet of the year 1715 by D. D.* The first relates to Queen Mary.

QUEEN MARY.

Century IV.—Quatrain 96.

La Sœur aisnee de L'Isle Britannique,
Quinze ans devant le frère aura naissance,
Par son promis, moyennant verrifique,
Succedera au Regne de Balance.

Translation.

The elder sister of the British Isle shall be born fifteen years before her brother ; true to her intervening promise, she will succeed to the Kingdom of the Balance.

---

* The full title runs : " The Prophecies of Nostradamus concerning the fate of all the Kings and Queens of Great Britain since the Reformation, and the succession of his present Majesty King George, and the continuation of the British Crown in his most serene Royal House to the last day of the world. Collected and explained by D.D., 1715." This book is in the British Museum. I do not know whether it is scarce or not. It is not common, for I never meet with it in booksellers catalogues.

This means that Mary, elder sister of Edward VI., shall ascend the throne of England. She was not born fifteen years before him. Her birth took place February 18, 1516, whilst Edward VI. was born October 12, 1537, over twenty-one years later. The fulfilment of her truthful promise lay in carrying out her vow to reinstate the Papists, causing even her sister Elizabeth to be imprisoned in the Tower on a charge of conspiracy. *Moyennant* seems to refer to the temporary nature and duration of her papal restorations ; *en la moyenne,* in the midst or interim, between the Protestantism of her young brother, and that of Elizabeth, who succeeded her. Mary's birth was an event actually contemporary with Nostradamus ; a very little inquiry, we may be sure, would have enabled him to have rendered it conformable to the facts of history. As exemplifying his method and procedure, it is very important to find that he took no trouble whatever to do so. It is evident that our prophet acted quite independently of external aids. He seems to have had methods and ways of his own, in which he had the most entire and implicit faith. In whatsoever manner the impressions reached him, he laid himself open to their reception, a reception to all appearance of pure passivity: he took the earliest moment of noting them down, more after the manner of an amanuensis under dictation than as being personally at all responsible for anything he committed to paper. The explanation of D. D. upon this passage is very singular, and implies somewhat of the insight of an adept into magical processes and fatidical language, of which we should be glad to know more.

We must, however, content ourselves with it as it is ; and even this little glimpse will be valued by those who love to study the human mind in all its byeways, and who are qualified to do so by thrusting aside from their own mind all private prejudice and vain prepossession. He says with regard to the discrepancy :

"But, if he has not known it, then has he either overheard it *in raptu*, whilst his genius dictated unto him one year and three *Heptades*, or forgot it *post raptum*, and did write one year and two *Heptades*. The *Lingua Demonum* uses *Septenarios in numerando*, as we do *Denarios.*"

Where he gets this intelligence from I have no idea. What he heard *in raptu*, could not have been one year and three heptades, for that would have represented twenty-two years, and we have to do with twenty-one years. What he might have heard, supposing we are right as to the *lingua demonum*, would be " one, plus two heptades," meaning *three heptades ;* and he might have supposed it to mean one year plus two heptades, or fifteen years. If not satisfactory, this at least, has something of plausibility about it.

The phrase *Regne de Balance* has much of importance attaching to it. Garencières translates the last line, " She shall succeed in the Kingdom of Libra," and he annotates that the princess, whom he does not recognize at all, born so long before her brother, shall be married to a King of France, which is signified by the " Kingdom of *Libra.*" He also says that Louis XIII. was called *The Just*, because he was born under the sign *Libra*. I give this for the sake of its being curious, though quite beside the mark, so far as I am able to see.

The phrase *Règne de Balance* is one of those pithy pregnant sentences, ever and anon dropping instinctively from the pen of Nostradamus, on all topics treated by him or glanced at. The whole bent of England's policy, from Henry VII.'s day to the Treaty of Vienna, has been to maintain a European equipoise, and to provide that no State should grow so strong as to overwhelm the rest. The wise counsels of the statesmen of Elizabeth were all directed in the hope of fortifying it ; and it was never seriously infringed until the first partition of Poland in 1772, which was completed by the third in 1795. Napoleon's false profession to restore it in 1806 may count—like all he said, " as false as dicers' oaths "—for nothing. England's permission of that crime,—that satanry of royal crowns, struck her with judicial blindness ;—and hired publicists, the venal reptiles that preceded the journalists, soon sprang up in abundance, to confuse and smoke-dry the moral sense of Europe. Poland had established that most unworkable of all governmental schemes, an elective monarchy ; an arrangement that insures periodical anarchy at every election, and generally a wrong choice at last. The satanry of Split Eagles gave out, that the Poles could not govern themselves. But the fourth article in Peter the Great's will shows that they were not to be allowed to govern themselves. They were to be kept in continual jealousy, whilst the other powers were to be corrupted by gold, and a share of the plunder ; till Russia could retake all. The bribers, the bribed, and the publicists succeeded so well that the very phrase " Balance of power " became, and still is, a topic of ridicule in common conversation. By this means its obvious rationality is excluded from any chance of a fair hearing. The Navigation Laws, Corn Laws, and Protection, have all been treated in the same way in our own time, and with the same revolutionary consequences, and loss of English supremacy. The Marquis de Bouillé, in his " Mémoires," ed. 1821, p. 8,—one of the few modern men who is entitled to be called a statesman,—says of England, that it is an empire whose support all other nations stand in need of, and that its happiness is intimately bound up with that of the world at large, but that if its thirst of gold should destroy its patriotism ; or that bold demagogues and orators should get power to meddle with its fundamental laws, it would soon become chaotic and fall, leaving nothing behind it but another great ghost of empire perished, to glimmer as an historical beacon through the night of time. Again he says, at p. 24, that for thirty years (speaking about 1783) she has been the happy rival of France, and in some sort the arbitress of Europe. A little later on, when we crushed Napoleon by sea and land, and yet preserved France, we rose to our highest ; but at Vienna the *Règne de Balance* * passed, probably

---

* Hume has very ably handled this important question in his Seventh Essay (Hume's " Philosophical Works," iii. 373, Edinburgh, 1826). He there sets out that it is no modern invention as some have maintained, for the Asiatics combined against the Medes and Persians, as Xenophon shows in his " Institutions of Cyrus." Likewise Thucydides exhibits the league

for ever, from the sceptre of England ; just twenty
years after the final partition of Poland.   Cursed are

formed against Athems, which led to the Peloponnesian war,
as being grounded on this principle.   Afterwards, when Thebes
and Lacedæmon disputed the supremacy, Athens always threw
her strength into the lighter scale to preserve the balance.   She
was for Thebes against Sparta till Epaminondas won at Leuctra,
and then she immediately changed sides, as of generosity, but
really jealous to preserve the balance.   If you will read
Demosthenes, he says, in the Oration for the Megapolitans you
may "see the utmost refinements on this principle that ever
entered into the head of a Venetian or English speculatist."
On the rise of the crafty Macedonian he again bugled the alarm
to Greece, which brought the banners together that fell at
Chæronea.   The principle was right, but the too great delay
had knit Fate's smile into a frown.   Envy (if you like to call it
so, but I call it a jealous prudence) must in a community of
States prevent any one from overtopping, as Athenian ostracism
expelled the citizen who grew too lush and vigorous for a communion in equality.   Hume points out with perspicuous beauty
how England went too far.   Her emulous antagonism to France
made her so alert to defend her allies that they could count
upon her as a force of their own.   The expenses consequent
upon this imprudent course led to funding, *i.e.* the *National
Debt;* and that has led us into an absurd meekness, a dread of
war, and the peace barkings of the Quaker Bright ; so that
England dares not fire a howitzer when Russia, contrary to her
most solemn pledges, annexes Merv, Bokara, and Khiva, and
cannot find one word to say when Germany has her foot on the
throat of France.   Blunders in extravagant advocacy, blunders
in parsimonious neglect of a principle, do not diminish its
importance ; they only emphasize it.   With a prophecy out of
dry reason Hume says it will become "more prejudical another
way, by begetting, as is usual, the opposite extreme, and
rendering us totally careless and supine with regard to the fate
of Europe."   That is how we now stand.   In a very recent
French cyclopædia, *l'équilibre Européan* is said to be quite
a modern idea, with nothing corresponding to it in antiquity.

those who, with arms in their hands, stand by and allow evil to be done! We repeated the cowardice when France was under the heel of Prussia. If no virtue remained, the common policy of equalization should have weighed, to throw in aid to the weaker side.

The writer pretends that it originated with the Church, and that Podichad the King of Bohemia sent Marini to Louis XI. to point out the necessity there was for a *Parliament of Kings* to adjust matters between the Church and people. This may be the first form of a Congress. Francis I. carried on the same policy, and Henri IV. extended it to an idea of a Christian republic of federated nations, as against a universal monarchy. This idea enabled Cromwell to meddle as European arbiter, whereas he ought only to have acted as moderator and equalizer of parties. Leibnitz called the House of Hapsburgh a continual conspiracy against the rights of the people, and Richelieu got the *equilibrium* established and introduced at the Treaty of Westphalia, as a principle of the law of nations, though with the concomitant of *Congresses.* The princes so assembled plotted against Poland, as might have been anticipated, and in the course of seventy years they were enabled entirely to break up the Balance of Power in Europe. Cromwell, Richelieu, Napoleon, and Bismark, by force, finesse, chicane, and brutal bluntness, have overturned the very groundwork of the principle. The English, having at first stirred up war by means of subventions, have now tumbled, only too laxly, into the stupid doctrine of non-intervention. Congresses should never have been allowed. These " Parliaments of Kings " can only do mischief, as they have no controlling power to refer to. They lack a *King* above the Parliaments, and as that is *impossible,* Congresses can only meet for evil. The strongest are irresistible in such congregations. The weaker can get no justice and no sympathy. If they take the field, everybody is against them ; if they submit, they are despoiled without hope of a remedy : whereas, formerly, a wrong done might excite a feeling of justice in a neighbour, and so induce him to help ; or, where justice was weak, fear of similar treatment might opportunely bring forth the required aid.

Queen Elizabeth (1533–1603).

Century VI.—Quatrain 74.

La dechassee au regne tournera,
Ses ennemies trouvez des conjurez ;
Plusque jamais son temps triomphera,
Trois, et Septante, la mort, trop asseurez.

Translation.

The rejected one shall at last reach the throne, her enemies found to have been traitors. More than ever shall her period be triumphant. At seventy she shall go assuredly to death, in the third year of the century.

Elizabeth was long withheld from the throne. When she reached it, of course all enemies were regarded as traitors, and no reign was ever more triumphant. She proved a thorn in the side of popery; overthrew the Armada; and crippled the power of Spain, despoiling it of a large tract of land in America, which has been called after her Virginia ; and under Essex, in 1596, inflicted on it a loss of twenty million ducats or pieces of eight, in the Bay of Cadiz. The next quatrain that we shall take seems to refer to the expedition by Essex.

The fourth line is a very singular one. It has no punctuation in the edition of 1558 ; so I introduce a comma between *trois* and *septante*. *Septante* is "seventy," a good old word that has dropped out of French usage, but which many French scholars think infinitely preferable to the clumsy circumlocution *Soixante dix*. *Trois* stands for 1603. Nostradamus often drops the thousands and hundreds from a date. We shall shortly come to a case in point, at the Fire of London, 1666. When Nostradamus describes the doomed city, he writes : " Bruslé par fond, de vingt-trois les six." The nought in 1603 cannot be given, so that, omitting the figures in the tens, hundreds, and thousands, the *trois* remaining gives the date ; so that the line remains " In the third year [of the seventeenth century] and seventy years old, assured death comes." Elizabeth was born September 7, 1533, and she died March 24 (April 3, N.S.), 1603 ; fulfilling to a nicety the conditions of the line as thus set forth.

ATTACK ON CADIZ BAY (1596).
Century VIII.—Quatrain 94.

Devant le lac ou plus cher fut getté
De sept mois, et son ost desconfit
Seront Hispans par Albanois gastez,
Par delay perte en donnant le conflict.

Translation.

Before the lake, where much treasure (*plus cher*) was stranded, after a seven months' voyage, and the host discomforted. Spaniards shall be worsted by the English, by time lost before giving battle.

Garencières here takes *Albanois* for Albanians, which of course prevents him from reaching any conceivable meaning. It stands for English, as Albanies, or Albions. The quatrain may reasonably enough be interpreted of the attack made by Essex, Howard, and Raleigh, June, 1596, on Cadiz Bay. They destroyed there thirteen ships of war, and forty huge South American galleons, part of the great " silver fleet," or " plate fleet." They had got stranded in their own harbour. Had the Spaniards been alert, they might have unloaded the treasure-ships, and so saved the cargoes. If they had attacked the English at once, instead of awaiting the onset, they might have beaten them off, or at least have kept them out of the harbour. But they were so supine that the Duke de Medina had at last to fire the ships to prevent their capture. The Spartans and Spaniards have been noted as being of small despatch : *Mi venga la muerta di Spagna*—" Let my death come from Spain, for then it will be sure to be long in coming" (Bacon's Essay on Despatch). Collins does not give this in his Spanish proverbs. But not only did Spaniards and Spartans procrastinate. " Business to-morrow," said the Theban Polymarch, in Plutarch, as he laid under his pillow some despatches relating to a conspiracy, and was killed before he read them. Copyslip wisdom saith " Delays are dangerous."

The bay and harbour of Cadiz may very well be called a lake, being twelve miles one way, and at least six the other, whilst the entrance to it from Rota to the Castle of St. Sebastian is a good six miles. When Essex got possession of the Castle of Puntales, he commanded the whole town and harbour. The idea of *lake* is actually expressed in the very name of Cadiz, which is derived from the Punic word *Gaddir*, an *enclosed place*. The Greeks corrupted this into γάδειρα, or γῆς δειρή, " neck of land." The Romans contracted either this or the Punic word into *Gades*, and the Spaniards into *Xerez*, by the help of their Arabic guttural.

Century VI.—Quatrain 22.

Dedans la terre du grand temple celique,
Nepueu à Londre par paix feincte meurtry :
La barque alors deviendra scismatique,
Liberté feincte sera au corn' et cry.

In the country of the great heavenly temple the nephew is murdered [by her who comes] to London under a feigned truce. The ship [of Peter] will then become schismatic, and feigned liberty become the hue and cry.

I cannot, I confess, altogether make this out. D. D. interprets it of the murder of Henry Stuart, 1567, and the final establishment of the Reformation. If it mean this, it will be a proof of the uncertainty, and almost caprice with which forecasts are concerned. It is strange that Henry Stuart's murder should find any representation, when, so far as I yet know, nothing is recorded of the fate of Mary Stuart herself. The heavenly temple is, according to D. D., the kingdom of the *Angeli*, Angels, or Angles, meaning the English. We are by no means forced to accept this interpretation, for *Celique* may stand for *luminous*, according to Le Pelletier's Glossary, where he derives the word from the Greek σίλας, though I see no such word. *Celique* is generally considered to stand for *celeste*, *cælitus*, from *cælum*. We might read it as a misprint for Celtique. Then *la terre du grand temple Celtique* would be the island in which is placed the great Druid temple of Stonehenge—the island of Apollo, *Templum Solis*, as Bath is the fountain of the sun, *Aqua Solis.* I record these hints, not as possessing much value in themselves, but as being possible aids towards future elucidation.

La Barque, in Nostradamus, is no doubt usually to be interpreted of the Popedom, the ship of St. Peter ; but if, as I think, the general reference of the quatrain be to England and English affairs, then I should

O

interpret *La Barque* as the Ship of State, becoming more and more schismatical, and in which the Puritans, Independents, and other Dissenters raise a great hue and cry about liberty, and liberty of conscience (*au corn' et cry*, or *à cor et à cri*, which is a variant of the early edition). The Puritans were becoming most troublesome both in England and Scotland all through the reigns of Elizabeth and Mary Stuart. Here D. D. insists upon what it is the business of his book to establish ; that the accession of the House of Hanover to the throne of England is one distinct topic of the prophecies of Nostradamus. James I. was the great-grandfather of George I. His daughter Elizabeth married Frederic, the Elector Palatine, and had issue the Princess Sophia, Electress of Brunswick-Lunenberg, the mother of George I.

England becomes Great Britain (1603).

Century III.—Quatrain 70.

La grand Bretaigne comprinse d'Angleterre,
Viendra par eaux si * haut à inonder
La Ligue neuve d'Ausonne fera guerre,
Que contre eux ils se viendront bander.

Translation.

Great Britain comprising England, will come to be inundated very forcibly by the waters. The new League in Italy will make war against all such as band together against any one of the cosignatories.

England was politically called Great Britain when Scotland was united to her at the accession of James I. in 1603. Still, in an indefinite way, the term, or kindred terms, had often been employed. To

* *Si*, for très.

go no further than the "Faerie Queene" of Spenser (Book III. c. ii. § 7), we find :

Far fro my native soyle, that is by name
The Greater Brytayne, here to seeke for praise and fame.

In this passage, Church says, it means Wales, as distinguished from the Lesser Brittany in France. The Greater Brytayne would hardly be Wales, but England and Wales together before the Saxon Heptarchy. This, however, in no way interferes with the propriety of the distinction drawn by Nostradamus. His allusion is clearly to the time of James I., who assumed the title of " King of Great Britain " on October 24, 1604.

The floods spoken of commenced about the end of January, 1607. The principal damage occurred in Somersetshire, where the sea broke down the dykes, and overflowed the country for thirty miles in length and six miles inland, to the destruction of all property and most of the inhabitants. Bristol suffered. The east coast by Norfolk suffered in like manner, though not quite to so great an extent. A long account of it, giving curious details of the calamity, was hunted up by Garencières, and found in an old, almost-forgotten Latin book, entitled "Rerum in Galliâ, Belgiâ, Hispaniâ, Angliâ, etc., *gestarum anno* 1607," à Nicolao Gotardo Artus Dantisco, VII., Book 2.

La Ligue neufve, D. D. says, was a renewal of the *Liga Sancta* first entered into in 1526 between the King of France, the Pope, and the Venetians. The renewal took place in 1606, and was simply defensive, precisely as the quatrain puts it. Thus the quatrain stretches over a space of three years, from October, 1604, establishing the title of "Great Britain;" the ratification of the *Liga Sancta* in 1606; and the inundations in Somerset and Norfolk in 1607. The alliance of 1526 goes by the name of the Treaty of Cognac (or *Holy League*). It was concluded on March 22, 1526, between the Pope, Francis I., Venice, Henry VIII., the Swiss, and Florence. The second or defensive alliance, according to D. D., was between three only of the original signatories; France, the Pope, and the Venetians. I do not find it mentioned, but presume he is right. Garencières evidently writes in entire ignorance of both these treaties; but he says that the League will be of Bordeaux, which is called *Ausone*, from Ausonius, the famous Latin poet, who was born there. Here it certainly means Italy; but I mention it, as it is quite likely that Nostradamus might so employ the word, though he does not on this occasion. *Ausone* occurs once again, at least, in Quatrain 22 of Century VII., which I do not know that anybody has yet interpreted.

CHARLES I.

Century V.—Quatrain 93.

Soubs le terroir du rond globe lunaire,
Lors que sera dominateur Mercure :
L'isle d'Escosse fera un luminaire,
Qui les Anglois mettra à deconfiture.*

Translation.

Under the jurisdiction of the round globe of the moon, when Mercury shall be lord of the ascendant : the island of Scotland will produce a luminary (prince) that shall throw the English into a great discomfiture.

* Read, *Qui mettra les Anglois en déconfiture.*

Garencières entirely misses the purpose of this, but remarks that the prophecy must of necessity relate to the past, for since the Union nothing of the kind has happened. Charles I. was born at Dunfermline on November 19, 1600; in astrological language, when Mercury, lord of the horizon, was combust and following Saturn cosmically with the sun : the sun leaning to a conjunction with Mars, and the moon, in her worst location, in quadrature with Mars. He succeeded to the throne in 1625.

D. D. translates the quatrain, oddly enough, as follows :

> In regione aëris sublunari,
> Mercurius shall govern,
> When a light shall be born in Scotland,
> Which will put England into great disorder.

We have here the stars in their courses fighting against King Charles, and, as soon as we had disposed of the historical remarks appended to the quatrain by D. D., our intention was to have thrown together some of the fatalistic signs of the time and the ill omens that attended this unhappy monarch almost throughout life, but unfortunately this intention must be laid aside for the present.

In 1609 James I. tried to induce the Scotch to conform to some sort of uniformity in Church ceremony, but he stopped short of endeavouring to thrust it down their throats. Archbishop Laud was less moderate. With the zealous persistency of a shard-borne beetle flying against a stone wall, he, in 1637 advised Charles to introduce the English Liturgy into the churches of Scotland, *auctoritate regis*. It was flying in the face of Fate. *Quem Deus vult perdere prius dementat.*

Next to the folly of establishing it, was the folly of its public withdrawal in less than twelve months' time. It was established by royal mandate, July 23, 1637, and by royal proclamation, June 20, 1638, withdrawn; a further undertaking being given that no English cere-monies should be thrust upon the Church of Scotland. Any tyro in statesmanship would have known that this course was doomed to fail utterly. Having taken the first inconsiderate step, it should have received no other impulse from England; private instructions should have been communicated to the chief clergy that no proceedings would be taken to enforce the law, and it would have died down of itself. As it was, the concession came too late, and gave the Scotch time to enter into a covenant never to permit the establishment of the English ritual; or, as they called it, the English *Service Book.* The fault was committed that, over and over again, the English commit as to Irish affairs; the yielding to outside pressure. Contentious opposition should be crushed by force first, and then conceded to as of grace. You will never get thanks from any party for having yielded to their threats. This only cemented dis-affection; and, in 1643, England, puritanically urged, went further still, and established the *Solemn League* to like effect. This was a pure piece of political claptrap intended to secure general disaffection.

In 1641 the discontent had spread into Ireland, and, as usual in such cases, English reasoning and Scotch logic developed into bloodshed on the other side of St. George's Channel. The English often content themselves with ink and oratory, but an Irish Celt prefers to record his dissent in a rubric of blood. During the first four months of antagonism, the rebellion under Phelim O'Neil caused the massacre of 40,000 English Protestants in Ulster : D. D. says 150,000, massacred by Papists, and they could be reckoned up by name. But where he got his list I do not know. His comment on this is : *Tantum religio potuit suadere malorum.* His quotation is not correct ; I hope the same may be said of his statistics.

As we all know, Laud expiated his mistake with his head on Tower Hill, and the King himself was to follow on five years later at Whitehall, after being surrendered for money by the Scotch to the English. As Nostradamus puts it [II. 53], *Du juste sang par pris damné sans crime.*

King Charles was only twenty-five when he ascended the throne, labouring in that respect under almost the same disadvantage as Louis XVI. Both of these kings could derive but little wisdom from the Council-table. Charles's early acts consequently were rash, and those of the French King speculative rather than practical. Clarendon, in his History (i. 23, ed. 1731), devotes a paragraph or two of great interest to the impeachment of the Earl of Middlesex (Lionel Cranfield). Clarendon admits him to have been "a man of great wit and understanding," and to have held every place with great ability. He had been raised by Buckingham from a city trader to a statesman, and in his success seems to have quite forgotten the patron to whom he owed it. The rash Buckingham, on his return from the Spanish Quixotism, influenced the House of Commons to impeach him; altogether overlooking the consequences of employing such a machinery to revenge a private pique, and he must needs drag in the young Prince Charles to help him. The King foresaw the evil. "The wise King," says Clarendon, "knew well enough the ill consequence,"* and he sent for these two,—his son and Buckingham —to lecture them if possible into wisdom. He pointed out that it wounded the Crown and shook his authority, as Ministers would thus have to look to the House, and not to the King alone, as heretofore. At last he burst out in choler: "By God, Steenie, you are a fool, and will shortly repent this folly, and will find that, in this fit of popularity, you are making a rod with which you will be scourged yourself!" He then turned to the prince, and told him: "You will live to have your bellyfull of Parliament impeachments; and, when I shall be dead, you will have too much cause to remember how much you have contributed to the weakening of the Crown by the two precedents you are now so fond of," *i.e.* engaging the Parliament in the war, and the prosecution of Cranfield. It was, indeed, to teach the many-headed (which is equal to no head) beast to taste blood. Here, indeed, a King turns prophet; foreseeing, from existing facts misdirected, what future evils will arise. This, of course, is quite different from Nostradamus.

* Observe here how very different is Clarendon's estimate of James I. from the trash that Sir Walter Scott indulges in at the King's expense, in those romances of his from which half the world draw their notions of history.

" Flambe exigue sortant de solitude " [I. 1], and all
that can be got out of visions of the night by *secret
estude* or otherwise.

CHARLES II.—CAPITULATION OF EDINBURGH (DECEM-
BER 12, 1650).

Century VIII.—Quatrain 40.

Le sang du Juste par * Taurer la daurade,
Pour se venger contre les Saturnins
Au nouveau lac plongeront la maynade,
Puis marcheront contre les Albanins.

The above is the reading in the texte-type, 1558.
D. D.'s version runs as below :

Le sang du juste, par Tore et les Torads,
Pour se venger contre les Saturnins :
Au nouveau lac plongeront la Menade,
Puis marcheront contre les Albanins.

He translates thus—

The blood of the righteous, for Torah and Torees' sakes, cries
for vengeance against the Saturnine rebels, who will plunge the
priestess of Bacchus, *la menade*, into the sea of their novelties,
and march afterwards against the Scotch.

D. D.'s idea of the interpretation of this is that, for
the sake of the law-abiding people (the Torah and
Torees), the King's blood cries for vengeance against
the Saturnian Roundheads. The intoxicated people
shall plunge into a new course of wickedness, and
will then march against the Highlanders. He considers that this was fulfilled in 1650, when, after the
capitulation, as he calls it, with the Scotch at Breda,
Charles II. landed in Scotland on June 23, and

* Latin, *per*, during.

joined the royal army, consisting mainly of High-landers. About the same moment Cromwell reached London from Ireland, and General Fairfax retired from the army. Cromwell, at this critical moment, jumps into his post, and, on June 29, heads the Parliamentary army against the Scots.

Without at all insisting upon the accuracy of this interpretation, I think it furnishes sufficient of curiosity to make it worthy of insertion. What follows, touching the Tories, I give in his own words :

"Some people stick to the Church of *England* discipline, even to a superstition, and to their last breath. These people had the nickname of *Tories*, cast on them by the Cromwellites ; which is as much as to say some have the law of the Church put upon them, from the Hebrew *Torah*, which signifies the *law*, or the *law of the Church of God.* Perhaps did Cromwell himself, or some of his confident advocates and ministers, designedly invent that cursed name ; as it is likely from what happened in the year 1651, when the Parliament ordered the law-books to be translated out of *Latin* into *English,* wherein the lawyers took a great deal of freedom by using the *verbalia passiva* very frequently, and almost on all occasions, according to their own fancy and pleasure. As, for instance, Apellans and Apellatus, they made an *Apealer* and an *Apealee ;* the *Arrestans* and *Arrestatus,* the *Challenger* and the *Challengee ;* as likewise the *Warranter* and the *Warrantee ;* the *Voucher* and the *Vouchee ;* the *Leaser* and the *Leasee ;* in which manner they used likewise the terms of *Torer* and *Toree ;* a *Torer,* in the first place—that is, a promoter of the Common Prayer and Church of England service; and an imposer of human traditions, instead of God's law; and, in the second place, a *Toree;* that is, one that submits and suffereth such laws to be imposed upon him. Which *nomina verbalia passiva,* so much in vogue amongst the English lawyers, are not at all English but mere French, and the *Participium Passivum* itself; and more proper to the neat *French* than the corrupted *Provincial Dialect;* which last our Nostradamus very often mixes with his style; wherein they commonly used to say, *Les confirmads, les restads, les escilads,* instead of *les confirmez, les restez, les exilez,* etc. And according to this *Dialect* one must say, LES TORADS, instead of LES TOREZ, and thus does our Poet."

If what he says above has any value, the *Toree* would be the prelates and clergy; the *Torads* the laity, who adhere to the Church of England and its discipline and ritual. This in the context would have a greater appropriateness than D. D. himself seems to be aware of, for the word it is contrasted with in the context is *les Saturnins.* This word in Nostradamus is constantly used for pagans, in contradistinction to *Albanins,* Christians, robed in white *albus.* In this quatrain also the men of Albany, if we take them for Scotch, are fighting on the side of Church and State against the Roundheads. *Saturne* is often put for Antichrist by Nostradamus.

The French of this quatrain, as it stands, does not appear to be correct. The first two lines require a verb understood to connect them : " The blood of the king [cries] for vengeance," etc. The third line has an embarrassed construction : "They will plunge the *Menade* into a new lake." If *Saturnins*, again repeated, be understood, it is difficult to see what plunging their mad priestess into the lake can effect. If it could be read as *les Menades*, then the frantic Bacchantes would plunge into a fresh sea of evil or troubles, and, in their wild intoxication, march north-wards. If we could put any interpretation upon *Taurer* that would be applicable to the rendering, the whole quatrain might then apply to the French Revolution, and not the English. I think that the *sang du Juste* furnishes thus much of certainty as to the interpretation. It must relate to one of two periods ; the death of Charles I. or Louis XVI. Then it would be that the Revolutionists, finding the Royalists to be seeking revenge, declared against the Church, and plunged madly into a new order of things. The *Menade* would be more appropriate to that period than to the earlier one. Bad as they were in England, there was more of lust, infidelity, and blood, corruption, vice, and madness, in France.

Menade. The μαινάδες were Bacchantes, the priest-esses who celebrated the festivals of Bacchus. Stephanus says that it is to be explained not only as Bacchic, but as frantic ; and this is unquestionably the meaning here. The Greek word appears to be con-nected with the Sanscrit *man*, to think ; and thence the word *manyu*, anger, is said to be derived. They used to run dishevelled, half-naked, and, brandishing the thyrsus ; in their fury they would kill and behead men whom they encountered by the way, and carry off their heads, leaping with rage and joy. According to Nonnus, they were virgins so careful of their chastity that they slept with a cincture of serpents. Juvenal attributes no great severity of virtue to them, but their pretensions to such superlative purism renders them all the fitter emblem of the canting Puritans who won Cromwell's battles for him. In Le Pelletier's Glossary *maynade* is given as a Romance word for "a child of four or five years;" but this throws no additional light on our difficulty.

The Battle of Dunbar (September 3, 1650).
Century VIII.—Quatrain 56.

La bande foible la terre * occupera,
Ceux du haut lieu feront horribles cris :
Le gros trouppeau d'estre coin troublera,
Tombe pres Dinebro descouvers les escrits.

Translation.

The weak band shall occupy the knoll (or, if preferred, it can be, occupy the ground or field [after the battle]). The Highlanders (*Ceux du haut lieu*) shall raise horrible shouts (before they engage, and also after their defeat). The large force shall be hampered or cornered (*d'estre en coin*), and fall close to Edinburgh, their papers even falling into the victor's hands.

This is a very important forecast indeed. The little band on the knoll—for I prefer that reading—is clearly enough Cromwell's small force, very much in the condition he describes it to be in, in his letter to Haslerig at Newcastle, September 2, 1650 (Carlyle's "Cromwell Letters," ii. 201):

"We are upon an engagement very difficult. The enemy hath blocked up our way at the Pass at Copperspath, through which we cannot get without almost a miracle."

* Variant, *le tertre*, the knoll or rising ground.

Before sunrise Lesley sends down on Monday his horse to cross the small Brocksburn. Whoso wishes to attack must first cross this little brook, in its deep *ditch*, as they then called it (the picturesque tourist would now say *glen*), forty feet deep. Lesley's army comes out and places itself in "rather narrow ground," says Carlyle (p. 202) in 1846 ; *d'estre en coin*, says Nostradamus in 1558 ; or 1546, if you like to have it so, for it was probably on paper a clean three hundred years before Carlyle commented ; you may even translate him, "takes the trouble to put itself into a corner." "Hampered in narrow, sloping ground," says Carlyle again (p. 206).

The reader who wishes for it can here leave off to peruse Carlyle's very celebrated prose lyric, as they call it, about this "Dunbar Battle," with its "moon" that "gleams out, hard and *blue*, riding among hail-clouds ;" whatever "a blue moon" may mean, or not mean. Carlyle makes Nol there, as the level sun shoots up over St. Abb's Head and across the sea, quote the sixty-eighth Psalm, in Rous's doggerel :

" Let God arise, and scattered
Let all His enemies be ;
And let all those that do Him hate
Before His presence flee ! "

Observe here that it is the *Saturnins*, in a frenzy of antichrist, who do this, according to Nostradamus. But you can take which side you please. " The Lord General made a halt," says Hodgson, "and sang the hundred-and-seventeenth Psalm " at the foot of Doon Hill ; to the tune of Bangor or other, says Carlyle, " strong and great against the sky," this grand strain arises, in which the metre, like the Lord General himself, makes a halt too :

> " O give ye praise unto the Lord,
> All *nations* that be ;
> Likewise ye people all, accord
> His name to magnify "—

which, to eke out the measure, has to be read, *nay-shy-ons*, and, for the rhyme's sake, *magnifee*. This energy is really not dramatic, but it *is* stagey ; on the border-land of sublimity, it curls the lip of humour to a smile.

The poor Highlanders taken prisoners were sold, " not," says Cotton, " to perpetual servitude, but for six, or seven, or eight years, as we do our own " (blessed are they who are of the household of faith) ; " which is really a mild arrangement," in the estimation of " the Sage of Chelsea " (p. 358).

But now back to our exegesis let us go. Cromwell captured, on this occasion, the whole of the papers of the Scotch War Office, as well as the Great Seal of Scotland, which he sent forward as a trophy to London. Cromwell's letter to Speaker Lenthall excuses his making " no more frequent address to Parliament," but " it hath now pleased God to bestow a mercy upon you worthy of your knowledge ; " and so he goes on, for a space occupying eight closely printed pages 8vo. He says he wishes to treat the Scotch very kindly, for that " God hath a people here fearing his name, though deceived ; " and he concludes, in the dirty language of the godly of his century, that he has " offered much love unto such, in the bowels of Christ." His bowels, to the Highlanders made prisoner, awarded slavery, not *perpetual*, but for eight years only. Here are tender mercies and bowels commiserate for contemplation! sufficient, as we have seen, to make Nostradamus shudder at their approach.

Son temps s'approche si près que je souspire (viii. 76, p. 177).

All that was done here, however, could not prevent Charles from being crowned on January 1, 1654, at Scone, in Scotland. In the next summer he penetrated into England, and was pursued by Cromwell and his Ironsides.

D. D. follows up the Quatrain 56, which we have just treated, with Century VIII., Quatrain 57, which stands next to it :

De Soldat simple parviendra en Empire. [II. 171.]

D. D. interpreting it of Cromwell, as was most natural at that time. Garencières does the same, saying, " I never knew nor heard of anybody to whom this stanza might be better applied than to the late usurper Cromwell ; " but unless it be a type of two handles, of the old ecclesiastical sort, I think it will apply still better to Napoleon ; and I shall so apply it further on, giving the reasons why it is more appropriate to him than to the Protector. Further than this, as a general rule in regard to the succession of the quatrains in Nostradamus, they have no more affinity to each other than that they lie together, as one bean touches another in a bushel measure. Still, the next we shall treat is in sequence with the two preceding.

CHARLES II. AFTER THE BATTLE OF WORCESTER. (SEP-
TEMBER 3, 1651).

Century VIII.—Quatrain 58.

Regne en querelle aux frères divisé,
Prendre les armes et le nom Britannique :
Titre Anglican sera tard avisé,
Surprins de nuict mener à l'air Gallique.

Translation.

When a kingdom in quarrel divided between two brothers
takes up arms, and the name of Great Britain : The King
(*Tiltre Anglican*) too late advised, surprised at night (is forced)
to seek the air of France.

It is rather harsh, but to make sense of this we
shall be forced to understand the two brothers to
be England and Scotland, or simply civil war.
When Charles at last made up his mind to visit
Scotland and fight for his crown, it was already
too late. The Parliamentary side had developed a
strength that he was never equal to cope with.
The loss of the battle of Dunbar was a disaster that
settled the question. He might as well have quitted
the field to Cromwell at once. Instead of that, on
the 3rd of September—ominous day! being the anni-
versary of the Dunbar fight—he engages him again
at Worcester. Charles was completely routed and
his cause hopelessly broken. He managed, under
the cover of night, to escape from the city of
Worcester, and, flying from place to place for weeks,
as most romantically chronicled in the Boscobel
Tracts, he at last, on the 20th of October, got well
shipped for Dieppe, and finally rejoined his mother
safely at St. Germain.

P

Death of Cromwell (September 3, 1658).

King Charles II.'s Flight and Restoration (September 3, 1651–1660).

Century X.—Quatrain 4.

Sur la minuict conducteur de l'armée
Se sauvera, subit esvanouy,
Sept ans après la fame non blasmée ;
A son retour ne dira onc ouy.*

Translation.

Upon the stroke of midnight, the leader of the army (King Charles II.) shall save himself (by flight), and suddenly evanish. For seven years longer that is, to a day, till the death of Cromwell, his reputation will survive unchallenged ; at his Restoration no one will say anything but yes.

In other words, Nostradamus tells King Charles II. to continue to hope on, for that though he will have to fly by night from Worcester, his memory will be preserved without diminution till the death of his victor, seven years later to a day. Further, that when the day of his Restoration does come round, he will be received back with universal acclaim. Had it been given as *neuf ans*, it would have been more complete as regards Charles II. personally. But, as it is, the date to a day coinciding with the death of Cromwell, makes one suppose it to have been given to point to that interesting coincidence. It would have been no more wonderful than are many others amongst the quatrains, had this been intended ; but whether it shall be so allowed or not rests with the reader,—now that he knows exactly how it stands,—to accept or to reject.

* D. D. reads here *ne dira t-on qu'ouy*, and I think the sense requires it.

The French used always to engage in a battle willingly on St. Louis's Day, April 11, and the English upon St. George's Day, April 23. But September 3, St. Mansuetus's Day, was ruinous to the Royalists and prosperous to Cromwell. The Battle of Worcester, so decisive in its consequences, was commenced at three o'clock in the afternoon on September 3, 1651 ; and at three o'clock in the afternoon of September 3, 1658, Cromwell died on what has been called his *Fortunate Day :* "Nature herself," says his last chronicler in the ninth edition of the 'Encyclopædia Britannica,' "seeming to prophesy, in the voice of the great tempest that swept over England, that a great power had passed away." * It was a tremendous tempest no doubt, and men at the time said the Devil had run away with Old Noll. Some say he died broken-hearted, when the last Parliament convened by him in January, 1658, refused to acknowledge his House of Peers. So great a burden "drank up his spirits," said Maidston.

* Historical discrepancies ought to be chronicled, for they confuse all investigation, and force every conscientious new comer to commence the whole work over again. A writer in the "Book of Days" pretends to be particularly accurate (ii 309), noting that "the storm in reality happened on Monday, August 30, and must have been pretty well spent before the Friday afternoon, when Oliver breathed his last." Rosse, in his "Index of Dates," says (v. *Storms*) that there was one on September 3. Carlyle ("Cromwell Letters," iii. 457) chronicles the stormy Monday, but not the stormy Friday. Hume says a violent tempest "immediately succeeded his death." Clarendon, who may be supposed to know better than any of them, writes (v. 648, ed. 1731 :) "And this now was a day (*i.e.* the Friday) very memorable for the greatest storm of wind that had ever been known, for some hours before and after his death."

CROMWELL DECLARED PROTECTOR (DECEMBER 16, 1653).

Century X.—Quatrain 22.

Pour ne vouloir consentir au divorce,
Qui puis après sera cogneu indigne,
Le Roy des isles sera chassé par force :
Mis à son lieu qui de Roy n'aura signe.

Translation.

The King will agree to the divorce of his crown, which would afterwards have been regarded as an unworthy action, and hence will by force be expelled from the island. One who will have no sign of kingship will be put in his place.

Garencières was alive to the true sense of this and its fulfilment. The Republicans murdered the king, gave the government, if not the crown, to Cromwell, and drove Charles II. into France.

CROMWELL THE FOX.

Century VIII.—Quatrain 41.

Esleu sera Renard, ne sonnant mot,
Faisant le saint public, vivant pain d'orge,*
Tyrannizer après tant † à un cop,‡
Mettant à pied des plus grands sur la gorge.§

---

* This, of course, is "living on barley bread," as everybody translates it. I think, however, it has reference to the phrase *faire ses orges*, to enrich one's self unscrupulously at the expense of others. If that be so, it becomes excellently applicable in the present context. [Noël.] He had sown his wild oats, and now began *à faire ses orges*.

† *Tant*, should, I think, be *temps*.

‡ Greek, κόπτειν, to strike = *coup*; it may even stand here for a *coup d'état*. [Borel.]

§ Construction is *mettant à des plus grands le pied sur la gorge*.

Translation.

A Fox shall be elected, uttering not a word, playing saint in public and helping himself to other people's property, in order to tyrannize after a while by a *coup d'état*, placing his foot on the throat of the greatest.

Garencières thinks this to apply to some Pope, but D. D. refers it much more aptly to Cromwell. If my proposed readings are allowed, the quatrain can fit no one so well, especially as it follows Quatrain 40, which we already have interpreted of the Commonwealth. D. D. reminds us that the Protector was a great Chiliast and Fifth Monarchy man, and certainly *Faisant le saint public ;* even so as to gull, in this our late day, Thomas Carlyle, who allowed the heroism of violence, in this case, to dazzle him into the belief that the hypocrisy of Saintship was Godfearing. As to Cromwell, D. D. says truly, that he was moderate in diet. This he says to strengthen the barley bread, though I feel very strongly that it is differently intended. It might even mean that he got his bread by barley, or John Barleycorn, from the Huntingdon brewery. He was more given to ambition than to pleasure, says D. D., as is the case with men of his saturnine complexion. This may, by such as choose to use it so, connect him with Quatrian 40 and *les saturnins.* " His fortunate star, Mars," writes D. D., " had brought him the glory of a valiant hero and general."

Here D. D. entertains us, somewhat at large, upon his notion of a " *wig*, or *trimmer*, that is, a wavering man or hypocrite, from the original words to *wag* and to *trim* about." We, however, know that this etymology is not worth very much.

Our next is a sequence of three quatrains, all of which seem to refer to English affairs.

THE FIRE OF LONDON—DUTCH WAR—PLAGUE (1665-1667).

Century II.—Quatrains 51, 52, 53.

Le sang du juste à Londres fera faute,
Brulez par foudres * de vingt trois les six ;
La dame † antique cherra ‡ de place haute,
De mesme secte § plusieurs seront occis.

Dans plusieurs nuits la terre tremblera :
Sur le printemps deux effors suite :
Corinthe, Ephèse aux deux mers nagera,
Guerre s'esmeut par deux vaillans de luite. ‖

La grand peste de cité maritime
Ne cessera, que mort ne soit vengée
Du juste sang par pris damné sans crime,
De la grand dame † par feincte n'outragée.

---

* *Foudre* metaphorically, saltpetre, here fireballs. The belief at the time was that the fire was the work of incendiaries, and it has never been disproved, though it has been ridiculed by those who set up for liberty and enlightenment. The Illuminati will not allow London to have been thus burnt by others ; and it is quite certain that they themselves will never set the Thames on fire. What Nostradamus asserts here, history has asserted. That is enough for the present purpose.

† *La dame.* Garencières takes this for St. Paul's, once dedicated to Diana, who is the ancient dame. We may take it for the mother Church, if we like ; and it would not be using much violence if we read *le dome*, for that might very well mean, as in the Latin, *doma*, house or church, as St. Jerome uses it—*Domus Dei*, in fact.

‡ *Cherra*, future of the verb *choir*, tomber, to fall.

§ *Secte.* By this Garencières thinks is meant the eighty-seven churches that were burnt with St. Paul's, belonging to the same Protestant sect. We might read *sorte*.

‖ *Luite*, Romance, for *lutte*, battle.

Translation.

The blood of the just shall be required of London, burnt by fireballs in thrice twenty and six ; the old Cathedral shall fall from its high place, and many (edifices) of the same sort shall be destroyed.

Through many nights the earth shall tremble ; in the spring two shocks follow each other ; Corinth and Ephesus shall swim in the two seas, war arising between two combatants strong in battle.

The great Plague of the maritime city shall not diminish till death is sated for the just blood, basely sold (for £2,000,000), and condemned for no fault. The great Cathedral outraged by feigning (saints).

The first quatrain deals most remarkably with the great fire of London ; noting the precise year, the burning of St. Paul's, and other injury to the Protestant interest.

The second shows that a bloody sea-war shall rage, the earth quaking under the cannonade from the ships, shaking the cliffs. There was such a war in 1665, 1666, and 1667, between England and the seven united provinces of the Netherlands. Cruising within the narrow seas, he likens to the Ægean waters between Corinth for England, and Ephesus for Antwerp. He describes them as they really occurred, commencing afresh with every ensuing spring,—*sur le printemps.* D. D. remarks that they were so obstinately contested, all these fights, that they would last for days on a stretch, or, as Nostradamus says, *nights : plusieurs nuits la terre tremblera*, according to the English custom of reckoning by a *fortnight*, and not fourteen days. Now the French reckon the fortnight as a *quinzaine*, that is, up to the fifteenth day, which of course contains only fourteen nights ; and you might say *la terre tremblera*, for the cannon reverberating between the cliffs would move them perceptibly. D. D. thinks that *la grande dame* in the last quatrain is the great city of London, the metropolis, or mother-city ; an Eastern way of speaking. In his learned way, he adds: "The great fire has only metamorphosed the city—*ex Ligneâ in Lateritiam*," converting it from wood to brick.

The distance at which sounds may be heard seems variable. Captain Parry, in his "Third Voyage," p. 58, relates, it is said, that at Port Bowen a conversation could be carried on distinctly at 6696 feet, which is over a mile. Dr. Clark, in his Travels (iii. 331), whilst sailing from the Gulf of Glaucus to Alexandria, heard the firing of the English upon the fortress of Rachmanie, upon the Nile. All on board heard it, at a distance of 130 miles. The earthquake at Sumbawn, in 1815, was heard 970 miles away (Elliot's "Horæ. Apoc.," iv. 218). In Dereham's "Physico-Theology" (i. p. 185, ed. 1786), a Dr. Hearn is quoted as certifying that guns fired at Stockholm in 1685 were heard at a distance of 180 English miles ; and in the above Dutch war, 1672, the guns were heard above two hundred miles (*vide Philosophical Transactions*, No. 113.) I remember reading, though I have not noted where, that the guns employed at Waterloo were heard, at Hythe in Kent, on the Sunday morning, so that it was known Wellington and Napoleon had engaged in battle somewhere ; the fact was confirmed by intelligence shortly after. The buzz of London traffic in 1820 could be heard by putting the ear to the ground on the top of Putney Hill, as Sir Richard

Phillips relates in his "Morning's Walk to Kew" (p. 152). But the whole south of Thames was then tricked out rurally in Nature's emerald vest, and, herself at ease, the earth could transmit vibrations from the troubled town ; but now she shudders with a like palsy of her own, and Putney is as rural as Clerkenwell Green. Much of the conveyance of sound depends upon the wind, no doubt. J. P. Malcolm ("Londinium Redivivum," iii. p. 117) has some interesting remarks upon St. Paul's bell. He lived in Somer's Town, and with a strong north-east wind he could hear every hour tolled as clear as if only a quarter of a mile distant, but with the wind east, south-west, or north, not a sound could be heard. Now Somer's Town is north-north-west from St. Paul's, which, in a straight line, is two miles and a half away ; so that a north-east wind should convey the vibrations to Lambeth. He found that this wind carried away all the smoke, and so left the air free for the sound to travel through it. A south wind overwhelmed him with noise. He could distinctly hear the guard at St. James's Park beat the tattoo at eight, nine, ten, and eleven, to each distinct roll of the drum. One would judge from this that the wind was blowing nearly due east at Waterloo on that famous Sunday, the 18th of June. It was an east wind at Baalzephon that ruined Pharaoh. I have dwelt thus episodically upon sound to show, if possible, that this *tremblement de terre* was an effect of sound arising on the waters but vibrating upon land, and not the convulsion of an earthquake.

Quatrain 80 of Century III. we have already treated

of by the help of Le Pelletier, and interpreted it of Charles I., and we there made the bastard to stand for Cromwell. D. D. takes the alternative reading of *l'indigne*, and understands James II. The bastard then is naturally the Duke of Monmouth, natural son of Charles II. ; but he was never *demy receu ;* and had it been intended to portray him, he would not have been mentioned after, but before, the abdication. Hence we to prefer to leave it as we placed it at first.

WILLIAM III. AND THE REVOLUTION (1688).

Century IV.—Quatrain 89.

> Trente de Londres secret conjureront,
> Contre leur Roy, sur le pont l'entreprise :
> Leuy, satalites là mort de gousteront,*
> Un Roy esleut † blonde, natif de Frize.

Translation.

Thirty of London shall conspire secretly against their King ; upon the bridge the plot shall be devised. These Satellites shall taste of death. A fair-haired King shall be elected, native of Friesland.

D. D. reads for *trente, trained.* Had the true reading been *trained* it would have been very wonderful, because the trained bands of London had not been thought of in Nostradamus's time. Garencières interprets the quatrain to refer to Charles I., and says it is well known that the plotters used to assemble at the *Bear at the Bridge foot.* This was a celebrated inn on the south side of London Bridge. It was pulled down 1761, when the houses were

---

* Variant, *Luy, satallites la mort degousteront.*
† Esleut, or *esleu.*

removed from London Bridge (*Public Advertiser*, December 26, 1761), "Hist. Sign.," p. 154.

The *Quarterly Review* (xxvi. 189), in some very disparaging remarks on Nostradamus, says of this particular quatrain that it predicts "the Revolution of 1688 with tolerable clearness," resting upon the last line, which it prints in *italics*. As, however, William III. was born at the Hague, he was not born in what is called Friesland, but South Holland. I do not know whether it formed a part of Friesland in Nostradamus's time. D. D. is puzzled with the word *blonde*, and suggests that perhaps William had fair hair in his youth, "or it might be an allusion to his name, Guillaume, because (*sic ?*) of *cil*, signifying *eyebrows*." This vermicular wriggle must be permitted to our highly excellent cleric, who is manifestly unable to get the quatrain to say what he wants it to say. We have had numerous quatrains that, when properly understood, have appeared to be clear enough, and which are disparaged as "perplexed verses" by the *Quarterly*. But this which they find expressed with "tolerable clearness," I do not find clear at all. I find no plot of *thirty*, no meeting of conspirators at the Bear at the Bridge foot, or at any other bridge, nor satellites who are executed, nor of a *blond* king, nor of a native of Friesland.

MARLBOROUGH AND THE CARDINAL DE BOUILLON.

Century VI.—Quatrain 53.

Le grand Prélat Celtique à Roy suspect,
De nuict par cours sortira hors de regne :
Par Duc fertile à son grand Roy Bretaine,
Bisance à Cypres et Tunes insuspect.

Translation.

The great Celtic Prelate suspected by the King,
Shall post with haste by night out of the realm,
Through Bisance, Ypres, and Bethune, undiscovered,
By aid of the duke fertile (in conquest) to the great King of
Britain.

This refers to the Cardinal de Bouillon, Great
Almoner of France, who was misrepresented to the
French King to such an extent that he could not
appear at Court. After some years he threw up his
charge and determined to quit France. He was related
to Prince Eugène, who was with Marlborough, near
Arras. The Cardinal came over to them under cover
of night, precisely as described by Nostradamus,
under the protection of a strong convoy, sent by
Marlborough to protect him from the scouts of
Ypres and the other places named. When he reached
Antwerp, he simply sent in his ribbon of the Order to
the French Court, accompanied with his resignation.
He is called "Prelat Celtique" as the Duchy of
Bouillon is in Gallia Celtica. D.D. holds that *grand
Roy* is an abbreviation of *Royaume*. But the sense is
better if taken literally as it stands.

I transcribe for the curious reader from D. D. the
following passage ; it is too singular to be neglected :

" But the allusion on the Duke of Marlborough is still prettier.
Had his [Nostradamus's] genius dictated unto him *Marnebourg*,
he might have understood and written down without hesitation,
for the English *Marl* and the French *Marne* are one and the
same. The Dœmons speak all sorts of languages, but Nostradamus did not understand the English, whence it came that at
the hearing of the name Marlborough, he startled, and thought,
' *Qu'est-ce que Marl ?* ' Thereupon it was inspired to him,
' *C'est une terre fertile et graisse,*' whereby he is ascribing to

him both *Nomen* and *Omen* at once : the Duke, by whose indefatigable zeal and incomparable valour the Kingdom of Great Britain should be fertile in conquests."

Century II.—Quatrain 68.

This has already been treated by Le Pelletier (i. 125) under Louis XIV., as fulfilled in the endeavour to re-establish James II. in Ireland. But D. D. refers it to March 23, 1708, when 'the Pretender cast anchor before Edinburgh, and nobody came out to him. He sailed away, narrowly escaping the English fleet. On this account an Act of Parliament was passed, declaring him a rebel, and setting a reward upon his head. D. D. says that from this time forth Nostradamus always designates him by the title of Rebel. As this quatrain, which we are upon, does not refer to the Pretender, the above remark would only show that Nostradamus always speaks of the Pretender as a rebel. Bouys interprets this, as we have said before, of Napoleon's victories at sea ; as also that Bouys was blindly prophesying after the battle of Trafalgar, and in ignorance that such a decisive engagement had been fought. Garencières interprets it as fulfilled in Charles II.'s times : so that with four interpreters we have four interpretations. Sceptics can employ this fact how they like ; I am pleased to furnish them with the opportunity. The total of the interpretations seems to me so astounding that we can well afford to submit to deductions such as this. Besides which, I am not endeavouring to establish any point ; I wish the facts to establish themselves. What they finally show to be tenable, let us adopt.

GEORGE I.'S SUCCESSION (OCTOBER 20, 1714).

Century VI.—Quatrain 64.

On ne tiendra pache aucune arresté,
Tous recevans iront per tromperie :
De paix et trefue, et terre et mer protesté.
Par Barcelone classe prins d'industrie

Translation.

They will keep no treaty fixedly (arrested). All who have gained by cheating will go (free). Peace and truce are proclaimed by land and sea. Barcelona captured by the perseverance of the fleet.

This quatrain is exceedingly obscure, and very difficult even to translate adequately. D. D., who is writing only a year after the actual events,—the publishing date of his book being 1715,—makes sense of it thus : George I. is proclaimed King, October 20, 1714, and Nostradamus notifies that there shall be a general liberation of all prisoners for debt. But it is hard to extract that sense out of the first two lines, especially as not a word occurs about England, a king, or a throne. The other two lines approach the period well enough. The Peace of Utrecht was concluded in 1713, and the peace between Germany and France at Radstadt followed in March, 1714. The war between France and Spain also was concluded before King George ascended the throne ; even Barcelona was taken, before he was crowned (October 20), by the French fleet for the King of Spain, September 12, 1714. At the intercession of Great Britain, honourable terms were conceded to the Catalonians in Barcelona, so that the mention of that city by Nostradamus comes with much felicity and appropriateness, if we decide that he refers to George I. at all here. D. D's book must have been written before October 20, 1714, as he says it is hoped that on the *Coronation Day* the King will empty most of the prisons.

GEORGE I. (1714.)

Century II.—*Quatrain* 87.

Après viendra des extrèmes contrées,
Prince Germain, dessus le throsne doré ;
La servitude et eaux rencontrées,
La dame serve, son temps plus n'adoré.

Translation.

Afterwards shall come, from a distant land, a German prince upon the gilded throne. The slavery and waters shall meet. The lady shall serve, her time no more adored.

D. D. considers this to relate to King George, and he remarks that the King exercised a stronger control than it was possible for Queen Anne to do. The German prince ascending the throne of gold certainly seems to point to George I. But Brunswick is not a very far country. It might be said that modern constitutional government was established first by the Georges, so serfdom and *les eaux*, or the people and their so-called rights, met together, but then you would have to interpret figuratively the last line : authority (*la dame*) serves, or is to become subordinate to, the phantom of Freedom, the time of reverence and good feeling having gone by. This, I say, might be so interpreted, but it does not carry much more conviction with it than does the meaning found by Garencières. He will have it to be a prophecy relating to Gustavus Adolphus of Sweden, called German because of German ancestry. His gilded throne was the gilded ship he sailed in. He made slavery and waters meet, because on landing he began to conquer Germania,—that lady who was no more worshipped afterwards as she had been before.

GEORGE I. AND PEACE (1714-1727).

Century X.—Quatrain 42.

Le regne humain d'Anglique geniture,
Fera son regne paix union tenir :
Captive guerre demy de sa closture,
Longtemps la paix leur fera maintenir.

Translation.

The human throne of English geniture will make its rule to maintain peace and union. War will be captive, or at least confined to half its usual area. (George will contend only with Spain. Peace abroad and an endeavour to maintain union at home, against the Pretender's efforts.) Thus peace will be secured to the country for a long stretch of years.

We have already given our interpretation to D. D.'s next quatrain (III. 57, p. 166). He discovers from it that George shall never want for an heir to the throne up to the Day of Judgment. Myself I see nothing of the kind to be warranted out of Nostradamus. He seems here to be contrasting the numerous changes in Britain with the happy stability of France. I should have made no reference to this, but for the opportunity it affords of introducing some of D. D.'s curious remarks upon the astrological portion of the verses.

At the Creation the Gemini stood in the house or sign Aries, near the equinoctial colure, which has but its own one pole ; but they are now in the fourth house called Cancer, near the solstial colure, which has a double pole, viz. *Mundi et eclipticæ.* *Basharion* is an Arabic word, and denotes *Humanus.* *Bashar*, a substantive *Caro, hominis cutis, homo.* In the three signs, Aries, Taurus, Gemini, which have successively formed the Caput Zodiaci, none but Gemini is of human figure ; that sign must be intended by the word *Basharion* (especially as the word is not *Basharion* at all, but *Bastarnan*) ; so that, till the age of the world is six or seven thousand years old, *i.e.*, till the Day of Judgment, this will last ; and when the great day comes there will be found a direct descendant of that great king sitting on the English throne.

He has taken no notice of the *Pempotam* and its duration of three hundred years, as a sort of measure of the seven changes, and Nostradamus nowhere says that the seventh change shall endure to the end of time. Like almost all interpreters, D. D. reads his own imagination into the prophecy.

The reader who cares about such explanations as these will find a great deal more of the same sort in Garencières' annotations upon this quatrain. He remarks that the sign of Aries doth govern France, and that by doubling his pole is meant his returning a second time to the same place, so that the stars do promise France a long continuance in exaltation. He adds that if he were a great astrologer himself he should work out exactly the whole calculation, and

Q

he thinks Aries should come to that pole in the year 1845. But Garencières seems to have had no inkling whatever of the French Revolution of 1789, as forecast by Nostradamus ; nor yet of the second Revolution of 1848, though he translated all the quatrains into English.

FRENCH REVOLUTION.

THE VULGAR ADVENT. [I. 160.]

Century VI.—Quatrain 74.

La dechassée * au regne tournera,
Ses ennemies trouvés des conjurés :
Plus que jamais son temps triomphera,
Trois et septante à mort trop asseurés.

Translation.

She who was proscribed will return to the kingdom,
Her enemies will be treated as conspirators ;
More than ever her time (or empire) will triumph ;
Seventy-three years its deathly domination is assured.

THE Revolution (*la dechassée*), repressed in 1816, shall again obtain the government. Its enemies will be treated as conspirators, and it will be stronger than ever. Seventy-three years are assured to its death-like rule. I give this as M. le Pelletier does, but I see no reason whatever to think that it is correct. Garencières makes it apply to Charles II. of England, and the seventy-three put to death are those who abetted the murder of his father. This is very vague. Garencières reads *Le dechassé*. Here we may remark that Napoleon himself [p. 289] dates his nobility from

---

* Romance, *dechassé*, driven away.

the battle of Montenotte, 1797. Seventy-three years added to this yields us the remarkable date of the fall of his dynasty at Sedan, 1870.

Century I.—Quatrain 3. (*September* 22, 1792.) [1. 162.]

Quand la lictiere du tourbillion versée,*
Et seront faces de leurs manteaux † couvers,
La republique par gens nouveaux vexée,‡
Lors blancs et rouges jugeront à l'envers.

Translation.

When the litter is turned topsy-turvey by the typhoon,
Men will mask their faces with the cloak of hypocrisy.
The republic will be troubled by new-risen men ;
The white and red will judge by contraries.

This means that the royalists (*les blancs*) and the republicans (*les rouges*) will judge of everything from utterly opposed points of view. What was top will become bottom, when the blast blows the litter over ; and, new men rising to power, the rest will cover their faces with hypocrisy, as men do with their cloaks in a storm. Compare the phrase *à l'envers* with p. 175.

Century II.—Quatrain 30. [1. 163.]

Un qui les dieux d'Annibal infernaux
Fera renaistre, effrayeur des humains.
Oncq' § plus d'horreur ne ‖ plus pire journaux
Qu'avint viendra par Babel aux Romains.¶

---

* *Versée*, for *renversée*.

† In this high-wind of revolution men will mask their countenances with the cloak of hypocrisy.

‡ Latin, *vexata*, troubled.

§ *Oncques*, never, *nunquam*.

‖ Romance, *ne*, *ni*, nor.

¶ The order is " *Qu'avint oncq'* plus d'horreur ni plus pire à Babel qu'il n'adviendra aux Romains par les journaux." This

Translation.

There will be one who will revive the infernal gods
Of Hannibal, a terror to mankind.
Never arrived by Babel more horror
Nor worse day's work than will fall upon Roman Catholics.

The meaning is, Napoleon shall arise, who will reawaken the solemn curse on Rome uttered by Hannibal, when he called the infernal gods to witness his hatred to her, to the terror of all mortals. Not Babel at the dispersion brought on the world more horror, nor days of more evil-ploughing for the present or seed-sowing for the future than shall fall upon the Roman world by him. This is much better than to limit it to an ecclesiastical area merely. We shall see that Charles V. is a sort of prototype of Napoleon, and Garencières adduces Charles V. as fulfilling this prophecy. Hannibal is also a prototype of Napoleon in attacking Italy by crossing the Alps.

Century I.—Quatrain 14. (1789-1793.) [1. 164.]

De gent esclave chansons, chants et requestes
Captifs par * Princes et Seigneur aux prisons,
A l'advenir par idiots sans testes
Seront receus par † divines oraisons.

is M. le Pelletier's reading, and he interprets it of Voltaire, the encyclopedists and journalists of the seventeenth century, who assailed the faith and the Church of Rome. But surely the one like Hannibal was Napoléon, and the *journaux* in this old speech does not stand for *journals* and newspapers that had no existence, and therefore no name in the time of Nostradamus *Journal* meant a day's work, such as could, in ploughing, be done by a man with two oxen.

* Latin, *per*, whilst.
† Latin, *pro*, for.

Translation.

Songs, chants, and refrains of the slavish mob,
Whilst the Princes and King are captive in prison,
Shall be received in the future as oracles divine
By headless idiots deprived of judgment.

Songs—such as the Marseillaise while the King and Princes are imprisoned in the Temple,—songs of the mob (*gent esclave*) are received by brainless fools for divine utterances, even prayers (*divines oraisons*). *Vox populi, vox Dei,* is always the fools' blasphemous formula, when swine chose Barabbas for Pontifex or Generalissimo. A cruelly entreated people; whose burdens are aggravated by wickedness in high places needlessly, above and beyond the grief, which every man is born to by the act of birth into a world of sickness, sorrow, and injustice; sighs heavily at this unduly heaped-up burden, and that sigh, that *vox populi,* runs upward like a lightning conductor to elicit fire from the clouds, coming back charged with electricity and thunder,—a *vox Dei* of terrible divinity. But when scum rises to the direction, as with the Revolutionists, and is followed by some brutalized *sabreur* aggrandizing himself as king of chaos and disorder, with shouts of subservient applause from the smutty mob, saying, " Herod, thou art a god," the *vox populi* that split the welkin once, is *now* the *vox infernorum demonum,* the whole upspring and outcome of which is bestiality and lawlessness enthroned in defiance of the decalogue and heaven. Thenceforth the appeal of all good men and sane is, " Ye who worship God, good and alone from eternity, down with them." The men must work and serve. This fiat is in the air, is in the sea, is on the earth. It is the *vox naturæ*, in comparison with which the people's voice, *vox populi*, is nothing, beyond a momentary troubling of the silences.

The following quatrain I give for what it may be thought worth. M. le Pelletier thinks it to relate to the creation of assignats, December 19, 1789. It would be a pity to lose sight of his identification, if even some should presume it to be incorrect.

Century I.—Quatrain 53. (*December* 19, 1789.) [I. 165.]

Las ! qu'on verra grand peuple tourmenté,
Et la loi saincte en totale ruine ;
Par autres loix toute la Chrestienté ;
Quand d'or d'argent trouvé nouvelle mine.

Translation.

Alas ! how great a people shall tormented be,
And holy law in utter ruin laid :
By newer laws all Christendom is vexed,
With a new mine of gold and silver found.

We shall see, alas ! the French people (*grand peuple*) agitated, the Catholic religion (*la loy saincte*) totally ruined, all Christendom put under new laws, when the National Assembly decrees that four hundred million assignats shall be issued (*nouvelle mine d'or*, etc.), secured on the property of the clergy, in the interests of the Revolution.

Older commentators applied this to the paper-money schemes of Law 1716 ; and Garencières finds the fulfilment in the discovery of the Spanish-American gold and silver mines.

A properly regulated paper-money issue, based on

the taxation of a State, having absolutely no intrinsic value whatever in itself, could undoubtedly be converted into a circulating medium that would work more smoothly than any metallic one can, because the market value of the ore, employed as now in coinage, is perpetualy introducing a fluctuation of values that conflicts with the nominal standard of the coin, so that the standard is never uniform. The currency required would never amount to a tenth part of the taxation leviable. Paper could therefore be destroyed at the Bank of England, or issued exactly according to the needs of trade and commerce. Fluctuation in the market value of metals would no longer affect the circulating medium in the least. Thus might one cause of recurrent panics be removed for ever. But can bank directors or ministers be trusted with such a responsibility? This hinges on honesty, and there is none to spare.

Century VII.—Quatrain 14.   (1789-1793.)   [I. 166.]

Faux exposer viendra topographie,
Seront les cruches * des monumens ouvertes,
Pulluler secte, sancte philosophie,
Pour blanches noires, et pour antiques vertes.

Translation.

Topography will soon be falsified,
The urns and sepulchres stand violate,
Sects swarm, and babbling sentiment
Black put for white, and green fruit for the ripe.

The curse be on them for changing old landmarks.
The provinces turned into departments (by decree of

---

* *Cruches* = urns, Cinerary urns.   Garencières read *urnes.*

the Assembly, December 22, 1789). The sepulture of Kings violated at St. Denis. Unholy sects will swarm, and a sentimental philosophy, of Rousseau and other maddened sophists, usurping the office of religion, black will stand for white, and green, crude fruit be substituted for the ripe.

Century IV.—Quatrain 24.

Ouy soubs Terre Sainte Dame * voix feinte,
Humaine flamme pour Divine voit luire :
Fera des sœurs de leur sang terre tainte,
Et les saints temples par les impures destruire.

Translation.
Hear from the ground a voice of Halidom,
A human flame pretending light divine.
The blood of sisters stains the earth to red,
And holy temples the impure destroy.

This, I think, refers to the sentimental advocacy of the Rights of man, as substitutionary of religion and, faith in the literary movement of the eighteenth century. It would comprise Rousseau's gospel of dirt and sentimentality, Voltaire's substitution of wit for wisdom, and the science of the encyclopædists floating disoriented upon the waters of uncertainty, in lieu of the deep thought of the solitary thinkers that

* *Sainte Dame* I take to be equivalent to our English *Halidom*, consisting of *Holy* and *Dome*—a terminative seen in kingdom and Christendom, and signifying rule or lordship. It has also been written as *Holidame*, as if referring to the Virgin Mary. Of course, if that were the correct etymology, it would furnish the exact rendering of *Sainte Dame*: but, as it is, it is equivalent. A voice feigning that of the Blessed Virgin may well be represented by a voice feigning that of religion and faith. I take this from Garencières, and not the *texte-type*.

preceded them. These last were men who, heretofore walking humbly and without association in conspiracy, interrogated the universe, divinely sown with riddles in great abundance by a hand invisible, until they fell asleep into that hand, and awoke to the illuminated answers.

The blood of sisters was the wholesale slaughter of women that distinguished the Revolution, whilst church altars were desecrated by naked women, set there to personate the goddess of impure reason, feigning *la sante dame.*

The quatrain 25 that follows this in the text of Nostradamus I now give ; but this verse 24, so far as I have seen, has never been commented upon nor has the connection been pointed out. Yet this stanza furnishes the reasons why the stars became overclouded to a people that were benighted, *par ces raisons,* as the reader will perceive by the second line that succeeds this.

Century IV.—Quatrain 25. [I. 167.]

Corps sublimes * sans fin à l'œil visibles,
Obnubiler † viendront par ces raisons.
Corps front comprins, ‡ sens § chief || et invisibles.
Diminuant les sacrées oraisons.

Translation.

The infinite stars are links that light to doubt,
And drop the pall of night upon the soul :
The eye and front of man,—and soul,—grown cerebral,
God and His host withdraw ; and with them prayer !

---

* *Sublimis,* high, elevated.
† Latin, *obnubilare,* to cloud, obscure.
‡ Romance, *comprins, compris,* contained in.
§ *Sens = sans,* without.
|| *Chief = chef,* God.

M. le Pelletier considers that Nostradamus attributes these effects to the reasonings hostile to the faith that improved optical instruments will introduce, as they suggest a plurality of worlds. I quite admit that in many minds this has been the tendency. Almost any discovery, giving a new hint as to infinitude, launches a number of inferior but vigorous brains into new lines of reasoning. We then get great multiplication of secondary volumes, which supply minced Aristotle or chaff to represent any amount of sausage-meat required by the reading public. Of course the further you can see by the telescope the further you put heaven away from the earth-dweller, and he loves it the less ; for it is the near things we love, and not the remote. The heart is not universal, and cannot be stretched to it. I look upon the telescope, to an ordinary man, as a drain-pipe, through which he can run off and lose the moisture of his soul and live the worse for it afterwards ; to the multitude of men, useless ; to the scientific man, a means of inflation and puffing up ; and to the really serious and isolated thinker, as the threshold of infinitude that may, though it has hardly yet done so, answer a few out of the ten million astral riddles sown in space. The last-named individual alone may benefit a little by it. But I question if anything at all of this was present to Nostradamus.

He seems to me, in these two closely interlinked quatrains, to enlarge much upon the theme of St. Paul (Rom. i. 28) that, as at the French Revolution, " they did not like to retain God in their knowledge, God gave them over to a reprobate mind ;" or one void of judgment, "to do things which are not convenient." So that the earth gave out deceptive voices to them, and false lights for Divine light, to slay women and desecrate the temples ; and then that the very stars visible to the eye, which should teach faith to all, will for these reasons veil themselves and leave nothing to mankind but the darkness of night.   Pure materialism follows, God and His host withdraw, and prayer is no more heard upon the earth.

Century I.—Quatrain 60. [I. 168.]

Un empereur naistra près d'Italie,
Qui à l'Empire sera vendu bien cher :
Diront avec quels gens il se ralie,
Qu'on trouvera moins prince que boucher.

Translation.

An emperor shall be born near Italy,
Bought by the Empire at a bankrupt rate :
You'd say the herd, he gathers to himself,
Denote him butcher rather than a prince.

An emperor shall be born in Corsica—Napoléon Bonaparte. His advent to the throne of France will prove prodigiously costly to her. It is enough to make one say, from the tribe he surrounds himself with, that he is more like a butcher far, with the steel dangling at his side, and slaughterman apprentices, than a prince.

It is natural that Bouys, who has hunted Nostradamus for quatrains that will serve for adulation of Napoleon, has passed this over, *sub silentio*, entirely. Garencières, speaking of this, says it is a prophecy for the future, for that until now (1672) no such emperor has been heard of, born near Italy, that cost so much and proved a butcher.

Century VI.—Quatrain 23. [I. 169.]

D'esprit de regne munismes *˙descriés,
Et seront peuples esmeus contre leur Roy :
Paix, sainct nouveau, sainctes loix empirées,
Rapis † onc ‡ fut en si trèsdur arroy. §

Translation.

The rampart of tradition battered down,
The people rise against their King anoint' :
Peace, a new Saint, and sacred laws made worse,
Paris was never in such disarray.

The traditions of the French monarchy are thrown
to the ground and the people rise against the King,
Louis XVI. Peace will succeed the anarchy when
Napoleon comes to power Pius VII., to flatter the
Emperor, will interpolate the ritual on the 15th of
August with a new saint, the fête of St. Napoleon,‖
who was martyred under Diocletian. The Emperor's

* Latin, *munimen,* rampart.
† Rapis, anagram, for *Paris.*
‡ Latin, *nunquam,* never.
§ *Arroi,* for *desarroi,* disorder.
‖ " On désigne quelquefois sous ce nom un habitant d'Alex-
andrie dont le véritable nom est Néopol, qui fut martyrisé sous
Dioclétien. Outre ce Saint, dont la vie est complètement in-
connue, les bollandistes font mention d'un Napoléon, brillant
cavalier, neveu de Cardinal Fossa-Nuova, qui se tua en tombant
de cheval à Rome en 1218. Saint Dominique, temoin de la
douleur du pauvre cardinal, ressuscita le jeune homme. Napoléon
reconnut ce bienfait en menant une vie fort chretienne et, quand
il fut mort pour tout de bon, l'Église le béatifia. Toutefois, il
n'avait pas sa place fixe dans le calendrier. Ce fut Pie VII. qui
lui assigna pour sa fête la date du 15 août, dans le but sans
doute de plaire à Napoléon Bonaparte."—" Grand Dictionnaire
Universel du dixneuvième Siècle," par M. Pierre Larousse, tom.
xi. p. 804. Paris : 1874.

interference will hurt the Church greatly, and foreign armies (1814–1815) will reduce Paris to extremities she has never before undergone.

As to the fête of St. Napoleon, the story runs that when it was first instituted its impropriety, if not blasphemy, was much discussed in Catholic circles. An Irish priest from Rome was one day communicating the strange fact at a dinner-table in Dublin, when an Irish gentleman exclaimed with vehemence, " What d—d impudence ! " " No, no ! " said the priest, " what you mean to call it is the Blessed Assumption," for that day falls on the 15th of August.

Century I.—Quatrain 31. [I. 170.]

Tant * d' ans en Gaule les guerres dureront,
Outre † la course du Castulon ‡ monarque :
Victoire incerte § trois grands couronneront,
Aigle, Coq-lune, Lyon-soleil en marque.

Translation.

War draws her length in Gaul for many a day,
Beyond the course of Castula the Queen ;
Uncertain victory will crown three thrones,
The Eagle, Cock-moon, Lion-sun, on coin.

Civil war and foreign will last in France long after the ephemeral Republic has perished. Victory, always uncertain, will crown three houses in succession. They

* Latin, *tantum*, so much.
† Romance, *outre*, beyond.
‡ Latin, *castula*, tunic. It was a kind of petticoat worn by women next the skin, and fastened under the breasts, which it left exposed. It stands here for the goddess of Republican Liberty, which is generally represented in this dress of the Roman virgins.
§ Latin, *incerta*, uncertain.

will coin money with the Imperial eagle of Napoleon ; the revolutionary Gallic cock appearing with the house of Orleans, instituted by revolution, and adding the crescent of Mahomet for successes in Algeria ; whilst the Lion represents Louis XVIII. and Charles X. of the Capetian Monarchy, with the sun representing Catholicism. Le Pelletier says the *Sun* symbolises Christianity, and the moon Mahomet or Antichrist. Myself I think it would be best to consider the *sun* as the symbol of Christ ; the *moon* as the symbol of atheistic democracy or Antichrist.

This Garencières thought to be interpretable in his time. He reads the second line,

" Outre la course du Castulon monarque,"

as, after the death of the King of Spain a Castilian monarch. The eagle as Charles V. [a further analogy with Napoleon], Henry II., contemporary with Nostradamus, and Soliman, which three crowns met under Leo with uncertain odds in war.

The quatrain that follows this is:

Century I.—Quatrain 32.

Le grand Empire sera tost translaté,
En lieu petit qui bientost viendra croistre,
Lieu bien infime d'exigue comté,
Où au milieu viendra poser son sceptre.

Translation.

The great Empire will soon be translated into a little place that quickly will expand. An unworthy spot, a mere county, from the midst of which he will come to lay aside his sceptre.

Garencières interprets this of Charles V., who, three years before his death, resigned Spain and the Low

Countries to Philip II., his son, and the empire to his brother Ferdinand. He then shut himself up in the Escurial, in Castile, a monastery; which the son afterwards enlarged into a grand palace, accounted by Spaniards as the eighth wonder of the world. But I am not aware that any one has yet pointed out that it fits Napoleon as patly just as it can Charles. His empire was cramped into Elba—Æthalia, the soot island (*lieu bien infime*); a mere countship was his monarchy there. It soon grew again into an empire, but he only came out of its midst to resign his sceptre a second time and for ever.

After these prelusory flourishes relating to the Vulgar Advent and French Revolution, we are now to enter upon a more special theme; the murder of the King, and the ragged beggars' festival and brawl, called the First Republic of the Sans Culottes.

LOUIS XVI.

WE enter now upon the lamentable period comprised in the reign of Louis XVI.—a period whose only parallel in history is the false and illegal trial of Charles I. of England ; the perfectibility of man being evinced only by the increased savagery and augmented moral turpitude exhibited at the later period. The first quatrain that has been adduced as pertaining to this period in the Centuries of Nostradamus is that of :

Century I.—Quatrain 57. [1. 173.]

Par * grand discord la terre † tremblera,
Accord rompu dressant la teste au ciel,
Bouche sanglante dans le sang nagera,
Au sol la face ointe de laict et miel.

Translation.

By reason of great discord the earth shall quake.
Revolt destroys the old order and lifts its head to heaven.
The [King's] mouth will swim in its own blood,
And his front, anointed with milk and honey, roll upon the sod.

* *Par = per*, Latin, by reason of.
† A variant is *trombe*. We are told that the modern commentators find in this word the anagram of *Rome*, by syncope of *t* and *b*. So you might in *rompu*, by substitution of *e* for *p* and the ellision of *u*. But as no good comes of doing either, I should suggest to leave them alone.

R

Tremblement de terre is earthquake, and from the time of Virgil, and much earlier than that, has been always taken to forebode convulsions of the State; disturbance of all things rooted and firm, and typifying upheavals of the populace. That it is the King's mouth shall swim in blood is shown unmistakably by the fourth line that follows, where the face is said to be anointed with the milk and honey of the holy ampulla. The Kings of France were crowned at Reims with the oil that was kept there in *la sainte ampoule* for this purpose. The milk and honey is merely a figurative expression; oil and wine, milk and honey, equally represent the fatness of the land.

Upon this quatrain, about the meaning of which he manifestly could know nothing, Garencières naïvely says: "The words and sense are plain, and I cannot believe there is any great mystery hidden under these words." Words put a slight upon men's minds to think they understand what they see written; from this it is clear that you may understand the words, and yet comprehend nothing from understanding them. Orators please take note.

Century III.—*Quatrain* 59. [Bouys, 55.]

Barbare empire par le tiers usurpé.
La plus grand part de son sang mettra à mort.
Par mort sénile par lui le quart frappé ;
De peur que sang par le sang ne soit mort.

Translation.

The rude empire is usurped by the third estate (tiers état).
It will put to death the greatest part of his [the Royal] family.
A quarter [of the kingdom] is struck with senile death ;
For fear of retribution of death, from children of those murdered.

This must relate to 1789, as in no country but in France had the third estate usurped exclusive power to itself. Since that period the House of Commons in England has pursued the same lines, in a more covert, gradual, and, as some would say, lawful manner. In the Lyons edition, 1558, the second line reads *mettra à mort*, which makes better sense, though it spoils the rhythm, unless the *a* in *mettra* may suffer elision in old French prosody—a question I lack knowledge to determine. The quarter being destroyed, as old age withers a man, is to be understood analogically of the lives of citizens removed by terror, or emigration, or spoilation of property, or revolutionary taxation, or by imprisonment.

Bouys tells us that *sang* is to be understood in Nostradamus of children, family, relatives, so that *que sang par le sang* here would mean, lest the families of the injured should rise against the assassins of their flesh and blood. Such a reaction actually took place in the South, in spite of all the truculent precautions taken. The quatrains exhibit no kind of method or chronological order in their arrangement. So that, out of the thousand and more that exist of them, the commentator must hunt at large until he comes upon something salient that enables him to attach the passage to some event, when often he will be led to the most extraordinary results. The usurpation by the *tiers état* here, with all but the very phrase supplied, and with the results that would follow from the usurpation so unmistakably set forth, fixes the pertinency of the quatrain almost as perfectly as if it had been headed *French Revolution.* Yet a reader of less observance and care than is requisite to stay the attention which leads to discovery, might readily pass it over as jargon and mere nonsense. But, once you have deciphered the quaint phrases and their connection, you cannot doubt the meaning, nor the author's vivid gift of expression in conveying ideas, with a terseness more than Tacitean, if less artistic. You discover that Nostradamus can hint in a phrase of three words what would require a long paragraph to make it explicit in an ordinary way. This is truly the language of prophecy. It becomes legible in the light of the event it prefigures, as characters written in milk upon paper become visible at the fire, or when placed in the hot light of the sun.

Century I.—Quatrain 36. [*Bouys*, 56.]

Tard le monarque se viendra repentir,
De n'avoir mis à mort son adversaire ;
Mais viendra bien à plus haut consentir,
(à ce) Que tout son sang par mort fera défaire.

Translation.

The monarch shall too late repent
That he hath not put to death his adversary ;
But he will have to permit later on,
That all his family shall suffer for it by death.

Taking this to be the meaning, it is clear that the adversary is the Duke of Orleans,—that centre of all plotting and intrigue against Louis,—who had so forgotten himself as, at a public bed of justice, in 1788, to shake his fist in the King's face with a most threatening expression of countenance. For this he was only sent into exile when he ought to have suffered death. In the last line *sang* again stands for family and relatives. This could scarcely be plainer if the names were given ; but, had Nostradamus here deviated from the secret idiom of prophetic language, he would have prevented the accomplishment of what he was asserting. Things like this may be happened on by chance, if you choose to say so, but the theory reels under the constant repetition of such chances. Men whose names are prominently before the world can hardly be introduced into prophecy. But we shall see shortly that Nostradamus is able to assign names with precision where the individuals are of a lesser rank, and that their names may so pass unobserved until history has recorded them with her iron pen.

Century IX.—Quatrain 20. (*June* 20, 1791.) [I. 174.]

> De nuict viendra par le forest de Reines,
> Deux pars, vaultorte, Herne la pierre blanche,
> Le moyne noir en gris dedans Varennes :
> Esleu Cap. cause tempeste, feu, sang, tranche.

Translation. [II. P., I. 174.]

> By night shall come through the forest of Reines
> Two parts, face about, the Queen a white stone,
> The black monk in gray within Varennes.
> Chosen Cap. causes tempest, fire, blood, slice.

In the translation of this, Garencières leaves the two words *vaultorte Herne* as in the original French, and does not attempt the translation. He also mistakes Reines for Rennes, the chief town in Little Brittany. He evidently has no conception whatever of the meaning of the quatrain. Bouys and Le Pelletier differ on minor points in rendering these words. *Forest*, Le Pelletier reads, in Latin, as *fores*,

gate, that is, by the Queen's gate, and he quotes
Thiers to show (" Hist. Révol. Fran." i. 309) that the
Queen made sure of a secret gate out of the Tuileries,
by which they escaped. But Bouys takes it for the
forest of Reines, which is on the road to Varennes.
Deux pars is husband and wife ; *voltorte*, or *vaultorte*,
is a cross-road, or a divergent road ; *vaulx*, a valley,
and *torte*, tortuous, says Le Pelletier. One does not
quite see how to educe cross road from this. Roquefort
gives *volt* for face, and *torte* would be turned, which
seems to me more likely. However, it stands for
the road through St. Menehould, on the way to Montmédi. This, it seems, they were forced into by post-
ing arrangements. Prudhomme (" Revol. de Paris,"
No. 102, p. 542) sets the divergence down to vacil-
lation or change of orders. If that be the correct
statement, then my etymology of *face about* for *vaultorte* fits it best. *Herne* is *Reine*, by metaplasm of
h for *i*. It was permissible in anagrammatic writing
to change one letter in a word, but not more than one.
The reader can refer for this to the " Dictionnaire
de Trévoux," under *Anagramme*. The white stone
stands for this royal or precious stone, the Queen,
who was dressed in white. The King was dressed in
grey. Prudhomme, in the work mentioned above
(p. 554), says he wore a round hat, which hid his face,
and had on an iron-grey coat (*gris de fer*), so he
appeared like a Carmelite.

There are nearly fourteen octavo pages of small
print (p. 411) of De Bouillé, which it might be well to
print, called " Détails du voyage du roi et de la reine
à Montmédy et leur arrestation à Varennes dans le

Clairmontais, le 22 juin, 1791," full of interesting
particulars.

VAULTORTE.

" Mais on verra que les circonstances changèrent entièrement
jusqu'au moment de l'exécution de son projet ; et ce qui était
possible au mois de janvier 1791, ne l'était plus au mois de juin."
—" Mémoires du Marquis de Bouillé," p. 195, ed. 1821.

" Il [le roi] m'informait qu'il partirait, avec sa famille, dans
une seule voiture qu'il ferait faire exprès. Dans la réponse que
je fis au roi, je pris la liberté de lui représenter encore une fois
que la route par Varennes offrait de grands inconvéniens, à
cause des relais qu'il fallait y placer pour suppléer à la poste. . . .
J'engageai donc Sa Majesté à prendre la route par Reims, ou
celle de Flandre, en passant par Chimay, et en traversant ensuite
les Ardennes pour se rendre à Montmédy. Je lui représentais
les inconveniens de voyager avec la reine et ces enfants, dans
une seule voiture *faite exprès*, et qui serait remarquée de tout
le monde," etc.—" Mémoires du Marquis de Bouillé," p. 217.

This flight occurred on June 20, 1791. On the
following day the National Assembly suspended
Louis XVI. from his functions. On the 1st of September they passed another decree, that should the
King surrender to the will of the people and become
a Constitutional King he might do so. This he duly
signed and attested on the 14th of the same month ;
so *Capet fut esleu.* The title of King of the French,
instead of the King of France, had been established
since October 16, 1789 (" Cyclopædia of Universal
History "), which virtually was the same thing. But
yet strictly it was not until after the flight that
he became *Esleu Cap.* Madame Campan, in the
" Mémoires de Marie-Antoinette," ii. 150, relates that
the Queen's hair had become white in a single night

and she had had a lock of her white hair mounted in a ring for the Princesse de Lamballe, inscribed *Blanchis par le malheur.* She had become *la pierre plus blanche encore.* Her dress was white, and her complexion too. The *tranche* stands for the slice, or *couperet,* of the guillotine. Bouys was amongst the first to explain this quatrain in print, and he says he owed the explanation to M. de Vaudeuil, of Nevers, who has written upon Nostradamus.

Century IX.—Quatrain 34. [I. 177.]

Le part * solus,† mary ‡ sera mitré
Retour : conflict passera sur le thuille,
Par cinq cents : un trahyr § sera ‖ tittré ¶
Narbon : et Saulce par coutaux avons d'huille.

Translation.

The husband alone afflicted will be mitred on his return. A conflict will take place at the Tuileries by five hundred men. One traitor will be titled—Narbon ; and (the other) Saulce, grandfather oilman, will [hand him] over to the soldiery.

The harness broke at Montmirail, and detained them two hours (p. 247). The King showed himself at

---

* *Le part* is the same word as in the last quatrain, and stands here for the husband.

† *Solus,* Latin for *seul.*

‡ *Mary,* or *marri,* is from the old word *Marrir, s'affliger,* and means afflicted, full of grief.

§ *Trahyr. Trahitor, trahiter,* from Latin *traditor = traître,* English traitor.

‖ *Coutaux* M. Le Pelletier takes as soldiers. *Par coutaux=per custodes.* They betrayed him into the hands of guards. I think it may also mean *coustiller,* a soldier armed with the *coustille,* a short, straight cutlass.

¶ *Avons = avus,* grandfather.

Chalons, and was recognized by the postmaster, who held his tongue. Everything went wrong owing to the change of date and loss of time on the road. At St. Menehould he was recognized again, and Drouet the postmaster's son, rode on to Varennes to betray him.

On the 15th of June the Marquis de Bouillé received a letter from the King, saying his departure would be delayed till the 20th, at midnight ; that he could not take the Marquis d'Agoult, recommended to him by Bouillé (as an "homme d'esprit, ferme et courageux, qui peut se montrer si les circonstances l'exigaient," p. 217), because Madame de Tourzel, the governess of the children, insisted on her right of place never to quit them ; and this consideration carried the decision. As if the King could not have let them follow in another vehicle ! Anything rather than be forced to show himself on the road as he did (p. 256).

How it all miscarried will be best understood by reading the whole of De Bouillé's account. His arrangements seem to have been masterly, like the noble soldier and statesman that he was ; the King's arrangements vacillating, foolish, and even perverse. In this account Monsieur Saulce is not seen at all.

This is to be filled in as follows. Louis XVI. alone, without his wife, will suffer the disgrace of being crowned with the red cap of Liberty, called the Phrygian bonnet or mitre, from its being the head-dress of the priests of Mithras. The five hundred Marseillais led the attack upon the Tuileries, a palace begun by Catherine de Medici (1564) on the site of the tile-kilns (*le thuille*), and not in existence when

Nostradamus wrote this (1555). The Count de Narbonne, Minister of War, was of the noblesse, and Saulce, father, son, and grandson, were chandlers and grocers, or oilmen, of Varennes. The father was *Procureur-syndic* of his commune. These oilmen betrayed him to the populace, and he was arrested *per custodes*. These sneaks stand as typical or representative traitors of the two classes of *noblesse* and *bourgoisie* paying cowardly court to the *prolétaire* class.

The Madame Campan before alluded to (ii. 158) relates that their Majesties alighted at the grocery shop of the Mayor of Varennes, Saulce; and he could have saved the King. The Queen was seated in the shop between two high-piled stacks of candles, and was talking to Madame Saulce.

The *Gazette Nationale*, June 25, 1791, reporting what took place in the Assembly the night before, announces that M. Martinet, in addressing the House, described Saulce's conduct as wise and *heroic*, replying as he did to the promises and caresses of the King and Queen, " J'aime mon roi ; mais je resterai fidèle à ma patrie." The result of his heroism was that two months later on the Assembly voted him twenty thousand livres as the reward of his exalted *vertue citoyenne*. Whether, in the scramble that so soon followed, he ever received the wasteful and ridiculous Judas-gift there is nothing to show ; but the bulletin recording the vote of these new-fledged statesmen, liberal of money not their own, still exists. We have here " *un Brute Français*," apeing the Roman, who loved Cæsar well, but blood better.

Thiers' account of the attack upon the Tuileries,

June 20, 1792 ("Révol. Fran.," ii. 152), furnishes
a pathetic picture of the afflicted King (*marri mitré*)
of the red nightcap, in which he was day-dreaming.
The palace was evacuated at about seven in the
evening by the populace, which had effected its entry
by main force ; but, when the crowd had now withdrawn peaceably and in good order, the King, Queen,
his sister, and the children, all met together, shedding
a torrent of tears. The King seemed stunned by
what had taken place ; the red cap was still upon his
head ; he now, for the first time for several hours,
noticed it, and flung it aside with indignation.

As to the five hundred men named by our oracle,
the historian of the French Revolution again comes
to our aid (ii. p. 209), saying that Barbaroux had
promised the Jacobins the co-operation of his Marseillais, who were on the way to Paris. The project
was to assemble at the Tuileries and depose the king
(ii. p. 235). They arrived on June 30, 1792, and were
five hundred men. Ils étaient *cinq cents*.

Those who care to see how Narbonne acted against
the King, can refer to the " Histoire de la Révolution,"
by Bertrand de Molleville, for satisfaction.

This stands out certainly as one of the most
startling of all the thousand quatrains of our strange
seer. It will henceforth and to the end of time
speak for itself without comment, if we merely
enumerate the historic facts as here anticipated in
four lines. The horror of the king at finding himself
mitré. The god Mithras is depicted on coins in this
very cap, and his priests made it their head-dress ;
further, it furnishes the lively etymology of the word

mitre itself. It was for ages, before the French took it up, the received emblem of that frantic crime that has been called *Liberty*. I will not say the result of this is, as poetry, artistically beautiful ; but, as a phrase of intense expression, it is so terse that at a stroke, beyond that of hydraulic power, it seems able to compress a truss of hay so as it may lie in a husk of beech-mast. I do say, nevertheless, that, thus regarded, Dante and Shakespeare can hardly furnish between them three sentences of such compressed force ; the matter in it seems to be condensed to adamant. *Mari sera mitré*, as it has been just explained, will be found, the more profoundly it is thought upon, to be an original miracle in phraseology. It is an actual and an awful prophecy in itself, but to devise a phrase to so convey the idea by human speech to the human mind of another is miraculous. It may sleep for centuries, as this has done, for lack of interpreta-tion ; but, when duly interpreted it cannot be resisted ; it storms the understanding ; and, as a phrase, seems to be a miracle begotten expressly to become the vehicle in which to convey another miracle. This horror of the King mitred is one distinct forecast. The second point is his return to Paris. There is, thirdly, the conflict of the five hundred. Fourthly, the spot, the Tuileries,—at Nostradamus' time, a thing of thin air, where the tiles were still baking, fire-hot to roof houses with, whilst the pen was writing this. Here again, if it is not poetry, it performs the poet's function, which gives to airy nothing a local habita-tion and a name. Fifthly, comes a titled name— Narbonne. Sixthly, that of Saulce ; and finally, the handing over to the custodians. Here are seven distinct prophecies of events historical : two of them, names of men yet to be born at a period two hundred years removed. And, behold, these seven facts are put before you in four lines!

There is a point of particular interest to be noted in that first line. Bouys (p. 62) remarks that, first line though it be, it should be the last, as the mitre was the closing act of the entire drama ; and he supposes that Nostradamus wanted to make the treachery most prominent to the mind of the reader. That is to talk like a chronologer. The first cause and the final are, in spiritual matters, one. The life and death of man are reduced to two points, and epitaphs give enough about most of the lives of mortal men when they chronicle the birth and death dates. "Alone he returned and was mitred." How, step by step, it all came about, *follows* necessarily ; and that is how Nostradamus puts it to us. If he had weighted himself with what science calls method, he would have destroyed his own instinct ; as science does, just as Saturn ate up the offspring of his proper loins. The soul that does this must grope to its results, but can never jump to them by prophecy.

Before we go to the next quatrain it may be instructive to note Garencières' treatment of the pregnant forecast we have just traversed. He translates thus :

> " The separated husband shall wear a mitre,
> Returning, battle, he shall go over the tyle,
> By five hundred one dignified shall be betrayed,
> Narbon and Salces shall have oil by the quintal."

"The verse signifieth, that some certain man who was married shall be parted from his wife, and shall attain to some great ecclesiastical dignity. The second verse is that, coming back from some place or enterprise, he shall be met and fought with, and compelled to escape over the tiles of a house. The third verse is that a man of great account shall be betrayed by five hundred of his men. And the last that, when these things shall come to pass, Narbon and Salces, which are two cities of Languedoc, shall reap and make a great deal of oil."

This shows some skill, but what an unintelligible total we reach. I merely set it down to prove to the sceptical, and those who incline to class Nostradamus authoritatively amongst impostors whose jargon is not worth the pains of interpreting, that they may look at this and learn from it two facts : First, that before the event forecast has happened, all the keys of interpretation are wanting, the prophecy looks like jargon, and is so for all practical purposes ; but that, secondly, once it has happened, or as we may say kissed sunlight, the keys appear with it, the light and the understanding awaken together. There is light in potence or *in posse* now ; but even then they will not unlock secrets, if the keys remain in the hands of ignorant or scientific persons [or self-sufficient, which is nearly the same thing as scientific], or in the hands of romance-readers and lazy dullards. You will not unravel "the words of the wise and their dark sayings" by reading a quatrain once through. The interpreter must approach the work in a simple, unprejudiced manner ; he must get light from history how he can,

—from memoirs, letters, books,—and learn by the
success and failure of past commentators. He must
be content to work very hard all the while, and with
little encouragement from others ; and then at last he
may so do something, that even his neighbours may
allow his work to be,—according to the bent or water-
pent of the particular mind of each,—some a discovery, some a revelation. He himself may probably
feel that a supreme patience has had more to do
with bringing the thing to pass than any other faculty
that could easily be named. Things of the spirit
must, of course, be spiritually discerned, and all talk
about faculties when the individual soul is treated of
must sound a little paradoxical. To divide the unique
and indivisible unity of the soul into parts and
pieces, betrays in the proposer himself perhaps some
"want of parts." But from the earliest time until
now, this has been the scientific way of treating the
human understanding ; so let us consider that it is right
enough. The soul has almost always been cut into
three, and then left to wriggle and wriggle, and at last
to join itself together again, as best it can, like a
worm in a garden. If this be according to Aristotle,
let all Sorbonne profess it for right. What does it
matter how we treat *one* thing, if only our method be
perfectly scientific and in accordance with all the
rest of the universal phenomena, and with a right
interpretation of nature? What can it matter about
the invisible, if only our eyes know how to take
account of the things that are seen ; that is, of the
only things truly subject to the cognizance of
man ?

Century IX.—Quatrain 92. [Bouys, 64.]

Le roi voudra en cité neufue entrer.
Par ennemis expugner l'on viendra.
Captif libère faux dire et perpétrer,
Roi dehors estre, loin d'ennemis tiendra.

Translation.

The King would enter into the city.
(By enemies expelled, France will obtain it [or] they will
arrive there ;)
It will be false to say and reiterate that the captive is free,
[And] that the King who is out [of Paris] will keep aloof from
enemies.

M. le Pelletier does not touch this quatrain. M.
Bouys gives his interpretation, which is not very
convincing, and I thought of passing it by altogether.
But the *captif libère* so links it with the journey to
Varennes of the Royal family, that it seemed preferable to include it, and leave it to the reader to
reject or accept it, as he might think fit. Another
determining influence was from my noticing that the
cité neuve, or Montmédi, which the King desired to
reach, was not French when the quatrain was penned.
The VIII., IX., and X. Centuries were not published
with the first seven, but were issued at Lyons from the
same press, namely that of Pierre Rigaud. Moreri
states that Nostradamus felt encouraged by the reception accorded to the seven Centuries to publish
three more (*i.e.* VIII., IX., and X.), in 1558. There is
a copy now in the Bibliothèque Royale, to which the
authorities give the date of 1558. Pierre Rigaud's
name appears 'on the title, but no date, which is
remarkable, as the first volume of 1555 has this
imprint : " *Ce present livre a été achevé d'imprimer le*

IIIIe jour de may MDLV," giving a date as if for a
nativity. M. le Pelletier demurs to the accuracy of
the pretended date, and thinks it must belong to the
edition of 1566, by Pierre Rigaud. If so, these three
Centuries scarcely appeared in the lifetime of Nostradamus, though they are dedicated to his patron,
Henry II.,—who died in 1559,—in an elaborate and
interesting epistle dedicatory. In opening this, Nostradamus says he has long been in doubt as to whom
he should devote (*consacrer*) these three Centuries, but
at last took courage to lay it at the feet of royalty.
Now, the edition of 1566 particularly states that the
prophecies *n'ont encore jamais esté imprimées.* One
cannot read the Dedicatory Epistle without feeling
sure it was written for the eye of the King, and therefore at least as early as 1558, but probably earlier by
a year or two. I therefore assume that he presented
them to the King in a fair manuscript, and that
having done that he remained content, and that the
family at his death, finding the original manuscript,
put it in Rigaud's hands to be printed.

My reason for thus inquiring into the dates is this :
that the investigation makes it extremely likely the
above quatrain was written before 1557, the year in
which Montmédi was taken by France, and, if so, it
explains the line that I have thrown into a parenthesis
in a manner in which it has never been interpreted
before. *Expugner* is not French now ; *expugnable* is
all that now remains of it in the language. So that

> Par ennemis expugner l'on viendra

may, I think, be regarded as a parenthetic explana-

S

tion referring to the *cité neuve*, which was not yet French territory, though on the point of becoming so, —*l'on viendra par ennemies expugner*, by expulsion of the enemy, in 1557. If this rendering be thought valid, it furnishes one reason the more for explaining this quatrain as one of the series belonging to the Revolutionary epoch, and one more redeemed from the maze of Nostradamus.

It would appear from Bouys, though he does not produce his historical authorities, that immediately the King escaped, France was flooded with announcements that the captive was free, and had their consent to hold himself aloof—*loin d'ennemis tiendra.* If this be established, it becomes certain that we can in the main determine this quatrain accurately. ("Histoire de la Révolution, par deux amis de la Liberté," in 7 vols., vol. vii. p. 126.)

Century VIII.—Quatrain 87. [I. 179.]

Mort conspirée viendra en plein effect,
Charge donnée et voyage de mort :
Esleu, créé, receu par siens, deffait.
Sang d'innocent devant soy par * remort.

Translation.

Death hatched by treason will take its full effect,
A charge imposed, voyage made to death.
Elected, created, received by his own, and undone by them.
The blood of Innocency (rises) before them in remorse (eternal).

Bouys thinks by the last line Nostradamus intended to convey, that the King felt poignant grief at the innocent victims his overthrow would leave without protection to the tender mercies of the States-General.

* A variant reads *pour.*

The other is better, connecting it, as it does, with that case analogous, where the mob cursed themselves out of their own mouth, and said "His blood be upon us, and on our children" (Matt. xxvii. 25).

Century X.—Quatrain 43. [I. 180.]

Le trop bon temps,* trop de bonté royale,
Fais et deffais, prompt, subit, negligence,
Legier † croira faux d'espouse loyalle,
Luy mis à mort par ‡ sa benevolence.

Translation.

Too much of good fortune, a too lax Royalty,
That makes and unmakes [appointments] sudden, hasty, negligent ;
Lightly believes his loyal Consort false,
And bids good nature lead the way to death.

This is a picture to the life of the fat-making King Louis Seize. The brush of a Velasquez, as it cannot paint the moral, could hardly so well place him before the eye, as in life. He is no picture well-framed, hanging for inspection in a gallery of pictures, but flesh and blood like one's self alive, and moving with us in the gallery a spectator and observer like ourselves. We have here Louis XVI. before us in the flesh.

" *He makes and unmakes appointments ;* yes, indeed." In a little more than eighteen years, sixty-seven ministers take office and relinquish it. Here they are alphabetically, as Bouys enumerates them.

* Construe Trop de bon temps.
† Legier, for légèrement. Romance language.
‡ Par, for Latin *per*, because of.

Amelot, Barentin, Bertrand de Molleville, Boyne, Breteuil, Brieune, Brogli, Beaulieu, Cahier de Gerville, Calonne, Castries, Champion de Cicé, Clavières, Chambonas, Clugny, Dabancourt, Danton, de Grave, Delessart, de Crosne, de Joly, d'Ormesson, Dabouchage, Dumourier, Duportail, Duport-Dutertre, Duranton, Foulon, Fourgueux, Fleurierès, Joly de Flemy, Lacoste, la Galaisières, Lailliac, la Jarre, la Luzerne, Lamoignon, Lambert, Laporte, Latour-Dupin, Lenoir, Liancourt, Leroux, Malesherbes, Maurepas, Miromeuil, Montmorin, Montbarrey, Mourgues, Narbonne, Necker, Pastoret, Puységur, Roland, Sartines, Ségur, Servan, Saint-Germain, Saint-Priest, Sainte-Croix, Taboureau, Tarbé, Terrier-Monceil, Thevenard, Turgot, Vergennes, Villedeuil. Several of these served twice, and Necker was in three times ; so that the number of ministries in the time mentioned is seventy-two—a thing not to be paralleled in history as a course of doing and undoing, of *fais and deffais.*

His temper was ungovernable and sudden, extending even to rough bathos, but was soon over. Maurepas always said, you must let the King have his first fling of humour out, and then he will soon recover. Secondly, his negligence let everything drift, finance included, till ruin brought collapse. You might think his economists had drawn their singular axiom for statesmenship, *Laissez faire*, from the example of their royal master. He fell at once into the intrigue of the diamond necklace belonging to Marie Antoinette, which was conveyed by the Countess of La Motte to the Cardinal de Rohan. Report runs that he even placed his wife under arrest in her own chamber for several days. "Lui mis à mort par sa bénévolence" displays a most wonderful forecast, and it is open to read it now LOUIS *mis à mort.*

Century VI.—Quatrain 92. [I. 182.]

Prince de beauté tant * venuste, †
Au chef menée, le second faict, ‡ trahy.
La cité au glaive de poudre face § aduste, ‖
Par trop grand meurtre la chef ¶ du Roi hay.

Translation.

The prince of very comely beauty (shall be)
Led to the head, and then betrayed to a second (place).
The city of the sword, with powder-torch, burns
The head of the King, hated on account of his illegal murder.

The edition 1558 gives the reading as above, but the line does not scan ; it wants two syllables. Bouys, without comment, reads *Prince sera*; Le Pelletier understands *menée* as a synonym for *intrigues.* But I should read it rather as a misprint for *mené.* The city of the sword is a graphic name for Paris, where the guillotine was first erected on September 25, 1792, having been perfected by Guillotin, the doctor, whose name was given to it. Roquefort gives the word *adusté* as *brûlé;* but Nostradamus uses it as a verb, *aduster,* in the third person of the present indicative. Paris burnt the king's head with a powder-torch, or burning powder, that is to say with quick-lime ; and, as having done him wrong, the people hate him, and wish to obliterate the traces of the murder perpetrated.

* *Tantum,* Latin, very. † *Venustus,* Latin, comely.
‡ *Faict,* Latin, *factus* made. § *Face,* Latin, *fax* torch.
‖ *Aduste,* Latin, *adustus* burnt. ¶ *Chef,* head.

The body and head of the King were placed in a basket of wicker-work, and carried, according to De Montgaillard ("Histoire de France," iii. p. 415. Janvier, 1793 *) to the cemetery of the Madeleine, and thrown into a trench twelve feet deep, which had been spread with quicklime ; more was thrown in upon the top of the body, so that decomposition would follow instantly. When the grave was reopened some twenty-four years after, to bestow a more decent burial on the relics, nothing remained but a few fragments of calcined bone.

Garencières reads *Princesse de beauté tant venuste,* which will not scan any better than the line of the edition of 1558 ; but he translates *au chef menée,* I find, as "shall be brought to the general," and the feminine termination is then right. This helps to confirm my rendering above. His annotation says that the only difficulty about the quatrain is as to what city is meant. As, however, he suggests no historical allusion whatever, he leaves every difficulty unsolved.

I think that most readers will be inclined to allow that this is a very extraordinary forecast, and that *La cité au glaive* as a name for Paris, and what has been perpetrated there, is both poetic and terrific in a very high degree—a sobriquet that, once heard, is likely

---

* "Le corps et la tête placés dans un panier d'osier sont à l'instant même portés au cimetière de la Madelaine, jetés aussitôt dans une fosse profonde de douze pieds, ouverte de six, garnie et recouverte de chaux vive, et dissous immédiatement. On l'inhume auprès des personnes qui avaient péri le 20 mai, 1770, jour de la fête donnée par la ville de Paris, à l'occasion de son mariage, et auprès des Suisses morts dans la journée du 10 août."

to cling in the memory for ever. To devise epithets of this simplicity and force constitutes an author at once master of utterance ; no matter what may be the shortcomings of the adjacent text. But, when you find these startling felicities perpetually recurring to illustrate facts historical,—facts that will not come into mortal ken for centuries after the death of the writer, —stiff, indeed, must be the reader's neck if he cannot bow it a little, as to a man of God passing by ; or, if he would rather have it so, to the occasional divinity shining through man's nature, that will not, cannot wholly die when death has done its worst. From Hecla to the tropics all rational creatures should rejoice at such a fact. What is the new world of Columbus to this? Why, nothing but a new hemi sphere of dirt. A spirit, that can read time future, must be a spirit whose habitation is Eternity. It is this hope kindles as we decipher, in the stillness of night, rune upon strange rune of the oracular sage of Salon.

Century X.—Quatrain 17. [1. 184.

La Royne Ergaste * voyant sa fille blesme
Par un regret dans l'estomach enclos :
Cris lamentables seront lors d'Angolesme,
Et au germain mariage forclos.

* *Ergaste* is *estrange* in Pierre Rigaud's edition. 'Εργαστήρ is a workman, and M. le Pelletier says *Ergaster* is Latin. It may be, but I do not find it in Facciolati, though *ergastulum*, a workhouse, is there given. When Marie Antoinette was in the Temple, she was reduced to working with her hands, like a workwoman (*ergaste*). But *ergaste* is the anagram of *estrange*, the one letter *n* excepted. Probably *estrange* is the preferable reading, inasmuch as Marie Antoinette was an Austrian, and so *étrangère*.

Translation.

The stranger Queen, seeing her daughter fading
By reason of the deep regret she endured inwardly :
The cries of Angoulême will be lamentable,
And the marriage with her cousin-germain foreclosed.

The Princess did marry the Duc d'Angoulême in
1799, but there was no issue,—*mariage forclos.* The
Queen wished to marry her daughter to a German
Prince : hence all the grief. The Abbé Torné-
Chavigny (" L'Histoire prédite et jugée par Nostradamus," ii. 28) had the merit, M. le Pelletier says, of
this learned interpretation. I cannot quite see this,
as M. Bouys gave the same interpretation as far back
as 1806, though with a particularity a little less
minute. The prophecy thus unravelled is the more
wonderful, as the event seems so little worth recording.
There is the same exactitude and precision shown as
where a kingdom is at stake.

Century IX.—Quatrain 77. [I. 185.]

Le regne prins * le Roy convicra,
La dame prinse à mort jurés à sort,
La vie a Royne fils on desniera,
Et la pellix † au fort de la consort.

Pierre Rigaud's edition reads *conjurera* for *convicra,*
and that, at least, makes the line scan, which *convicra*
does not. Bouys says that some ancient editions
read *conviera, commitari per viam,* and then it would
mean to arrange the funeral cortège of the King. I
think *conjurera* the best reading, for that might be

* *Prins,* Latin, *prensus,* taken, captive.
† *Pellix,* Latin, *pellex,* prostitute.

taken to mean that they condemned the King by jurors, or jury, as the Queen was in the next line.

Translation.

The assembly will condemn the King taken,
[And] the Queen taken to death by jurors sworn by lot ;
They will deny life to the Dauphin (*à Royne fils*),
And the prostitute at the fort will partake of the same fate.

Upon the word *jurés,* in the second line, M. le Pelletier remarks that the Convention, erecting itself into a supreme court of justice, proceeded to condemn the King to death. But the judgment upon Marie-Antoinette was passed by the *Tribunal révolutionnaire*, newly set up, which proceeded by jurors chosen by lot, *jurés à sort.* He further says that this *jury* is an institution borrowed from England, and he erroneously fancies that it had been first introduced into England at the Revolution, and had no existence there, even by name, during the lifetime of Nostradamus. This shows how little a Frenchman, when even well read, cares about English institutions. Pettingal almost proves that the Roman *judices*, and Greek δικασταί, were jurors. There has been great and profitless dispute, as to whether the Anglo-Saxons had juries, or whether they came in at the Conquest. If they did it would be strange, for they died out in Normandy. If the practice be Roman, it would have prevailed in England as in Normandy, both having been under Roman law forms. Coke, Blackstone, and many others, confidently maintain its existence here prior to the Conquest. If Anglo-Saxon it would still be Roman. Were it Scandinavian in origin, or were it Teutonic, it would equally have prevailed

here before the Conquest. So that the whole dis-
cussion has an interest merely archæological; and
leaves the *trial by jury*, no matter what its orgin, a
thing of immemorial usage in these islands. You
might as well try, by chemical analysis, to ascertain
when oxygen first entered as a component part into
the air men breathe. If you could settle the question
it would be no use; whilst the time lost in discussing
it might otherwise be well employed. But the
forensic usage was not so in France itself, as modern
Frenchmen think, for in old Glossaries, like Roquefort's, you find *jurie*, not *jurée:* "Assise où l'on pro-
nonce sur le rapport des jurés."

They delivered the poor Dauphin to the *cordonnier*
Simon, with orders to let him die slowly. The inhuman villains seem to have felt they could not
condemn a child to public execution; so they give
orders to a murderer to make away with him by ill
usage and starvation, a process that would have
rendered the guillotine welcome and a boon.

The last line admits of three interpretations. M. le
Pelletier takes the *pellix* to stand for the National
Convention itself, saying that it had prostituted
justice in condemning an innocent prince over whom
it had no jurisdiction. But clearly it had no jurisdiction over the King or Queen. He then takes the
fort to be the *Conciergerie*, to which it consigned its
own members, *consorts*, as an introduction to the
scaffold. This is very striking, but the quatrain does
not appear to me to threaten members of the Assembly
at all. The unity of conception is best maintained by
limiting its meaning to the fate of Royalty; and

Bouys places an excellent and forcible interpretation upon it without breaking the unity of purpose. He says that it relates to the Dubarri, the King's courtesan, and that the fort is her palace of Luciennes, which had anciently been a strong place or fort. This is good, if the Château de Luciennes bears it out ; but the *fort* may so easily be *sort* with the old *s* type, which is scarcely distinguishable from an *f*, that I think we might very well substitute it. We should then construe the last line

" And [consign] the prostitute to the fate of the Queen consort."

This interpretation requires less force to be employed upon the line, and less explanation than any of the others. The forms of the *s* and *f* are nearly identical. The reading that brings simplicity with it, and removes stumblingblocks out of the way, usually proves the safest and the best. Here we remove the complication introduced by the word *fort*, which otherwise requires explanation, and it runs : *The courtesan shares a like fate with the Queen.* It is now for the reader to select the best.

Sixaine 55. [I. 186.]

Un peu devant ou après très-grand' dame,
Son ame au ciel, et son corps soubs la lame,
De plusieurs gens regrettée sera,
Tous ses parens seront en grand' tristesse,
Pleurs et souspirs d'une dame en jeunesse,
Et à deux Grands la deuil delaissera.

Translation.

A little before or after a very great lady,
The soul [of Madame Elizabeth shall rise] to heaven, her body
under the blade,

She will be grieved for by many persons ;
All her family connections will be cast into deep sorrow,
One lady very young [Duchesse d'Angoulême will shed] tears
     and sighs,
And two great ones will be depressed with mourning.

This can be mistaken for no one but Madame
Elizabeth, the sister of Louis XVI., her niece, the
Duchess d'Angoulême, and the two brothers of
Madame Elizabeth, the Count of Provence and the
Count of Artois. This is not one of the very striking
stanzas, but the forecast is still notable, and occupies
its position very well as one in a considerable series.

Century I.—Quatrain 58. [1. 187.]

Tranché le ventre naistra avec deux testes
Et quatre bras : quelques ans entiers vivra,
Jour qui * Alquiloye † celebrera ses festes,
Fossen, ‡ Turin, chef Ferrare suivra.

Translation.

The belly cut shall spring again with two heads
And four arms : *Aquiloye* shall live several years,
In great force (*entiers*) what (*jour qui*) time he holds.
Fossen, Turin, Ferrara shall fall under his domination (*suivra
     chef*).

This is a very crabbed, but very wonderful quatrain.

The elder branch of the Bourbons was cut short in
the person of Marie-Antoinette (*le ventre tranchée*) ;
shall spring up again in two heads, Louis XVIII. and
Charles X. The two heads being crowned, the four
lesser princes are called arms and uncrowned. They
are counted thus : The Duc de Normandy, who died

---

* Qui = Latin *cui*, to which.
† Alquiloye = *Aquilæ lex*, law or rule of the Imperial Eagle.

in the Temple, June 8, 1795 ; the Duc de Berri,
assassinated January 13, 1820 ; the Duc d'Angoulême ;
and the Duc de Bordeaux, exiled August 16, 1830,
who, though he had so many close chances, died
without the crown,—an arm only, not a head, a hand
tenaciously to the last holding to its white hand-
kerchief as a flag. Zurich and Fossano stand, by
synecdoche, for Piedmont, and Ferrara for the Papal
States.

This brings us to the end of the Louis Seize series.
Let us, before passing on to a fresh series, just give a
glance at the ground we have traversed; and endeavour
to estimate the value of the historical facts prefigured
for us by Nostradamus in his book more than two
hundred years before the earliest of them began to
take effect upon the stage of actuality.

First, we beheld a section of the nation, the third
estate, usurping the sole authority of government,
and bringing down upon the whole the desolation
that was witnessed in Europe in 1789. Then the
intriguing Duc d'Orléans was portrayed, and the poor
King was seen repenting that he had not, when
insulted by him, publicly punished him by death.
The next picture was that of the remarkable flight to
Varennes, in which the very travelling habits of the
King and Queen, to their respective colours even,
were minutely given, and the precise name hinted of
the fallen Capet on the road,—fallen, though elected
by the people, *eslen cap*. At the very last moment
we are told their destination was changed by the
King, where changing meant his destiny. He was
then depicted as betrayed. He had run into the jaws

of death, and the very names of the traitors, Narbonne and Saulce, were given ; with the further detail, that he was taken back to Paris and mitred with the Phrygian cap, in the desecrated Tuileries, at the dictation of five hundred Marseillais. In another quatrain that journey is called a voyage of death, and in one line is laid before us all that happened to Louis the Unfortunate. He is elected, created king, received by his own people, and undone. To this succeeds that extraordinary picture of the King himself : his best friend could scarcely have portrayed the man so truly to us. Too prosperous at the outset, too good-natured a royalty, sudden in temper, yet dilatory in act, making and unmaking ministries quarterly, and finally done to death by his own benevolence. We then have a stanza devoted to him. We see him as a beautiful youth made chief, then deposed, and his head rolling from the scaffold in the City of the Glave, even to his burial in quicklime at the Madelaine, a procedure so unheard of in the case of kings. Then that curious reference to *La Royne Ergaste* and the little incident touching her daughter's marriage to D'Angoulême. Then follows the Queen's death, brought about by a jury, a novelty imported from England by the innovators of that period ; crowned by cruelty to the Dauphin. There follows a more or less curious sixaine, conveying the fate of Madame Elizabeth, the King's sister ; till we close with a brilliant quatrain that exhibits, in a symbolical fashion, the Napoleonic interregnum, when the severed Bourbon race puts out again its last two crowns, above the Eagle-law or *Alquiloye,*—probably the last appearance it will ever make upon the stage of history. I think we may agree, that it would not be easy to parallel such a series of verified forecasts relating to the most striking historical incidents, that bear upon a single reign, from any one book existing in the world.

THE NATIONAL CONVENTION.

W E now reach a fresh division, and shall treat of
the National Convention,—a period of about
three years.

Century VIII.—Quatrain 17.　[I. 189.]

Les bien aisés subit * seront desmis ;
Par les trois freres le monde mis en trouble.
Cité marine saisiront ennemies ;
Faim, feu, sang, peste, et de tous maux le double.

Translation.

The well-to-do [members] shall be suddenly dismissed,
On account of three brothers the world shall suffer trouble.
Enemies shall take possession of the marine city ;
Hunger, fire, slaughter, plague, of evils all the double.

Privilege is to be abolished suddenly.　The three
brothers who trouble the world are the Royal trio,
Louis XVI., Louis XVIII., and Charles X.　Toulon
is the maritime city.　We shall come upon it again,
further on, in Century VII. 13, where it is treated of
more fully.　M. le Pelletier interprets *feu* as being
war, and *peste* as standing for irreligion.　As goods
were all doubled to Job, so here all evils are to be

---

* *Subit* stands for *subito,* suddenly.

doubled. On the night of August 4, 1789, feudal privilege was abolished suddenly (*subit*). The clergy and nobility were dispossessed of property and title. Toulon, taken by the English, is the *Cité marine.* It was retaken, in the name of Louis XVII., on August 23, 1793, by the French ; on the 19th of December, Marie-Antoinette and Égalité, Duc d'Orleans, being both executed during the British tenure.

Century IX.—Quatrain 17. [1. 191.]

Le tiers * premier pis que ne fit Neron,
Vuidez † vaillant que ‡ sang humain respandre !
Rédifier fera le forneron, §
Siecle d'or mort, nouveau Roy, grand esclandre !

Translation.

The third become first does worse than Nero,
See how much valiant human blood it squanders !
It will rebuild the old tile kilns,
The age of gold is dead, a new dynasty, and great scandal.

This interprets itself. M. le Pelletier explains the rebuilding of the kilns as setting up the scaffolds to consume the clergy and nobility. I do not myself see the force or necessity of this. The age of gold yields to that of iron or the sword ; the new dynasty (the Napoleonic) is a vast scandal, and reintroduces pomp and ceremonial at the Tuileries.

* Tiers = third.
† Vuidez = Latin, *videte*, see.
‡ Que = how much.
§ Forneron = Latin, *fornax*, furnace.

T

Century VIII.—Quatrain 19. [1. 192]

A* soustenir la grand' cappe † troublée,
Pour l'esclaircir les rouges marcheront :
De mort famille sera presque accablée,
Les rouges rouges la rouge assommeront.

Translation.

They will *not* sustain the great but troubled Capets,
The reds will take steps to purge their number,
They will almost exterminate the family with death,
The red of reds will overwhelm the red.

This very forcibly announces the Reign of Terror
to have set in.   The reds will do what in them lies to
crush the Capets, till they have almost annihilated the
family in death ; and, then the reddest reds will
guillotine the reds,—the Montagnards the Girondists.
Bouys does not allude to this, though one would
have thought it must strike every reader as far as
what is said relating to the conduct of the double-dyed
reds against the moderate reds.   Garencières' mistakes
serve to show how impossible it was to guess at the
meaning of a quatrain in the seventeenth century.
He fancies this to refer to some conspiracy of red
Cardinals against a Pope, to be designated the Red
one.

Century VI.—Quatrain 69. [1. 193.]

La pitié grand' sera sans loing tarder,
Ceux qui dônoyent seront contraints de prendre :
Nuds, affamés, de froid, soif, soy bander,
Les monts passer commettant grand esclandre.

* *A* is the Latin *a*, privative.
† *Cappe*, is put for *Capet*.

Translation.

A sight of pity will not long delay,
The almoners will soon be forced to beg :
Hungered, athirst, naked, proscribed, and cold.
In bands they cross the Alps, a scandal to be seen.

This conveys a forcible picture of the calamitous emigration the clergy of France would undergo between 1792 and 1801. Once the clue is supplied, it leads so naturally, that one almost finds insight from it into the manner in which these representations presented themselves to Nostradamus. One feels, that he must have seen the events passing before the field of sight as visions, sometimes accompanied with uttered words ; otherwise how could he get intimation of names ? But, if it was thus that intuition came to him, the quatrains, that he now scattered up and down throughout the Centuries in utter disorder and disconnection, must have come to him in a sequence, rendering them comprehensible ; more or less, indeed, in the very order probably into which the chronology of historical record enables the careful student to replace them now, as soon as they are understood by him. If this be so, a rather curious fact presents itself, in a form approaching to something like a certainty, which is this : disorder must have been the method of the book. We know that generally his practice was to write down the matter in prose, and at leisure convert this into separate quatrains rhymed ; these he must afterwards have shaken up in a bag or hat, and when inextricably mixed have counted them out into hundreds. I think it quite possible that he found his forecasts became too intelligible when put together in their natural order, and in the sequence of events. No doubt, with regard to those events of his own time and to be soon fufilled, he first began to perceive the necessity for inverting or displacing the order. Consecutive and interlinking stanzas would form a kind of commentary, and throw mutual light one upon the other ; so that the adoption of disorder would follow as a measure of personal security. He thought that his sayings should be dark, as becometh the words of the wise ; and that it would be quite time enough, should they grow clear when fulfilled to a reader, who would take sufficient trouble to elucidate them and bring out their meaning.

Century I.—Quatrain 44. [I. 194.]

En bref* seront de retour sacrifices,
Contrevenans seront mis à martyre ;
Plus ne seront moines, abbés, ne† novices,
Le miel sera beaucoup plus cher que cire.

This quatrain exhibits the suppression of the Catholic worship in France, which took place November 10, 1793. What they called the worship of the goddess of Reason was set up ; and a return to Paganism is what the first line means.

Translation.

For a short time there will be a return to [Ethnic] sacrifices,
And those who oppose will suffer martyrdom :
There will be no more monks, clergy, nor novices ;
Honey will fetch more than wax.

The last line means that wax will be cheapened, as

---

* *En bref, temps,* understood.
† *Ne,* again used for *ni.*

none will be consumed in the churches. The rest explains itself. Garencières can see the meaning of the last two lines ; but the first two he considers to have been fulfilled in the time of Henry V. of France and Henry VIII. of England.

Century II.—Quatrain 8. [I. 195.]

Temples sacrés * prime † façon Romaine,
Rejetterons les gofres ‡ fondements,
Prennant leurs loix premieres et humaines,
Chassant non tous des saincts les cultements.§

Translation.

The temples consecrated in the fashion of early Rome,
They will reject the deep foundations [of Christianity].
Returning to their first and human laws,
They will not entirely abolish all saint-worship.

This M. le Pelletier explains to be a forecast of the *Fête de l'Être Suprême,* which was appointed by decree of the Convention May 7, 1794, and celebrated on the 8th of June of the same year with great pomp.

Century V.—Quatrain 33. [I. 196.]

Des principaux de cité rebellée.
Qui tiendront ‖ fort pour liberté r'avoir,
Detranchés ¶ masles, infelice ** meslée,
Cris, hurlements, à Nantes piteux voir !

* *Sacrés,* for *consacrés.*
† *Prime,* Latin, *prima,* first.
‡ *Gofres* is deep, profound.
§ *Cultements,* Latin, *cultus,* worship.
‖ *Tiendront fort,* will struggle hard.
¶ *Detranchés,* Romance for *tranchés, tête* understood.
** *Infelice,* Latin, unhappy.

Translation.

The chief citizens of the revolted city,
Who will struggle hard to recover liberty.
The men beheaded, an unhappy mixture,
Cries, howlings, at Nantes piteous to see.

This was realized at Nantes, in Britany, under the Proconsulate of De Carrier. The town had, in 1793, become the focus of the Vendean reaction against the National Convention. The men were beheaded generally, but many men and women were stripped naked. They were then tied together, a man to a woman, in couples, or pairs, which their fiendish tormentors styled "republican marriages." In this diabolic connection (*infelice meslée*) they were precipitated helplessly into the Loire, amidst heartrending cries and howlings. No viler crime was ever committed on this earth, nor can ever be ; the infamy of man and the revengeful filth of lust can no further go. From that extraordinary coinage and coupling of words, *infelice meslée*, you know, or seem to know, that Nostradamus beheld the horrid spectacle in vision—

Estant assis de nuict secret estude (Century I. 1).

Those who believe this to be a recital at haphazard are of a brain-formation singularly constituted.

Century VIII.—Quatrain 88.

Dans la Sardeigne un noble Roy viendra,
Qui ne tiendra que trois ans le royaume.
Plusieurs couleurs avec soy conjoindra,*
Luy mesme après soin sommeil marrit † scome.‡

* *Le* to be understood before *conjoindra*.
† *Marrit*, afflicted.
‡ *Scome*, Latin, *scomma*, gibe, taunt.

In Sardinia a noble King shall come,
Who will only hold the kingdom during three years.
The tricolour will annex him [the King] to itself;
He after much pains will sleep afflicted and ridiculed.

This is Charles Emmanuel IV. The Republic of the tricolour, "le drapeau tricolor," will despoil him of his continental estate; and he will withdraw to his island, ruling for three years, 1798–1802. He then abdicates to his brother, Victor Emmanuel I., and, *après soin* much care, will sleep [as regards governing], and, residing at Rome, sad and humiliated, will assume the Jesuit robe, and die in 1819.

PIUS VI.

THE next four quatrains refer to Rome and Pope
Pius VI.

Century V.—Quatrain 57. [I. 199.]

Istra * de mont Gaulfier † et Aventin,
Qui ‡ par le trou advertira l'armée.
Entre deux rocs sera prins § le butin,
De SEXT ‖ mansol ¶ faillir la renommée.

Translation.

When a [French] army shall go from Mont Gaulfier to the
    Aventine,
There will be a man advising them from under the hole.
The booty shall be seized between the two rocks,
And the glory of the sixth celibate shall wither.

This is a very curious stanza. The name of Montgolfier, the aeronaut, is visible enough in the two
separate words, *mont Gaulfier.* M. le Pelletier calls
it the grammatical figure of metaplasm ; but it is not
strictly so. Metaplasm is the forming of cases from a
non-existent nominative. This is making two words for

---

* *Istra* = *ira*, will go, or will go forth.
† *Mont*golfier, the inventor of ærostatics.
‡ *Qui*, Latin for who, a man who.
§ *Prins*, taken.   ‖ *Sext*, for *sextus*.
¶ *Mansol, man, sol. Manens solus* means celibate, or priest
under vows.

things non-existent to represent a proper name. But
there is a still greater singularity in the employment of
it here. For Nostradamus, as I understand him, makes
this fictitious mountain contrast with the real Mount
Aventine. He makes it stand, as I think, for one of
the two rocks between which the booty is secured.
The brothers Montgolfier were paper-makers at
Annonay Ardèche, and they gave their own name
to their discovery, which dates June 5, 1783. Their
balloons opened at the bottom to be filled, so that a
man placed in them was under the hole, *par le trou.*
I do not know at what point the Montgolfier was
floated to furnish military information to the French,
but I suppose on the Italian side of the Alps, so that
from that rock or mountain to the Aventine rock
would be the points between which the booty was
seized. But the former of these Nostradamus seems
to me to designate by the man's name, which lends
itself to a play upon the word, rather than by a peak
of the Alps. M. le Pelletier says that the two rocks
refer to Peter, *pierre* being *rock*. One is Avignon, in
France, and the other Rome, in Italy, and the booty
was obtained by the treaty of Tolentino, under date of
February 19, 1797. By this the Pope lost Avignon
and Venaissin in France, Bolognia, Ferrara, and the
Romagnia in Italy, and this he calls the two rocks.
The balloon was first used to reconnoitre the position
of the Austrians at the battle of Fleurus, June 16,
1794. Almost immediately after the treaty, the
Pontiff was dragged from Italy to die at Valence:
thus was fulfilled the prophecy of *faillir la renommée.*
Interpret how you may, the mention of the name of

Montgolfier so appropriately in this connection, must always stand as proof of the most solid kind that Nostradamus's foresight was miraculous.

Century V.—Quatrain 30. [i. 201.]

Tout à l'entour de la grande cité
Seront soldats logés par champs et villes :
Donner l'assaut Paris Rome incité,*
Sur le pont † lors sera faicte grand pille.

Translation.

Compassing all round the great city
There shall be soldiers camping in the fields and towns :
A Frenchman [Paris will take] Rome excited ;
There will then be perpetrated on the Pope a great pillage.

The Executive Directory, in defiance of the Constitution which formally forbade it, encamped troops around Paris, *la grande cité*, on September 4, 1797. This was to quell, or keep in awe, the counter revolution. A Frenchman [*Paris*], General Berthier, took Rome by assault, February 10, 1798, the pretext being that General Duphot had lost his life in an *émeute* [*dans Rome incité*]. Pope Pius VI. was dispossessed of his states, arrested in his palace, and subjected to general pillage.

Century VIII.—Quatrain 46. [i. 202.]

Pol ‡ mensole § mourra trois lieües du Rosne ;
Fuis ‖ les deux prochains ¶ tarasc ** destrois : ††

* Latin, *incitatus*, agitated.
† *Pont*, pour Pontificat, or Pontifex.
‡ πολύς, grand, considerable.
§ *Man. sol., manens solus*, as before.
‖ The ordo is, les deux prochains destrois fuiront le tarasc.
¶ *Prochain* = proche parent, who partakes in a heritage.
** ταραχή = tumult.
†† Romance, *destrois*, afflicted, dejected.

Car Mars * fera le plus horrible trosne
De Coq, et d'Aigle, de France Freres trois.

Translation.

The grand Celibate shall die three leagues from the Rhone ;
The two dejected brothers shall fly tumult :
For war shall make a most horrible throne
For the three brothers of France by the Cock and Eagle.

The Pope, that is, shall die at Valence, a few leagues from the Rhone. The two brothers [afterwards Louis XVIII. and Charles X.], alarmed at the movement of the populace, take flight. War inflicts sad havoc on the throne of the three brothers [Louis XVI., Louis XVIII., Charles X.] by the Orleans Cock, and Napoleonic Eagle.

Century II.—Quatrain 99. [I. 203.]

Terroir Romain qu'interpretoit Augure †
Par gent ‡ Gauloise par trop sera vexée :
Mais nation Celtique craindra l'heure,
Boreas § classe ‖ trop loing l'avoir poussée. ¶

Translation.

The Roman territory that the Pope governed
The French will cruelly vex :
But that Celtic nation should fear the hour
When it has advanced its army too far to the north.

I render this in the main in accordance with M. le Pelletier ; but perhaps some may think that the

* *Mars*, god of war. † *Augur*, for Roman priest.
‡ *Gens* is Latin for *nation*.
§ *Boreas* is north wind, or north.
‖ *Classis*, Latin, is a body of men, used here as army.
¶ The ordo is, [où elle] aura poussé son armée trop loin vers le nord.

Pope cannot be called an augur without great
violence. *Interprétoit* can hardly stand for spiritual
government. It is also difficult to make *classis*
into army. *Classis* represented the orders of the
people of Rome; that divided them into bands and
companies for governmental and electoral purposes,
not for war. The only *classis* of war was the *fleet*, and
Garencières renders it by *navy*, although he is entirely
abroad in every other respect in his interpretation of
the quatrain. Though he forces a fulfilment upon it
in the time of Henry II. of France, still, evidently
Rome is meant, whatever the Augur may interpret.
The Roman territory was twice trampled on by the
French: first by General Berthier against Pius VI.,
and again by General Miollis, who in 1809 removed
Pope Pius VII. The closing couplet is clearly a
forecast of Napoleon's defeat in Russia. That will
not be affected by the manner in which we interpret
classe; but I cannot imagine for a moment that
Nostradamus would employ the Latin *classis* so
erroneously for an *army*, which no Roman would ever
use it for. *Certamen classicum* is a sea-fight, but never
employed for engagements on land. The result of
this minute verbal inquiry will, I think, end by establishing the more remarkably the prescience and forecast of this consummate seer. He uses the word
classe in one of its late eighteenth, or early nineteenth
century acceptions, for that body of young men,
which is called out every year in France by lot to
serve in the army; or all those called to the colours,
who are drawn for service in the same year. It is an
administrative word, that sprang into use out of the

conscription, and which will die out again when that fraud, passed upon the nations of Europe, has been detected and abolished ; that institution which fosters war and makes its otherwise intermittent evils permanent and perpetual upon humanity. To enlarge the area of this view is to doom conscription to death and sure oblivion. Conscription is an invention of Beelzebub, when seeking his bath of blood, under the euphonic guise of a patriotic defence of the mother soil. *Mourir pour la patrie* is the glozing lie of Roget de l'Isle, that supplements, or drowns, the true cry of " Blood for Moloch." So we will read, for the first time now, the passage thus : But let the Celtic nation beware the hour when her *conscript columns* are pushed too far to the Boreal north-east. In brief, beware of Moscow. If this sixteenth century anticipation of a nineteenth century idiom be nothing, then let the Alps be called a molehill, and the hollow sea a cup. Here we close the prefiguration of the Papal torment appropriately enough ; it closes with a terrible hint to its tormentor.

NAPOLEONIC RULE.

Century III.—Quatrain 35. [I. 205.]

Du plus profond de l'Occident d'Europe,
De pauvres gens un jeune enfant naistra,
Qui par sa langue seduira grande troupe,
Son bruit au regne d'Orient plus croitra.

Translation.

In the Southern extremity of Western Europe
A child shall be born of poor parents,
Who by his tongue shall seduce the French army ;
His bruit shall extend to the kingdom of the East.

IN the island of Corsica was born, of an ancient but impoverished family, a child, Napoleon Bonaparte, whose proclamations electrified the French troops. His expedition, by order of the Directory, to Egypt, which was meant to ruin his career, conferred upon him a world-wide renown. This man was not eloquent as orators are eloquent ; verbosity is their gift. Even the endowment of Cicero lay much in words ; and in their multitude, which wanteth not folly : Solomon says sin. A plethora of words becomes the apoplexy of reason. But this man's phrases are all portable, made for the knapsack : they fly to the lip as lightning does to metal ; poetry, passion, and energy are in them, but fused to an aerolite, till they fall like a luminous bolt, only to burn in man's memory for ever after. They are not winged, but lightning-shod. Fulminants are matter etherealized to an interlinking with spirit. But this man's words are spirit itself, and burn their niche in Time, to last as long as that will. Take two of them : " Soldiers, forty centuries look down upon you ! " and again, " Behold the sun of Austerlitz ! " When you speak, speak thus to men ; such words are deeds ; and come not as from one who beateth the air to the pitchpipe of the tibicen Cice-ronical, but as the bullet to its butt ; speak sword-points, that press between the joints and marrow. But I will stop here, to escape oratory. That may still fetch its price, and seduce the zebra troup in the courts of legal falsity, or in the Babel-room down by the river-Minster.

Century I.—Quatrain 76. [I. 206.]

D'un nom farouche tel proferé sera,
Que les trois seurs * auront fato † le nom ;
Puis grand peuple par langue et faict dira, ‡
Plus que nul autre aura bruit et renom.

Translation.

Of a savage name there shall be such publishing
That the three sisters shall have by Fate the same name :
Then he will lead a great nation by tongue and deed,
And have more glory and fame than any other.

Here M. le Pelletier takes *le proferé* for a thing placed before, and understands it as being the pre-nomen of Bonaparte, viz. Napoleon. But I cannot

---

* *Seur* = sœur.　　　　† *Fatum*, Latin, fate, destiny.
‡ *Duira*, for conduira.

see how that is shown to be the meaning of *proferé*.
That word, if from the Latin *proferre*, never was used
for *cognomen* or *prænomen*.   One of the meanings of
proferre is *palam facere*, to make public or publish, and
I think it would be safer to render it as I have done.
It will still equally draw attention to the name
Napoleon, in contradistinction to the name of Bonaparte ; because, when he mounted the throne as
Emperor, he adopted the new name and abandoned
the previous one.   This selection of a new name
seems to be a natural instinct of humanity on entering
upon a new phase of life.   The popes take a new
name on assuming the pontifical rank ; monks and
nuns do so on entering the religious life ; commoners
leave their name behind when created peers ; women
do so when they marry ; and here Napoleon does it.
But I do not think it desirable to consider this to be
indicated by the word *proferé*.   Nostradamus says
that it is such a fatal name that the Parcæ themselves
will adopt it.   He then repeats that he will lead,—I
think it should be seduce (*séduira*),—the *grande nation*
by speech and deeds, and raise a name unrivalled in
the universe.   This was certainly true, and the prefiguration of it is, beyond the denial of prejudice,
marvellous.

We have now to deal with the word itself, which
will furnish to investigation a few interesting hints.
Of course some may think them intricate and far-
fetched.   There is no great importance to be attached
to them perhaps, but they must interest the curious ;
and curiosity that is innocent has a value of its own.
Who could see in Sloane's strange Chelsea gallery

the shape, dimension, and value of the museum of
Bloomsbury and its affiliations?

Century IX.—Quatrain 33. [I. 208.]

Hercules Roy de Rome et D'annemarc,*
De Gaule trois Guion † surnommé,
Trembler l'Italie et l'unde ‡ de Sainct Marc,
Premier sur tous monarque renommé.

Translation.

Hercules, King of Rome and Denmark,
Surnamed the triple Giant of France,
Shall make Italy tremble and the wave of St. Mark,
First in renown of all monarchs.

There was a Celtic Hercules fabled to draw men
by their ears · *Par langue et faict il conduira*, as we
have just seen, so that this Hercules means the
Napoleonic dynasty. As to King of Rome, Napoleon
actually assumed that title, and later on he conferred
it upon his son by Marie Louise. In the " Mémorial
de Sainte-Helène," 1840 [i. 79], by Las Cases, it is
said that during his consulate somebody published a
genealogy connecting his family with the ancient
kings of the north. This Napoleon ridiculed in the
public journals, stating that his nobility dated only
from Montenotte or the 18th Brumaire. Things
were not yet ripe for royal pretensions. The Bonaparte family in Italy can trace to the thirteenth
century. One branch was settled at Treviso, the other
at Florence, and both held an honourable position ;

---

* Δαν-αρχή, Princedom of Dan. The old Kings of Denmark
pretended to derive from Dan, seventh son of Jacob, it is said.

† Γῆς υἱός, son of earth. *Terræfilius*, giant.

‡ *Unda*, wave, *onde*.

a third was at Sarzana, in Genoa. A Charles Bonaparte settled in Corsica in 1612, and lived in obscurity,
says Le Pelletier, till this family of kings was born.
Taine has discovered that the family was of *condottiere*
stock, and De Staël and Stendal had, before that,
both of them found Napoleon's character more
analogous to that, than to any other type known to
them. Taine finds him to be a Sforza or a Malatesta
born belated by three centuries. He is as unscrupulous, searching, and ambitious as Macchiavelli ;
and, curiously enough, the only book * he is known
to have ever annotated profusely is Macchiavelli's
" Prince," which was found in his baggage at Waterloo,
and has since been published ; and an intensely

---

* The title of this book is " Machiavel Commenté par N⸰⸰
Buonaparte," 1816, published by H. Nicolle, 12, Rue de Seine.
I have a copy, but there is none in the British Museum. The
Preface and the Introductory Discourse on Macchiavelli are
full of ability. The translation of the " Prince " in French
occupies the left-hand column of each page, and seems well
done ; on the right-hand column are given the emperor's annotations, where they occur, otherwise it stands blank. They are
severally initialled G., R. C., or E—General, Republican Consul,
Emperor,—according to the period at which Napoleon may
be supposed to have written them. Some of the remarks are
clever, but perhaps scarcely show the grip of Napoleon ; which,
whether right or wrong, was always that of an iron vice. I
now imagine it to be an ingenious forgery, but it is quite curious
enough to merit further inquiry. This footnote, it will be seen,
does not correspond with what I have said in the text. I wrote
that under the impression that the document was genuine, and
it would be just, if the book were true. But I leave it as it
is, though it tells slightly against myself, as the contrast, between
the first and second thoughts seems to me instructive. It
shows that, let a man walk by right faith or by wrong, he must
steer by the belief that is present with him.

interesting book it is ; enormously wicked and shrewd, but diabolically wise in the Devil's gay antics. It is a scientific treatise on government without God in the world. Its moral axiom would seem to be that even murder should be directed by good sense in the hands of a craft-master. In this respect I think it is even superior to the clemency of Cæsar. The " Prince" evidently fascinated him deeply. He treats his author quite imperially, as Bentley or any other great critic might do, and points out condescendingly where the priest is but a theorist and errs for want of knowledge, such as can only be gained from the practical handling of affairs by a man of the Napoleon calibre. I don't know that you can read so deep into the very spirit (for I will not mention heart in the same breath with Napoleon) of the man of blood and brain, as you may by the pencil interlineations by him jotted down in this his Italian *vade mecum ;* from time to time as he recurs to the book, enlarging in view from general to first consul, and from first consul to emperor. You seem to sit with him, as in a magical cave, with terrible writings that come and go upon the wall before you, writings which are the words of this book, and are lit up with a lurid phosphoresence, the light of which emanates from his own putrescent brain.

It is not historically true to say, as M. le Pelletier does, that the family lived in obscurity in Corsica. The house at Ajaccio was the largest in the place, a palace even as compared with the other residences. The title of King of Rome was precious to Napoleon, as it enabled him to claim succession to the Empire of Charlemagne. Although Garencières, in his interpretation, fails of attaching any individual fulfilment to the words, he is able, from this title, to say that whoever it belongs to will attain to the Roman Empire.

Guion is equivalent to Terræfilius or Earthborn, and means giant; in fact, it almost seems a variant of *géants;* but why *three giants of France?* I do not know that this has ever been explained. Hercules mythologically was distinguished by three symbols (Martinii, " Etymologicon," *s.v. Hercules),*—a lion's skin, key, and three apples. The three apples were, not to get angry, not to love money, not to love pleasure. This need only be mentioned for the sake of the double triplication and as marking so far the propriety of the term Hercules. Master of Rome, *i.e.* Italy; of Venice, *i.e.* Austria; of Paris, *i.e.* France; as ruled over by Napoleon as General, Consul, Emperor. That he was " the first of monarchs over all renowned " needs no elucidation.

Century VIII.—Quatrain 61. [I. 209].

Jamais par le descouvrement du jour
Ne parviendra au signe * sceptrifere †
Que tout ses sieges ‡ ne soyent en sejour,§
Portant au coq‖ don du Tag ¶ armifere.**

---

* *Signum,* ensign, standard, or perhaps symbol of rule or domination.

† *Sceptrum ferre,* sceptre-bearing, reigning.

‡ *Siége,* position, situation.

§ *En séjour,* permanent, durable.

‖ *Coq,* the Gallic cock.

¶ *Tago,* or *tango,* to touch or take, le Pelletier says; but it does not yield very good sense. Perhaps τάγμα, a regular body of soldiers, in Dion Cassius it stands for the Roman *legion.* Garencières reads here Tag *à misère,* "The *tag* to misery," and

Translation.

Never shall he in broad daylight
Reach to the symbol of sceptre-bearing rule.
Of all his positions none will be of a settled permanency,
Conferring on the Gallic cock a gift of the armed Legion.

In other words, the Emperor will never enjoy a
settled seat of firmly established government, and he
will confer upon France, either the ruinous legacy or
bequest or gift of the legionary conscription, which
converts Europe into an armed camp,—an evil gift,
indeed ; or those who prefer it, may render it as the
gift to France of a huge burial-place in Spain and
Portugal, where so many thousands of men, her best
blood, fell. But conscription is of the wider issue,
and the more permanent evil, as it affects Europe to
this hour. It makes peace an interlude to war, and
very little less costly than war.

Our next quatrain is a great rarity, for it seems to
be in pure Provençal, and extremely pleasing it is, a
great deal more honied, to the ear in sound than the
present French language ; which is excellent for conversation and the *salon*, where society grimaces, but
where true souls are struck dumb and poetry has
ceased to be possible ; or only possible to rebellion,
such as that of Victor Hugo.

Century IV.—Quatrain 26. [I. 211.]

Lou grand eyssame se lèvera d'abelhos,
Que non sauran don te siegen venguddos.

says it is wretchedness to come from Portugal to France, *Tag*
being the *Tagus*, on which Lisbon is situated. This might be
interpreted well to mean the mischief arising to the empire
from the successes of Wellington in the Peninsular war.

De nuech l'embousq. Lou gach dessous les treilhos,
Ciutad trahido per cinq langos non nudos.

The great swarm of bees shall rise,
That none can tell from whence they came.
Night's ambush. The jay * beneath the tiles,
City betrayed by five tongues not naked.

The bees stand for the Bonapartist army and the
Empire. The second line is understood, by M. le
Pelletier, to refer to the origin of the family, and it
may be so ; but I think it refers to the surprising
suddenness with which the rouges, *sans-culottes*, and
republicans,—in pretended love with equality and freedom,—were found to welcome tyranny and Rule of

* The jay, of course, is Esop's Fable of that bird, tricked out
in finer feathers than its own. The elegant rendering by La
Fontaine [iv. 9, Ed., 1838] of *Le Geai paré des plumes du Paon*
had, when Nostradamus wrote, not then taken shape. The
original is so accessible, that it may suffice to give here the
English version.

> " A peacock moulted, and a jay
> 　　Assumed the feathers fine,
> And, strutting in a peacock-way,
> 　　Thought ' now I look divine.'

> " The first who met him laughed outright ;
> 　　Others he found to sneer ;
> The peacocks voted him a fright,
> His brother jays all quizzed ' the sight,'
> 　　But none would have him near.

> " Of biped jays like this, there are
> 　　Thousands from here to Zanzibar ;
> 　　We call them ' plagiarist ! '
> But hush ! For setting souls ajar
> 　　Is not my line, I wist."

One, that used to be spoken of as Monarchy. Guillotined in that form, Frenchmen hailed it as a sword-saviour in the new dictator. It seems to me to be the sudden conversion of such opposed principles to Bonapartism on the night of the 18th Brumaire [November 9, 1799],—*De neuch l'embousq,* an ambuscade of night,—that startles Nostradamus. Certainly there was no doubt whatever whence the Napoleon family sprang ; a family with a history more or less traceable for five hundred years can scarcely be described with propriety as one "whose origin is *lost* in the night of time." Yet this is the meaning M. le Pelletier would have us put upon it.

Next, like the jay in the fable, tricked out in peacock feathers and spoils of the Capetian kings, Napoleon makes their palace of the Tuileries [*Treilhos*] his head-quarters. The city is given over to him by *cinq langos,* five prodigious talkers of the long robe. Far from naked as to words or clothing were they, but as to principles very nude and bare, quite unable to cope face to face with the audacity of this unscrupulous cut-throat, this gunner of Ajaccio.

The men of no principles and no practice were simply ciphers before this man of practice, *par langue et faict ;* this ethnic Hercules of tongue and sword ; this servant, as Daniel has it, of "the God of Forces ; " this fly-pest Beelzebub, man of *Vespres et mouches,* grown to a dynamic King. Where men have lost their virtue, the poor sceptics are given over to believe a lie of their own making ; tongues have they to lie withal, but never a hand amongst them to furnish help at need.

Century VII.—Quatrain 13. [I. 213.]

De la cité marine et tributaire
La teste rase * prendra la satrapie :
Chasser sordide † qui puis ‡ sera contraire ;
Par § quatorze ans tiendra la tyrannie.

Translation.

The short-haired man shall assume authority
In maritime Toulon tributary to the enemy :
He will afterwards dismiss as sordid all who oppose him ;
And for fourteen years direct a tyranny.

The English had seized Toulon in the name of Louis XVII., and held it a few months till Bonaparte retook it. He overturned the Directory (*sordide*), and suppressed its partisans with the Republic, and enjoyed the tyranny for fourteen years, from 18th Brumaire, November 9, 1799, to April 13, 1814. We have already seen (p. 272) that the *cité marine* is Toulon. Garencières fancies this to have been fulfilled when Richelieu made himself governor of *Havre de Grace*, where he kept his treasure and tyrannized for about fourteen years.

* This curious phrase manifestly points to Napoleon wearing short hair, in military fashion, as distinguished from the flowing locks of the line of Capet,—shaven as contrasted with bewigged. This is one of the many coincidences that connect the Commonwealth of England with the French repetition of it at the Revolution. Croppies, or Roundheads, distinguished the sanctimonious insurgents of the Commonwealth from the cavaliers with their flowing locks. The Tory cavaliers wore wigs ; the Whigs undermined the bewigged.

† *Sordide* should be written *sordid'*, and *teste*, *test'*, if we wish the line to scan.

‡ *Puis*, for *depuis*.

§ Latin, *per*, pendant.

Century VIII.—Quatrain 57. [I. 214.]

De soldat simple parviendra en empire,
De robbe courte parviendra à la longue :
Vaillant aux armes, en Eglise, où plus pire,
Vexer * les prestres comme l'eau fait l'esponge.

Translation.

From a simple soldier he will rise to the empire,
From the short robe he will attain the long:
Able in arms, in Church government he shows less skill ;
He raises or depresses the priests as water a sponge.

This is a very remarkable quatrain, that Bouys and Le Pelletier, and I suppose all French commentators, pronounce to belong to Napoleon ; and it certainly fits him very well. But, with almost as little injury to historical fact, it may be applied to Cromwell, and accordingly Garencières does so apply it. He writes :

" I never knew nor heard of anybody to whom this stanza might be applied, than to the late usurper Cromwell ; for from a simple soldier he became to be Lord Protector, and from a student in the University he became a graduate in Oxford, he was valiant in arms, and the worst Churchman that could be found ; as for vexing the priests, I mean the prelatical clergy, I believe none went beyond him."

The circumstances of the French Revolution and the English Commonwealth times are so much alike in many respects that it is not surprising that such a description as this of a soldier who seized power and afflicted the clergy should fit both the usurpers, Napoleon and Cromwell, almost equally well.

Napoleon was a plain lieutenant in 1785, Consul for life in 1799, and Emperor from 1804 to 1814. He

* Latin, *vexare*, raise, inflate, according to Le Pelletier ; but Facciolati gives no such meaning. "Vexed Bermoothes" gives it.

changed the short robe for the long, is understood by
M. le Pelletier as being the consular robe for the
imperial.   There is no need to interpret thus.   The
military dress or that of the civilian is the short robe.
Nostradamus takes but little heed, so far as we have
yet seen, of the consular dignity.   In the last quatrain
he designates the duration of the tyranny, not as one
of ten years, which would represent the Empire, but
of fourteen, which regards the consulship and empire
as one period.   If we take Cromwell's protectorate,
however, from the death of Charles I. to the death of
Cromwell, the term will correspond with Napoleon's
imperial career.   But the interregum in England was
a period of twelve years, and that in France under
Napoleon was of fourteen (*quatorze ans*) ; hence this
quatrain must not be applied to Cromwell, though it
in other respects is as true of him as of Napoleon.

Valiant in arms, but in ecclesiastical matters less
successful, still he thoroughly vexes them, penetrating
into every place and corner, as water does into a
sponge.   We cannot accept M. le Pelletier's rendering
of *vexare* as meaning to raise and cast down.   It was
used in the sense of to trouble, *cruciare ;* to anger,
commovere ; or to harass with care, *curarum æstu
fluctuare ;* but never to alternately swell and depress,
as in filling or squeezing out a sponge.

Century II.—Quatrain 69.   [I. 215.]

Le Roy Gaulois par la Celtique dextre,*
Voyant discorde † de la grand Monarchie,

* *Dextera*, Latin, right hand, or sword hand.
† *Discorde* should be *discord'*, or the line will not scan.

Sur les trois parts fera florir son sceptre,
Contre la Cappe * de la grand Hierarchie.

Translation.

The Gallic King by means of the Celtic sword-hand,
Seeing the discord of the great monarchy,
Shall make his sceptre flourish by restoring the three parts,
As against the Capets, and the Popedom.

Garencières understands as "the Cap of the great Hierarchy," Spain in the Netherlands, which was the great upholder of the Popedom. His application of this to history is of no value. But if we understand Cap as Capet, and the ancient connection of the French crown with the Papal Hierarchy, I think we elicit a better sense than that of M. le Pelletier, which makes the Capet and the Hierachy one. The three parts restored, M. le Pelietier makes to consist of clergy, nobility, and tiers état. I feel that the three parts under Napoleon were Emperor, Senate, and Chamber of Deputies, which would be head (or Caput instead of Capet), Senate representing the higher classes, and the Chambers the people. That would constitute *les trois parts* of the quatrain.

These may be minor matters, but those who think them unimportant are not wise. It is an excellent rule in literature to let nothing remain wrong that can be set right by a little scholarship and industry. In the world it is very different ; there you should never put anything right, for everything wrong has a host of latent friends, that will fight very savagely in its defence.

* *Cappe*, for Capet, says M. le Pelletier. The texte-type gives a variation here as *la Chappe*. This yields no help at all, except as showing by the variant that there is something wants altering. The line will not scan as it is. I think it should be altered to *le Cap*. If it stands for Capet it is masculine, and when it occurred before, in Quatrain 20 of Century IX., it was given as *Esleu Cap*.

Century I.—Quatrain 88.   [I. 216.]

Le divin mal surprendra le grand Prince,
Un peu devant aura femme espousée : *
Son appuy et credit à un coup ‡ viendra mince,‡
Conseil mourra pour la teste rasée.

Translation.

He shall have married a woman just before
The divine wrath falleth on the great Prince ;
And his support shall dwindle in a sudden atrophy ;
Counsel shall perish from this shaven head.

This divine evil that surprises the Prince a little
after his marriage with Marie-Louise of Austria and
his mean-spirited repudiation of Josephine, is most
excellently rendered by Garencières as "*the falling
sickness,* called by the Greeks *Epilepsia,* and by the
Latins *Morbus sacer.*" Garencières was a Fellow of
the London College of Physicians, and a man versed
in the medical nomenclature of his day ; so that *le
mal divin* should here be rendered epilepsy. It has
never yet been so rendered, except by Garencières, and
he has no application to make of it whatever, though,
as a mere matter of translation, he says, "the construction of the whole is easie." It strikes me that
this forecast, thus interpreted, will throw light from
Nostradamus on what history has heretofore over-

---

* These two lines furnish an hyperbaton and will be best
transposed, that the great Prince will have married a woman
before the divine wrath falls upon him.

† This is equivalent to *tout d'un coup*, suddenly.

‡ This line is too long by a foot ; *appuy et credit* mean the
the same thing, and one should be omitted.   The line should be
corrected thus :

Et son appuy à un coup viendra mince.

looked, and will necessitate the re-writing of Napoleon's life from the date of his wicked prostitution of the marriage rite. Napoleon, Cromwell, Mahomet, Cæsar, were all epileptic, and probably Alexander. But this particular scoundrel first committed, from the purely sordid motive of self-aggrandisement, a moral crime, and that brought on the convulsion of the brain, that practically discharged for ever the mighty Leyden jar or electric battery, with which this potent brain-fiend had dealt out merciless torpedo-shocks to Europe, and death as from the hot wind Samyel. Inflated vanity, the epileptic stroke, the reaction of external forces on the weakened centre, made the cerebral pap, still of gigantic power, entertain new phantasms huger than ever, with a terribly diminished power of reason, to bring them to birth by the practical handling of circumjacent facts and time-tendencies. Now, said the fool of this western parable, now am I master of events, and may swim against the sea,—not with it, as I and common mortals heretofore have done, but against it, and to win. Well, he did carry the big dream into Russia, and as far as the nightmare of Borodino. He also still found a mighty utterance of lurid glory, with which to pin that evil minute in letters of fire and phosphorus upon the curtain of eternity, " Behold the sun of Austerlitz ! " The looming *mot d'ordre*, the old work, the old guards, and the old drillings, guided once again to a Pyrrhic victory; two such will damn a kingdom. Reader, read Ségur [Comte de Ségur, "Napoléon et la Grande Armée," liv. vii. ch. viii. p. 179], and there perceive the giant unbrained and drivelling about his bastard boy called "King of Rome," and what else belongs to *mon étoile effacée.* "All the supports dwindle," says Nostradamus, "and counsel will perish from the shaven head." Garencières is right, and the diagnosis true. It is the falling sickness. It is not Jove fulminant that strikes the reeling Pagod from without, as with Cæsar 'twas, but an epiletic withdrawal of electricity from within, backwards. Emperor and empire will soon roll together in the dust ; man's posthumous analysis, and that of all the evil works wrought by him, though the good live after.

Century I.—Quatrain 4. [I. 127.]

Par * l'univers sera faict un monarque
Qu'en † paix et vie ne sera longuement :
Lors se perdra la piscature barque,
Sera regie en plus grand detriment.

Translation.

Throughout the universe a monarch shall arise,
Who will not be long in peace nor life ;
The bark of St. Peter will then lose itself,
Being directed to its greatest detriment.

The Emperor Napoleon, reviving pretensions to the old Roman empire or universe, will neither enjoy peace nor life for very long. In his time the Holy Seat, *la piscature barque*, shall so guide itself to greatest detriment as to be cast away and lost (under Pius VII.).

Pope Pius was made a prisoner by General Miollis, July 6, 1809, and carried to Savone, then to Fontainebleau, and kept under strict guard by Napoleon till March 10, 1814, when he was set at liberty. Garen-

* Par is Latin, *per*, throughout. † Equals *qui en.*

cières interprets this as being fulfilled in the time of Henri II. of France, who was slain by Montgomery in the tilt yard. Through all his reign he was at war with the Emperor Charles V. This Emperor sacked Rome, and Pope Clement VII. was made a prisoner (*vide* Garencières, " Tiber," p. 77).

Century V.—*Quatrain* 60. [I. 218.]

Par teste rase viendra bien mal eslire,
Plus que sa charge ne porte * passera ;
Si grande † fureur ℮t rage fera dire
Qu'à feu et sang tout sexe tranchera.‡

Translation.

In the shorn head France will have made so bad a choice ;
It will be heavier than its force will enable it to endure.
So great fury and rage will make men say
That he will exterminate the male sex by fire and sword.

The period of the fulfilment of this event M. le Pelletier gives as extending from 1813 to 1815. It asks no further interpretation than that afforded by the translation.

Century IV.—*Quatrain* 82. [I. 219.]

Amas s'approche venant d'Esclavonie,§
L'Olestant ‖ vieux cité ruynera,

* The texte-type furnishes *porter*, with *porte* as a variant. M. le Pelletier embodies this in his text. I should replace the word that he excludes. Further, I should regard *passera* as being a form of the Latin *patior*, and the French *pâtir*, and therefore read *pâtira*. *Porter pâtira* will then mean suffer it to bear. *Charge*, for the scansion, should be *charg'*.
† *Grande* should be *grand'*, for the scansion.
‡ *Tranchera* should read *il tranchera*.
§ *Esclavonie* is put for modern Hungary.
‖ *Olestant* is another variation of the nom fatidique de Napoleon, p.171, from ὔλλυμι, to destroy, ὀλλέσθαι.

Fort desolée verra sa Romanie,
Puis grande flamme esteindre ne scaura.

Translation.

A troop approaches, coming through Sclavonia ;
The destroyer will ruin an old city ;
He will see all Romania desolated,
Nor will he know how to extinguish such a blaze.

A mass of troops is wending from Sclavonia. The destroyer, Napoleon, will ruin old Moscow altogether, and see Roumania desolated ; such a conflagration he will not know how to extinguish. It was Rostopchin, in 1812, fired Moscow to prevent the French from wintering there, and it settled the fate of the campaign.

Century II.—Quatrain. 44. [I. 220.]

L'aigle poussée * entour † de pavillions,
Par autres oyseaux d'entour ‡ sera chassée,
Quand bruit des cymbres § tube, ‖ et sonnaillons ¶
Rendront le sens de la dame insensée.

Translation.

The eagle, drifting in her cloud of flags,
By other circling birds is beaten home.
Till war's hoarse trumpet and the clarion shrill,
Recall her senses to th' insenate dame.

This is one of the few quatrains that lend themselves freely to a poetic rendering. The Napoleonic

---

* *Poussée*, for *repoussé.*
† *Entour* should be *entour'*, for *entouré.*
‡ *Entour* here is for *entourage.*
§ *Cymbres*, κύμβη, cymbals.
‖ *Tube*, *tuba*, trumpet.
¶ *Sonnaillons*, literally, bell-ringing, but perhaps clarion may serve.

eagle driven back to France with all its retreating flags about it, or chased by a surrounding of other eagles, Austrian, Russian, Prussian. The din of cymbals, trumpets, and clarions restore France to reason, the insensate dame.

Garencières's annotation here is extremely funny, and should not be unrecorded. He says : "It is an eagle driven from the tents by other birds, when a mad lady shall recover her senses by the noise of cymbals, trumpets, and bells."

Century X.—Quatrain 86. [I. 221.]

Comme un gryphon viendra le Roy d'Europe,
Accompagné de ceux d'Aquilon,*
De rouges et blancs conduira grand † troupe,
Et iront contre ‡ le Roy de Babylon.

Translation.

Like a griffin the King of Europe will come,
Accompanied with those of the north.
Of red and white there will be a great number,
And they will go against the King of Babylon.

The King of Europe is Louis XVIII. ; shall come like a griffin (Griffon, γρύψ γρύπος, a fabulous animal, with hooked beak: *v.* Liddell and Scott; *v. Griffe,* Noel; *Griffeau,* Roquefort, Littré, Gwillim, Brunet, etc.), accompanied with those of the north. He will conduct grand battalions of red and white uniforms, *i.e.* English and Austrian, and they will march as one against the King of Babylon, which is Paris. Louis, as the de-

---

* This line cannot be scanned ; we must read *de l'Aquillon.*
† This requires, for both grammar and scansion, *grande.*
‡ The *E* in *contre* must suffer elision, thus : *contr'.* It is right in Garencières's.

X

scendant of Hugh Capet, may be styled the first of European Kings. The King of Paris is Napoleon, who ruled the Revolution there, and brought order to confusion or Babel. But we can bring it home to Paris even more intimately than this, for the old name of Paris was Lutetia, or mud-place, where the toads, *crapauds*, or Frankish frogs dwelt, and out of whose mud, or *bourbe*, came the Bourbon family. So that Paris, their chief city, *en calembour*, yields *Bourbe ville, Babyl, Babel.*

Garencières thinks to see Gustavus Adolphus here as the most eminent King of Europe in his day, and he came from Aquilon, the north, and warred upon the Emperor, who was King of Babylon, from propping the popedom, or from the Babel of confusion. He had regiments red, white, blue, and yellow and green, in the hope of creating emulation amongst them. If he had only had regiments red and white we might have hesitated, and gone further to examine where the clue would lead to. But what begins by proving too much is like other overshooting, and misses the mark entirely.

Century VI.—Quatrain 89. [I. 222.]

Entre deux cymbes * pieds et mains attachés
De miel face oingt et de laict substanté,

---

* κύμβη, is a cup, usually, in Greek. M. le Pelletier gives κύμβος as a cavity or precipice. I find no such meaning as precipice. There is a great difficulty to settle the meaning here. Κύμβη means a cup, a boat, a wallet, and also, is like κύβη, the head. We should perhaps simplify the issue by confining ourselves strictly to the Latin word, *Cymba*, which is boat or skiff. Always a light boat, as in the Georgics, i. 136, where the little boats were made of *alnos cavatas*, the riverside alders hollowed out.

Guespes et mouches, fitine,* amour, fachés,
Poccilateur † faucer ‡ Cyphe § tenté.

We have now rather laboriously cleared the way for a

Translation.

Between two prisons, bound hand and foot,
With his face anointed with honey, and fed with milk,
Exposed to wasps and flies, and tormented with the love of his
child,
His cupbearer will false the cup that aims at suicide.

It is rather a craft for a small lake than for the sea ; as Ovid
charmingly puts it :

"Non ideo debet pelago se credere, signa
Audet in exiguo ludere cymba lacu."

But, then, what sense would it yield, "a man being between two
boats, tied hand and foot?" Between two abysses, M. le Pelletier
interprets ; but, then, we do not find that, either in Greek or Latin,
the word yields that meaning. He interprets it of Elba and
St. Helena. But was an island ever called an abyss ; I think as
seldom as ever κύμβη meant one. Hesychius gives κοῖλος μυχός, a
hollow recess, the penetralia of the women's apartments, and he
adds also βυθός, the depth of the sea, to explain κύμβος. In
Martinius's "Lexicon Etymol.," there is a very curious quotation
from Isidore, Bk. 19., which makes the *cymba* to be the space
occupied by a ship in the displacement of the water beneath it.
I think out of all this we may extract a meaning for the *deux
cymbes.* As two places, or recessed prisons, hollowed out of the
sea, he shall be put, bound hand and foot. The line, to scan
correctly, should have the word *et* left out.

* *Fitine,* φυτόν, plant, scion, child.

† *Pocillator* is cupbearer. ‡ *Faucer* is fauser, to trick.

§ *Scyphus,* cup. There is a singular appropriateness in this
word, whether intended or not by Nostradamus, for Athenaeus
describes the Bœotians as first using huge silver drinking-cups,
or scyphi, which were denominated Herculean, because Hercules,
who was very fond of feasting, used such, and first invented the
cry of "no heel taps!" *ut libantes nihil in calice vini relinquerent.*
The reader will bear in mind the *Hercules de Gaule* of a former
quatrain.

M. le Pelletier renders this: Napoleon, after being consecrated by Pius VII., and anointed from the sacred ampulla with honey and milk, underwent a double imprisonment in Elba and St. Helena. The imperial bees—for so he translates the wasps and flies—are desolated as to their love for the child, and his surgeon, Yvan (*pocillator*), has falsified the death by poison, on the night of April 12 to 13, 1814. Now, as it was not his own soldiers that tormented him, I think we ought to read it *faché:* he was desolated by wasps, flies, his child, and love. His soldiers are called *abeilles* before, never *guêpes;* these are the enemy tormenting, who will not let him abdicate in favour of his son (φυτόν). We shall do better here to follow Garencières's example, drawn from the life of Artaxerxes, King of Persia. The Persians used to punish poisoners by laying them between two troughs, here called boats, with their face uncovered, bedaubed with honey to attract the wasps and flies, and fed them with milk to prolong the torment, which if they refused, they ran needles into their eyes most persuasively, and then left them till vermin ate them up. So that it means: he was tormented between two prisons bodily and mentally, with the ruin of his family, insomuch that he would have been glad to have escaped it all by poison. Whenever Napoleon was thoroughly frustrated in his plans, he evidently tried to fall back upon, what he had never deserved, human sympathy; which in prosperity he had never thought of nor desired. He first showed this softening, rather of the brain than heart, at Borodino, as we have said before.

We will now take the substance of what happened at the abdication, as given by M. le Pelletier from the *Manuscrit de* 1814, by the Baron Faim. He abdicated [here may we say, " Woe unto him that buildeth a town with blood " (Habakkuk, ii. 12)] at Fontainebleau April 4, 1814, reserving the Regency for the Empress Marie Louise, and his son. He was thrown into despair when he found the allies to be masters of Paris, and to reject any such conditions. Baron Faim was his private secretary, and describes what occurred on the night of the 12th and 13th of April, before the day of his unconditional abdication. Fontainebleau really became a prison under the surveillance of strangers. There were no terms left to him to save even his life. Still he let the day close without yielding.

For some days previously he had seemed altogether preoccupied in revolving some design. His conversation turned always upon the voluntary death that the great men of antiquity courted when in situations such as his. The Empress had reached Orleans on her way to rejoin him, but he had given orders not to allow her to do so. He dreaded such an interview as likely to unman him for the resolution he meditated.

It was a terrible night of suspense ; the long corridors of the palace resounded with the footsteps of servants going and coming, the candles were burning in the private apartments. Doctor Yvan is suddenly called upon to attend, the Duc de Vincence is sent for, and they hurry to fetch the Duc de Bassano from the Chancellory ; they are all taken to the bedroom as they drop in one after another. Sobs and sighs escape, but not a word is yet dropped to satisfy curiosity. On a sudden the doctor leaves the apartment, descends to the courtyard, finds a horse ready saddled, and quits the place at a hand-gallop.

All that transpires on the occasion is that, at the retreat from Moscow, Napoleon had provided himself with a means of escape, should he fall alive into the hands of the enemy. Yvan, his surgeon, had given him a packet of opium, which he had ever since carried round his neck. The valet heard him rise in the night, and saw through the half-opened door that he mixed something in a glass of water, drank it off, and returned to bed. He quickly felt that his end was approaching, and had his most trusted followers called to his bedside, Yvan amongst the rest; but, when he heard Napoleon complain that the action of the poison was too slow, he precipitately quitted Fontainebleau, as we have seen.

A very heavy slumber supervened, accompanied with profuse perspiration, and when he awoke the symptoms had disappeared, the dose having proved of insufficient quantity, or time had deprived it of its efficacy. Napoleon, astonished at the failure, simply exclaimed, " *Dieu ne le veut pas !* " and professing, perhaps for the first time in his life, to yield to Providence, resigned himself quietly to his new destiny. On board the *Northumberland* he strongly reprobated suicide. It would have been instructive to have heard the arguments employed by this intellectual giant, merely as a mental acrobat exhibiting, and as showing how far the intellect may be effective in illustrating the path of duty. But on nothing could Napoleon's opinion be worth so little as on a question of morals, where the soul's instinct is chief guide. The rats ate his heart, it is said, in an interim of the medical dissection. I doubt it ; he had eaten it himself long before he left Brienne.

On the morning of the 13th, Napoleon rose and dressed as usual. His objections had vanished, and his next act was to ratify the treaty—a solemn act, which he took the earliest opportunity that offered to betray and break.

Century X.—Quatrain 24. [I. 227.]

> Le captif prince aux Itales * vaincu
> Passera Gennes par mer † jusqu'a Marseille,
> Par grand effort des forains ‡ survaincu,
> Sauf § coup de feu,‖ barril liqueur d'abeille.

Translation.

The captive prince, conquered, is sent to Elba ;
He will sail across the Gulf of Genoa to Marseilles.
By a great effort of the foreign forces he is overcome,
Though he escapes the fire, his bees yield blood by the barrel.

He ran the blockade, March 1, 1815, and landed at Cannes, close to Marseilles, crossing the Gulf of Genoa, till defeated at Waterloo on the 18th of June, "seeking death," says Le Pelletier, "without being able to find it," (*où il sera sauf de coups de feu*). When the smoke rises from the bottomless pit, "shall men seek death and not find it ; and shall desire to die, and death shall flee from them " (Rev. ix. 6). Napoleon

---

* Itales, *Ætalia*, Elba.　　† *Par mer*, Gulf of Genoa.
‡ *Forains*, Latin, *foris*, strangers.
§ *Sauf*, Latin, *sabous*, English, safe.　　‖ *Sauf de* coup de feu.

comes out of the island Æthalia, or metallic smoke, and escapes the murderous artillery that kills his men, though it were far fitter he should die. His beehive is not burned with fire, but other liquor than honey flows freely,—the life-blood of his bees.

Century II.—Quatrain 70.

Le dard du ciel * fera † son estandue,‡
Morts en parlant, grande execution.
La pierre en l'arbre, la fiere gent § rendue,
Bruit humain monstre ‖ purge expiation.

The third and fourth lines will neither of them scan. *La fiere gent* should be written *la fier' gent, fier* being read as one syllable.

Bruit, in the fourth line, is to be read as one syllable. Garencières has *Brait*, which, though it have no meaning, shows perhaps that it was one syllable.

Translation.

The thunderbolt shall strike his standard ;
He shall die speaking proud words, great is the execution.
The stone is in the tree, the proud nation yields,
The monster purges his human fame by expiation.

The thunderbolt from heaven shall strike down his standard, and he fails or dies ¶ uttering haughty words. There is terrible execution done. The stone ** is in the tree. The proud nation yields. The hero purges by expiation his human renown.

* *Le dard du ceil* is the thunderbolt.
† Latin, *ferire*, to strike.   ‡ *Estandue* is standard.
§ Latin, *gens*, nation.   ‖ Latin, *monstrum*, prodigy.
¶ *Morts* should be read *Meurt*, perhaps, as referring to Napoleon, who showed great delight, it is said, when he found that Wellington intended to fight him. It cannot refer, as Le Pelletier would have it to do, to the celebrated *mot* of Cambronne or General Michel, as it has been proved that it was never uttered at all, but manufactured by a wit *après coup*.
** The stone is in the tree. Le Pelletier would here understand

In spite of all these doubts interposed, this yields us a quatrain of a sufficiently clear sense, in conveying two leading ideas ; a providential and mighty overthrow of a giant leader and braggart of swelling words ; and of a proud nation split in battle, as a tree is by thunder-stroke. The forcible picture is not unworthy of Waterloo or the Battle of Mont Saint-Jean, as the French call it ; even though it may not be impossible to find some other battle since the death of Nostradamus that it might represent almost as well, if not quite so fully, as the tremendous day of Waterloo, June 18, 1815. Englishmen seem half afraid now to mention the day with pride, for fear of hurting French susceptibilities. To mention it insultingly, or in a hostile spirit, is unpardonable ; but to speak of it modestly and thankfully, and of Wellington as a great soldier and benefactor to us, is only manly and proper. The man who has not the courage to do this firmly and inoffensively in the company of Frenchmen is only one of the many cowards amongst us, who lead the French to think that, however great things our fathers may have done in the past, the spirit has fled from us that would repeat them in the future.

Century IX.—Quatrain 86. [I. 230.]

Du Bourg la reyne parviêdront droit à Chartres,
Et feront près du pont Anthoni pause :

silex, the flint axe of primitive ages. This seems to me to be very far fetched, and I would rather read, with Garencières, the stone into thunderstone or aerolite, which seems to be far less forced.

Sept pour la paix cauteleux comme martres,
Feront entrée * d'armée à Paris clause.†

Translation.

From Bourg la Reine they shall march on Chartres,
They shall camp close to Pont Anthony :
Seven chiefs for peace, cautious as martens,
Shall enter Paris cut off from its army.

The generals of the seven nations coalesced shall, under pretext of peace, but really out of jealousy of France, says M. le Pelletier, and in virtue of the capitulation of the 3rd of July, enter Paris ; now cut off from her army (*clos d'armée*), which retreats upon Chartres, passing by Bourg la Reine and Pont d'Anthony, where it camps. The quatrain does not at all obviously read so, but we must suppose that it is the French army which goes to Chartres. We are not, however, bound to believe that the marten-like and cunning seven only pretended to establish peace out of jealousy to France. All Europe and France herself sighed for peace ; and if, when victorious, the enemies were inclined to take back what France had robbed them of severally, that would not be very wonderful. The seven nations signatory to the treaties of 1815 were England, Austria, Prussia, Russia, Spain, Sweden, and Portugal.

This is a very remarkable forecast, and shows that although Nostradamus is a national prophet of France, and nearly all his one thousand quatrains turn upon her and her interests, he seldom exhibits a particle of

* Hyperbaton : the construction is *feront entrée a Paris clos d'armée.*

† Latin, *clausus,* shut, cut off from the French army.

partisanship, and you would not know he was a Frenchman from any word that he lets fall. He strictly limits himself to the utterance of his vision in the tersest phrase, and the most forcible words that he can bring to bear for that purpose. I think there is no other instance known of such inviolable temperance. A man sits down in his study and prophecies ; commits his visions to paper in prose ; turns them deliberately afterwards, and in cold blood, into the pithiest poetry he knows how ; shakes up in a hat, as we have previously remarked, all the quatrains together, and, when he has effectually destroyed all sequence and order, counts them out into even hundreds ; then, without a word of note or comment, he sends them forth in type into the world to sink or swim ; be ridiculed or admired, be understood or mistaken, perish or endure ; until such period as their fulfilment in the centuries of time is realized, and the sleeping world awakens to the miracle, that has slept also, beside the sleeping world, till light arose to make both clear at once.

Century II.—Quatrain 67. [I. 232.]

Le blonde au nez forche * viendra commettre †
Par ‡ la duelle § et chassera dehors :
Les exilés dedans fera remettre,
Aux lieux marins commettant ‖ les plus fors.¶

* *Forche*, fourchu, or forked.   Latin, *furca*, hooked.
† *Commettre*, ellipsis for *se commettre*, to come to blows with any one.
‡ Latin, *per*, through, or by means of.
§ Latin, *duo*, a second repetition.
‖ Consigning.   ¶ *Plus fors*, read *plus forts*.

The light-haired one will come to blows with the hooked nose
For the second time, and chase him out :
The exiled will replace him within,
Consigning the strongest of the party to a fortress in the sea.

Louis XVIII. is designated *Le blond au nez fourchu*
according to Le Pelletier. *Le blond* is, no doubt, the
sign of the Capets, as shown by several other stanzas
in Nostradamus, but not the aquiline nose, I think ;
that, I believe, is intended for Napoleon. So that
Louis XVIII. comes to blows with the hooked nose,
or Napoleon, for the second time and drives him out ;
he who was exiled before now replacing him within.
The strongest, that is Napoleon and his officers, are
committed *aux lieux marins ;* which either means to
the English, who go down to the sea in ships, or else
to St. Helena, a prison in the sea.

Century X.—Quatrain 90. [I. 233.]

Cent fois mourra le tyran inhumain ;
Mis à son lieu sçavant et debonnaire :
Tout le senat sera dessous sa main,
Fasché sera par malin * temeraire.

Translation.

The inhuman tyrant shall die a hundred times ;
A learned and debonnaire King shall take his place :
All the senate shall be under his control,
And he shall be grieved by a bold criminal.

Napoleon is the inhuman tyrant to die a hundred
deaths : one his suicidal attempt ; another Elba, with

* *Malignus,* Latin, a criminal.

its cinerary and fuliginous ashes; another Waterloo; and lastly St. Helena, with its ten times ten remorseful hours, regrets, and studious falsifications of the history of his life. *Debonnaire* is, with Nostradamus, an epithet of the Capet family, and stands doubtless for Louis XVIII. put into his place. The King finds the Senate quite submissive to his will, but he is cut to the heart by the daring attempt of the criminal Louvel upon the Duc de Berri, February 13, 1820.

This is the excellent interpretation of M. le Pelletier. Bouys (p. 80), writing in 1806 under the full influence of the demon of Napoleon, gives it a very different reading. The inhuman tyrant with him can be nobody but Robespierre, who, with a pistol shot, endeavoured to put an end to himself ineffectually, but blew away half his face, suffering thirty hours of fearful torment, and finally was dragged to the place of execution amidst the maledictions of the populace. The *sçavant et debonnaire* to Bouys is, of course, Napoleon. The *malin téméraire* is a forgotten Georges, whose conspiracy gave a little momentary anxiety to Napoleon. Here terminate the oracles assigned to Napoleon by M. le Pelletier. But Bouys adduces several others, which sufficiently relate to the Emperor to be enumerated here. It is painful to see how men manipulate these things to suit their theories. We will give now a quatrain that Bouys cites, as he thinks it favourable to Napoleon; but he carefully omits the one next to it in the same Century, purely, as it seems, because it is unfavourable to Napoleon.

Century II.—Quatrain 29.   [Bouys, 82.]

L'oriental sortira de son siège,
Passer les monts Apennons voir la Gaule :
Transpercera le ciel, les eaux et neige,
Et un chacun frappera de sa gaule.

Translation.

The oriental will quit his post,
To cross the Apennines and see after Gaul :
He will transfix the heaven, the mountain ice and snows,
Striking each of them with his magic wand.

The Oriental, *i.e.* Napoleon in Egypt, will leave his army behind there, after almost turning Mahometan ; return and cross the Apennines and Alps to look after the Directory and their doings in France. He will soon even subdue the elements and Nature by his marvellous roads over the mountains of ice and snow, and will strike each as with the rod of Moses, or the wand of a magician ; for the archaic and unusual word *gaule* may mean that, as well as a riding switch. Bouys misses the plainer meaning of the first line, but is determined it shall represent Napoleon, so he takes *Oriental* to be Corsica, as being east of Toulon. The passage of Mont St. Bernard with cavalry and artillery he gives rightly enough ; the Alps have to be introduced for the Apennines. The quatrain following next to this he passes *sub silentio*, for the reason above assigned, though it is pregnant with meaning ; and how this should have been overlooked by M. le Pelletier, I cannot quite understand ; but so it is.

Century II.—Quatrain 30. [II. 45.]

Un qui les dieux d'Annibal infernaux,
Fera * renaistre, effrayeur des humains.
Oncq' plus d'horreur ne plus pire journaux,
Qu'avint† viendra ‡ par Babel aux Romains.

Translation.

One whom the gods of Hannibal from the lower regions
Shall cause to be born again [shall be], a terror to mankind.
Never will more horror, nor more evil days,
Come upon the Romans. The confusion will be like that before
from Babel.

Hannibal and Napoleon are the only great
generals who ever forced their military way over the
Alps successfully ; Hannibal, with his *acetum*, vinegar,
or hatchet, as some have interpreted Livy ; and
Napoleon for cavalry and heavy pieces of artillery.
He seemed to be the marvellous Carthaginian born
again out of the shades of Hades, a scourge and
flail of men : Babel itself not worse in the confusion
that fell upon Rome, and the Church of Rome
through him. We have given this before, at p. 228,
but repeat it here with further enlargement, as it
belongs more to Napoleon than to the Revolution.
Garencières thinks it was fulfilled when Charles V.
sacked Rome. If we consider, as I do, that the two
stanzas are inseparable, they will fit only Napoleon.

We come now to a quatrain that M. le Pelletier
has overlooked, but which Bouys (p. 83) with some
reason attributes to Napoleon.

* *Fera* should be *feront*, I think.
† *Avint* I take to mean *avant.*
‡ *Viendra* for *viendront.*

Century IV.—Quatrain 54.

Du nom qui onque* ne fut un Roi Gaulois
Jamais ne fut un foudre si crantif.
Tremblant l'Italie,† l'Espagne et les Anglois,
De femme estrangiers ‡ grandement attentif.

Translation.

Of a name that never belonged to Gallic king,
Never was there so terrible a thunderbolt.
He made Italy tremble, Spain and the English.
He wooed a foreign lady with assiduity.

Bouys introduces into his interpretation of this a
good deal of foolish adulation of Napoleon; pretending that he was not only *crantif* towards his
enemies, which we must render *a cause of terror*, but
also that he was himself *crantif*, very tender of the
lives of his troops. To prove this monstrous proposi-
tion, he quotes the claptrap uttered by him before
the battle of Austerlitz: " I regret to think how many
of these brave fellows I shall lose. I feel for them as
if veritably they were my own children. Indeed I
sometimes reproach myself for this sentiment of
tenderness; I sometimes fear it may end in rendering
me unfit to carry on war." This was, indeed, an
heroic fear, says Bouys. We are content to let its
heroism wrestle with its hypocrisy; we foresee which
will come by the first fall.

Garencières translates that the warrior, whoever he
may be, will follow after strange women; and that

* *Onque* should be *oncq'*, to scan.

† *Italie* is the reading of the *texte-type*. Bouys reads *Itale*, and
then the line will scan.

‡ *Estrangiers* was probably pronounced as of two syllables
only, but it is difficult to make this line scan.

would fit Napoleon, though not specially. But we think it better to render it with Bouys as indicating the Empress Josephine, who was of Creole blood, and therefore foreign ; or Marie Louise, equally foreign. If the latter, *Estrange* would stand for Austrian (*v.* Century I., Quatrain 83).

Century VIII.—Quatrain 53. [I. 269.]

Dedans Bolongne voudra laver ses fautes,*
Il ne pourra au temple du soleil
Il volera faisant choses si† hautes,
En hierarchie n'en fut oncq un pareil.

Translation.

In Boulogne he would make up for his shortcomings,
But cannot penetrate the temple of the sun.
He hastens away to perform the very highest things.
In the hierarchy he never had an equal.

This is a singularly interesting quatrain. It has received three different interpretations ; all three somewhat curious. Garencières opens the ball. He says there are two towns called *Bolloin*, one in Italy, one in France ; that is, Bologna in Italy, and Boulogne in France. He thinks Boulogne is intended, and that Richelieu, a man of high things, and beyond the hierarchy, vowed, a little before his death, that if he recovered he would make a pilgrimage to Boulogne ; to the Temple of Miracles there, dedicated to the Virgin, here described as the *Sun*, from that passage in the Revelation, "And there appeared a woman clothed with the sun ; " but the cardinal took the road

* *Fautes*, to be taken as shortcomings.
† *Si* — very.

Y

of death, which led, not through Boulogne, to the
shades below, and certainly not to the Temple of the
Sun. This has an interest of its own, but, as an interpretation, is utterly wide of the mark. Richelieu on a
repentant pilgrimage to the Temple of the Sun would
have been admirable as a caricature in Rabelais ; but,
would be no fitter subject for Nostradamus's pen, than
if a lady of title went to Aix-les-Bains to take the
waters there. And observe, he had to invent a
Temple of the Sun to send him to, for never was
there such a temple at Boulogne.

We have also Le Pelletier trying his hand, and he
realizes it in Louis Napoleon, in his escapade of 1840.
When he was made Emperor, his Italian exploit is
represented as a flight to the *Temple of the Sun*. But
how he could suppose *that* inferior mortal, to be
referred to in *n'en fut oncq un pareil*, I cannot divine.

Bouys and others attribute it to Napoleon, and his
intention to descend upon England from Boulogne in
the flotilla. Is there not a column there, ridiculously
built to commemorate the failure ? Is there not also
a Boulogne medal struck (Ford's "Spain," i. 272)
with one of the Napoleonic falsehoods (an endless
series) imprinted on its face, which runs, " Descente
en Angleterre frappé à Londres " ? These are the
ridiculous touches ; but now let us enter on the
serious interpretation and see what that will yield us.

At Boulogne the Emperor will endeavour to blot
England from the map of Europe, and so redeem all
his previous shortcomings in that direction. He
promises himself the satisfaction of dictating his
terms in London, and possibly entertained, in that

strange brain of his, some dream that he would be crowned on that royalty-confirming stone of Scone in Westminster Abbey; where, tradition tells, the Temple of Apollo was shaken down by earthquake, A.D. 154, the Temple of the Sun. But *Il ne pourra au temple du soleil,* says Nostradamus : and history has thought fit in this as on so many other occasions to endorse the forecast of the prophet. Bouys adds, " Napoléon finira par faire la conquête de l'Angleterre ; " but Bouys is not Nostradamus ; and Napoleon, like Richelieu, went to the shades below from St. Helena, and did not go to the Temple of the Sun nor to the Stone of Scone. He went away, however, from Boulogne to very great things, as men count greatness ; and was quite without an equal in the hierarchy of kings.

LOUIS XVIII. AND LOUIS PHILIPPE.

W E now come to the Restoration of Louis XVIII.

Presage 38. [I. 235.]

Roy salué Victeur,* Impereateur,†
La foy faussée. Le Royal fait ‡ congnu : §
Sang ‖ Mathien ¶ Roy fait ** supereateur,††
De gent ‡‡ superbe humble §§ par ‖‖ pleurs venu.¶¶

This is a very crabbed quatrain.

Translation.

The King is saluted victor and dominator,
The oath falsified : The King makes himself known again :
Grandson of Louis XIV. becomes King,
Is called back by the proud people humiliated to tears.

Louis XVIII. is proclaimed King, May 3, 1814,

* Latin, *victor*, conqueror.   † Latin, *Imperator*.
‡ Latin, *factum*, action, act.   § *Congnu* = connu, known.
‖ *Sang*, son or grandson.   ¶ *Mathien*, Æmathien.
** Latinism, *factus*, made, become.
†† Latin, *superator*, rule, dominator.
‡‡ Latin, *gens*, nation.
§§ *Humble* = humiliated, perhaps *humblée*.
‖‖ Latin, *per*, by reason of.
¶¶ The order is, " venu à cause des pleurs de la superbe nation humiliée."

but the people take up Napoleon from Elba, March 1, 1815, thus breaking faith. Louis XVIII. (Le Royal) is again recognized, July 8, 1815 ; the grandson of Louis XIV. (*sang Æmathien*), a name conferred by Nostradamus on Louis XIV., who assumed the emblem of the Sun, Æmathien being son of Aurora, who opens the gates of the morning sun. This grandson becomes now undisputed King, the humiliated French nation recalling him with tears.

Century X.—Quatrain 16.   [1. 236.]

Heureux au regne de France, heureux de vie,
Ignorant sang, mort fureur et rapine,
Par nom flateur * sera mis en envie :
Roy desrobé,† trop de foye en cuisine.

Translation.

Happy in the kingdom of France, happy in life,
Free from blood, violent death and angry rapine,
He will have a flattering name, and be an object of desire :
A King retired, with too much faith in the kitchen.

Here we are to take Louis XVIII. as restored to the throne of France : his life passes happily, without violent experiences of blood, death,¹ rage, or rapine. The flattering name was given to him of *Desiré*, that is prophetically hinted in the words "*il sera mis en envie.*" He will not devote sufficient attention to his public duties, so that he may be described as *desrobé*, retired or retained at home ; and he will be too much addicted to enjoyments of the table,—*trop de foye en cuisine.* The gastronomy was proverbial ; the obesity conse-

---

* The original text is corrupt here, but this yields the best sense.

† *Desrobé*, withdrawn, or shut up.

quent upon it made him grow inert, so that he gradually let the affairs of State drift without giving them due attention.

Century III.—Quatrain 96. [I. 238.]

Chef de Fossan * aura gorge couppée
Par le ducteur † du limier et levrier ;
Le faict patré ‡ par ceux du mont Tarpée,§
Saturne en Leo ‖ 13 de Fevrier.

Translation.

A prince of Fossano shall have his throat cut
By the keeper of his hounds and greyhounds :
The attempt will be made by those of the Tarpeian rock,
Saturn being in Leo on 13th February.

Fossana is put, by synecdoche, for Sardinia. A prince, therefore, of Sardinia shall be stabbed by the Keeper of the Kennel, instigated by Republicans, when Saturn is in opposition to the sign of the Lion, on February 13, 1820. M. le Pelletier, who seems somewhat learned in the houses of the stars, says that Saturn was in opposition to, and not in conjunction with, Leo on this occasion. But Nostradamus leaves it open. The Tarpeian rock is figuratively employed to signify the *Mountain,* or the demagogues and the Republicans generally. The Mons Tarpeius was first named from murder, and was

---

* Fossano is the alternative reading, a town in the Sardinian States.
† Keeper of the hounds and greyhounds.
‡ Latin, *patratus,* done, committed.
§ The Tarpeian rock at Rome.
‖ Latin, *Leo,* the astronomical sign of the Lion.

for ages a scene of murder. Tarpeia, who betrayed
the Capitol to the Sabines, was crushed by their
shields at the gate, and her father, Spurius Tarpeius,
was thrown over the battlements by order of Romulus.
Children ill-formed at birth were flung from its
heights. It was better known as Capitolinus, so called
(*caput Toli*) from the head of Tolus, found there when
digging foundations for the Temple of Jupiter : thus
the place of the skull, a Golgotha from the beginning
of Rome. Later on criminals were sentenced to be
thrown from it. Many of these deadly associations
were, no doubt, present to the mind of Nostradamus,
and made this mountain of death seem to him fit to
foreshadow the death that should emanate from the
French mountain. To dwell upon this is of physiological interest, as showing how very closely the
natures of the poet and the prophet overlap each
other ; so that, as in the rainbow colours, there is no
line to be drawn as to where one begins or another
ends :—they may be seen, but not severed.

The Duc de Berri was the son of Marie Thérèse of
Savoy, married to the Comte d'Artois, she being the
daughter of Victor-Amédée III., King of Sardinia.
This Sardinian was to have ruled France, and, with
but one intervening, to have followed the Corsican in
the occupation of the throne. Louvel, the murderer,
stabbed him coming from the opera, and wore the
King's livery at the moment of the attempt. The
forecast is again wonderful in prefiguring every particular short of the names of the two individuals.
The nationalities are given, the calling of Louvel, and
the day of the month. If all this be Chance, some

hare-brained few would prefer it to what they know of Certainty.

Century V.—Quatrain 4. [I. 240.]

Le gros mastin de cité dechassé,*
Sera fasché de l'estrange † alliance :
Après aux champs avoir le cerf chassé,‡
Le loup et l'ours se donront § defiance.

Translation.

The great mastiff chased from the city
Will be afflicted by the strange alliance :
When the stag is driven to the fields,
The wolf and bear will commence to mistrust each other.

The Duc de Bordeaux is the great mastiff, dethroned August 9, 1830, by Louis Philippe, in the dog-days, when the star *Sirius* is in opposition. *Le Grand Chien* burning in the horizon is a synonym for the *gros mastin ;* the city, of course, is Paris. Charles X., who was fond of the chase, is turned from the great huntsman to the stag. The wolf is Louis Philippe, a name which lends itself to Lou. P. The bear represents, according to M. le Pelletier, *la Montagne,* in the assembly, because bears make their lair in the highest situations. We need not insist on this resemblance or characteristic pointed out by Le Pelletier.

There are six quatrains devoted by Le Pelletier to the Duc de Bordeaux,—the Henri Cinq that was never to be,—that Royal Prince whom all the Princes

* *Dechassé* = chassé, chased away.
† *Estrange* has again the meaning of foreign, or out of the family.
‡ The order is *après avoir chassé le cerf aux champs.*
§ *Donront* = *donneront.*

should see to be heaven-descended. But as we, who are not royal, have seen that nothing came of him ; and that, being now dead, nothing can come of him, we shall pass over the six quatrains in silence. The quatrains of Nostradamus lend themselves most kindly to elucidation once you find the clue, but they most persistently refuse to have a meaning read into them from without.

M. le Pelletier has elaborated the meaning of the six quatrains, about Louis Philippe with so much ingenious learning that we must give the whole of them, and let the reader take them at his own valuation.

Century VI.—Quatrain 84.

Celuy qu'on * Sparte Claude † ne peut regner,
Il fera tant par voye seductive,
Que du court, long le fera araigner, ‡
Que contre Roy fera sa perspective. §

Translation.

He who will cause that the lame cannot reign in Paris,‖
He will effect so much in his seductive way

---

* *Celuy qu'en = Celuy qui fera qu'en.*

† Latin, *Claudus*, lame. This Le Pelletier has before endeavoured, with surprising dexterity, to show to be the Duc de Bordeaux.

‡ This whole line is difficult. *Araigner*, in the Romance language, is said to mean to plead and gain a cause against another. The *court* and *long* we had before, in Century VIII., 57, applied to Napoleon, as rising from a soldier to the long-robed Emperor ; here he had to refer to Talma to teach him how to carry it. Now, again, it means the rise from a mere dignitary to Kingship. § Latin, *qui*.

‖ *Sparte* = Paris. The letters *te* may be considered as one letter, the *e* being mute. It will then convert, according to the rule of the anagram.

That from the short to long he will attain,
Who has brought to bear his deception against the King.

The meaning of this is that Louis Philippe d'Orléans will cause the Duc de Bordeaux to be unable to hold the reins of government in Paris. The anagrammatic substitution of Sparte for Paris is doubly ingenious, inasmuch as Lycurgus at Sparta established a double kingship so-called. Of course the office could not be that of king at all, but there was the name if not the fact, and that suffices for this prince of dexterous analogists, Nostradamus. Louis Philippe will achieve this by the byeways of seduction, and will usurp successfully his nephew's throne (araigner), putting himself in opposition, says Le Pelletier, to his lawful King. *Faire sa perspective* he renders opposition. I do not think this is the meaning of the phrase. There is an extract from Fontenelle (I cannot refer to it in his works at present), in which he speaks of a perspective that will make an emperor or a beggar out of the same figure, according to the point of view from which you regard it. That is an optical illusion. Descartes, in his "L'Homme," mentions the pictures placed at the end of corridors to cheat the eye agreeably, and adds, "L'exemple des tableaux de perspective montre combien il est facile de s'y tromper." And then there were those perspectives that Holbein and his contemporaries used to introduce into their pictures, of a skull, or death's head, so painted that you could not quite tell what it was till you reached the right point of view, when it would suddenly contract and draw its elongated self together to a true skull by a process the reverse of foreshortening. By the words *sa perspective*, I conceive that Nostradamus meant that Louis Philippe brought his deception to bear against the King.

Century V.—Quatrain 69. [1. 250.]

Plus ne sera le Grand en faux sommeil,
L'inquietude viendra prendre repos :
Dresser phalange * d'or, azur, et vermeil,
Subjuger Afrique, la ronger jusques os.

---

* *Phalange*, flag, standard, writes M. le Pelletier. As far as I can discover anything, this statement appears to be entirely erroneous. The word "phalanx," as connected with matters military, always signifies a body of men in military order. It may in the plural even stand indefinitely for armies. In the singular it is very confusing. It may stand for a party of twenty-eight men or eight thousand (Potter's "Antiquities," ii. 56). Danet says six thousand men. Gibbon introduces one of his constantly recurring slovenly phrases about it,—absurd in fact, but philosophic in form. He is comparing the legion with the phalanx (i. 22), and tells us, "It was soon discovered by reflection, as well as by the event," that it could not contend with the legion. It is obvious here, that if it had been discovered by reflection it would never have been tried by the event. This somewhat justifies the sarcasm of Porson, that schoolboys ought to be set to translate Gibbon into English. As a pleasing variety, Smith sets the number when complete at about sixteen thousand men. One feels inclined to say that these classical guides are conveying us to that ditch, which is never far to seek, when the blind are leading the blind. Martinius, in his curious "Lex. Phil.," cites Pliny to show that the Africans first fought the Egyptians *fustibus*, with staves, which they called *phalanges* in the plural, or *phalanx* in the singular, so that it is an African word. פלג, in Hebrew *phalag*, is a staff. Also there is a spider called *phalangion;* and as the pikes of the first five ranks in a *phalanx* were interlaced, they were somewhat like a web of staves. Many may regard all this as extremely useless ; perhaps

Translation.

Le Grand will pretend no longer a alse sleep ;
His disquietude will now lull itself n security,
Arrange his army under gold, blue, and red,
Subjugate Africa, gnawing it to the very bone.

Louis Philippe, now King, and so become *le Grand*,
says M. le Pelletier (though, as applied to the individual, it looks quite like a misnomer), will now unmask
his designs, and take his repose in security. He will
adopt the tricolour of the Revolution and complete the
conquest of Algeria ; Pelissier roasting the refugees
in caves, to the very bone. Everything but the word
Grand justifies the interpretation to a nicety.

Century I.—Quatrain 39. [I. 251.]

De nuict dans lict le supresme * estranglé,
Pour avoir trop sejourné blond esleu,
Par trois † l'Empire subrogé ‡ exanclé §
A mort mettra carte || et pacquet ne leu.¶

Translation.

When France shall be dominated by three parties,
The last of the family shall be strangled at night in bed,
For having lent too much to the fair Capet.
Put to death because a paper and packet were not read.

---

they will concede that it is curious ; if so, I shall consider it to
be useful. I have long found that whatever is very curious is
useful. It sets the mind agreeably in movement, and often
throws a new light on things that previously had no interest
and seemed obscure. At any rate, we have now established
that *phalange* is not to be rendered *standard*, but troops, army.

* Latin, *supremus*, the last.

† The order is, " Quand l'Empire sera exanclé par trois
subrogés."

‡ Latin, *subrogatus*, substituted ; read *subrogés.*

§ *Exancillatus*, subdued to, under the yoke of.

|| Latin, *charta*, paper.   ¶ Romance, *ne leu*, not read.

When France is dominated by three alternately (Orleanists, Republicans, Bonapartists), the Prince de Bourbon, Condé, last of his race, shall be strangled, at night in his bed, for desiring to follow in the suite of the Duc de Bordeaux. A new will, duly sealed up, in favour of the Bourbon, but not read, is the cause of his death. The "not read" means, not read by the Duc de Bordeaux, in whose favour it was drawn. The Baronne de Feuchères, whose interests were allied to those of Louis Philippe, defeated this by the murder. M. le Pelletier acquits Louis Philippe of complicity in the crime, but he remarks that the interest of the baronne was incidentally that of the King. Her crime was incited by the desire to do away with the new will, by which she would be a heavy loser. It is curious that Garencières considers this quatrain to have been fulfilled in Philip II. of Spain, who had his own son, Don Carlos, strangled in bed. The coincidence of the name Philip is singular, but the remaining two lines he does not attempt to interpret.

Century VIII.—Quatrain 42. [I. 253.]

Par avarice, par force et violence
Viendra vexer les siens chef d'Orleans ;
Près Sainct Memire * assaut et resistance,
Mort dans sa tante,† diront qu'il dort leans.‡

Translation.

By cupidity and abuse of power, force, and violence,
The chief of Orleans will come to vex his own ;

---

* *Sainct Memire* is the anagram of S'Meri. To make this pass, M. le Pelletier drops one *m* and one *e*.

† *Tante* is to be read *tente*.

‡ *Leans* is an old word for *là dedans.*

Near St. Memire resistance will be made ;
Dead in his palace he will ever after sleep.

Avarice was always the fault of Louis Philippe.
By extortion and abuse he raised resistance at Saint
Meri ; in and near the church he forced the republicans
to submission, *dort leans* a play upon the name,
never again showed energy, but slept a sleep as of
death in his palace (*dans sa tente*). The insurrection
that was quelled took place on June 5 and 6, 1832.

Century IX.—Quatrain 89. [1. 254.]

Sept ans sera Philipp ; fortune prospere :
Rabaissera des Arabes l'effort ;
Puis son midy perplex * rebors † affaire,
Jeune Ognion ‡ abismera son fort.

Translation.

Seven years will Philip's fortune prosper well ;
He will defeat every effort of the Arabs ;
In his embarrassed middle period all goes against the grain,
Young Ogmion will overwhelm his fort.

Fortune will favour Louis Philippe for the first
seven years. He will repress the Arabs. But in the
middle of his reign the Eastern question will spring

* Latin, *perplexus*, troubled.
† *Rebors = rebours; à rebours* is against the grain.
‡ *Ognion* is *Ogmius*, the Celtic Mercury or Gallic Hercules.
It has figured in 1792, 1848, and again after the German war,
1872. At the two first periods they put the figure of this
Hercules on their five franc pieces, with that idle exergue,
Liberté, Égalité, Fraternité. This vocable, *Ogmion*, is equiva-
lent to *Oignon*, onion, or bulbous root of the lily. If there could
be any doubt at all about this, Nostradamus has taken care to
remove it, calling it *le grand mercure d'Hercule fleur de lys*, in
Century X. 79.

up, and cover him with disgrace (this culminated July 15, 1840). For the next seven years all will go against the grain, and the new Republic (*jeune Ogmion*) will overturn his throne and his Bastille ; the Paris he thought he had so strongly fortified.

Garencières again introduces Philip II. of Spain, and there seems to exist some analogy between these two kings. The Spaniard also was prosperous for some seven years, and in the person of his brother, Don Juan of Austria, beat the Turks in the Battle of Lepanto. Garencières reads *Barbares* for Arabs. Later on he had to put his son to death, and was opposed by young Ogmion ; the King, Henri Quatre, of France and Navarre.

Century V.—Quatrain 92. [1. 255.]

Après le siege tenu dix-sept ans,
Cinq changeront en tel revolu terme :
Puis sera l'un esleu de mesme temps,
Qui les Romains ne sera trop conforme.

Translation.

After the throne has been held for seventeen years,
Five shall change when that term has run out :
Then, at the same time, one shall be elected,
Who will not be very conformable to the wishes of the Romanists.

After the reign of Louis Philippe, during seventeen years, five of his sons lost the throne with himself ; and with much manœuvring have never been able to reapproach it. They were the Comte de Paris, representative of Chartres, Duc de Nemours, Joinville, Montpensier, and Duc d'Aumale. The election that followed was that of Louis Napoleon, whose mixed, or no policy, suited neither the Revolutionary party nor the Roman Catholics. There is nothing here but the seventeen years to connect this with Louis Philippe. For the five who changed with the revolt would be six if Louis Philippe himself were counted, and he certainly ought to be. The concluding two lines are very vague, and may or may not belong to Louis Napoleon. I merely cite it, as one of the ingenuities of M. le Pelletier.

There are three prophecies cited relating to the Duc de Chartres, which seem fairly well interpreted ; and very wonderful they would be if they stood alone or related to any one whose fate was of any importance in the opening scroll of history. All the little interest of Louis Philippe is centred in himself, and therefore I omit the three quatrains relating to his son, not because they are not curious, if rightly interpreted of the son, but that, even supposing them to be so, the Duc de Chartres is a person and a character not deserving of serious mention in history. The gossip of a barber's shop in Nostradamus's own day would be even more interesting to any rational investigator of human affairs.

REPUBLIC, 1848, AND NAPOLEON III.

Century IX.—Quatrain 5. [i. 261.]

Tiers * doigt du pied au premier semblera,
A un nouveau monarque de bas haut : †
Qui ‡ Pyse et Luques tyran occupera,
Du precedent coriger le deffaut.

Translation.

The third § shall be a stepping-stone to the throne,
To a new monarch from low position to the top ;
He will as tyrant have taken a military post in Tuscany, ‖
And will seek to correct the defects of his predecessor.

THE National Assembly of 1848 shall serve as a foot to Louis Napoleon to step from private life into a conspicuous position. He had in his youth been concerned in the Revolution of Tuscany, and purposed correcting the defect of his predecessor.

* *Tiers*, pour *le tiers* État. The third order now claiming to govern itself.

† *De bas haut*, for *de bas en haut* elevated from a low to a higher and conspicuous position.

‡ Latin, *qui*, he, who.

§ The third estate will serve, as a toe of the foot to the first rank, a stepping-stone to place.

‖ Lucca and Pisa stand for all Tuscany, where, in 1831, Louis Napoleon and Charles Bonaparte, his elder brother, had, with one cannon served by himself and a few Italian partisans, possessed himself of *Civita-Castellana*, in the Pontifical States.

Z

This might mean that he purposed to guide France better than Louis Philippe had done, or than in four years the Republic had done, or, which is most probable from his *Idées Napoléoniennes*, to carry to completion the policy of his uncle Napoleon I. I cannot think it refers to Napoleon II., Duc de Reichstadt. The entire application of the quatrain is neither very clear nor very important.

The quatrain on Cavaignac, I think, is hardly made out satisfactorily, so I omit it.

Century VIII.—*Quatrain* 43. [I. 265.]

Par le decide * de deux choses bastards,
Nepveu du sang † occupera le regne : ‡
Dedans Lectoyre § seront les coups de dards,
Nepveu par peur pliera l'enseigne.

Translation.

By the fall or ruin of two bastard things
The nephew by blood will occupy the empire ;
In Lectoyre there will be deaths by arrow,
The nephew will fold up his standard for very fear.

By the overthrow of Louis Philippe and the Republic, two bastard governments, Louis Napoleon will now succeed to the throne, a nephew by blood

* Latin, *decidium*, a word not of classical usage, signifying ruin, or a fall.

† Romance *sang*, family.　　　　‡ Latin, *regnum*, empire.

§ *Lectoyre*, a town in France, in the department of **Gers.** Garencières adopts the variant Lectoure, which he says is a town in Gascony. The word occurs again, Century VII. 12, and there he says it is a city of Guyenne. *Lectora* was the Latin name. It was a place of great strength, and picturesque ; but, unless we can find it to be an anagram, there is nothing to connect the town in any way with the fortunes of Louis Napoleon.

of Napoleon Bonaparte; and, what is not generally known, he was the only one of the Bonaparte family born in the Palace of the Tuileries. In battle afterwards at Lectoyre (*coups de dards* must be taken simply as battle) the nephew will furl his standard through fear.

Writing in 1866, M. le Pelletier particularly remarks that the epoch is left undetermined, and, as to the enigma of *Lectoyre*, nothing can be known till the event has transpired. It may then be interpreted, he thinks, in some of the idioms known to Nostradamus —Greek, Hebrew, Latin, Celtic, Languedoc, etc. He considers the standard to present a further enigma, and asks "What standard?" This difficulty I do not quite recognize. The imperial standard that is adopted by him, whatever it may be. To furl a standard is to close and shut it up, so that no one will rally to it any more. It symbolizes that the cause it represents is brought to the ground finally, and that it is no longer flying.

As to the word *Lectoyre*, we now know that, if it is to be interpreted at all, it will have to be found in connection with Sedan,—the noblest reminiscence connected with which is that it was the birthplace of that great soldier and greater man, Marshal Turenne. He may well be called *La gloire de Sedan*, whilst as appropriately may Napoleon the Little be designated as *Cédant de la gloire*, with that furled ensign, *qu'il par peur pliera.**

---

* The word *pleira*, is of course, only an archaic transposition of *pliera*. The line here can in no way be made to scan, being two syllables or one whole foot short. I would suggest it be read Nepveu (du sang) par peur pleira l'enseigne.

After much difficulty and searching I have at last come upon two old maps, printed at Amsterdam by Blaeuw; the one dated 1620 and the other 1650, styled "Les Soverainetez de Sedan." In both of these the embattled town of Sedan is given, as seated on the right bank of the river Meuse, whilst on the left bank is shown an extensive territory named *Grand Torcy* and *Petit Torcy*. In another map it is given as *Torsy*. These maps give no indication of the points of the compass. But from another map, indicating them, the river-bend on which the town is seated appears to run from east to west; and, if so, Torcy lies south or south-west of Sedan. In a more modern map it appears as *Le Grand Torcy* and is described as lying "sur la route impériale de Mezieres à Sedan." Evidently therefore we are entitled to place *Le Torcy* at Sedan. The French must determine for themselves, by their military bureau, whether the French camp was pitched in the meadows of *Le Torcy ;* but nothing can alter the great fact, as now for the first time made plain, that the *Nepveu du sang* furled his standard for ever at Sedan or *Lectoyre,* as the oracle gives it. Now *Lectoyre* is the precise anagram, letter for letter, of *Le Torcey*, though the commoner spelling is without the second *e*, *Le Torcy*. If we are to reckon this as being a chance coincidence, my only furthur comment will be, that such chance as this is quite as miraculous as any miracle in the world could be.

As regards the words "*nepveu du sang*," there was a caricature very popular in France at the time of the candidature for the French presidency, consisting of two pictures. In one the Prince de Joinville was commending himself to the French people for election, having the young Comte de Paris by the hand, and saying, "I am the uncle of my nephew." On the other side Louis Napoleon presses his suit by pointing to a statuette of Napoleon Bonaparte and uttering the words, "I am the nephew of my uncle;" showing how characteristically *nepveu du sang* designates Prince Louis Napoleon. He may almost be said to have chosen it himself as a cognomen.

Century VIII.—Quatrain 44. [i. 267].

Le procreé naturel d'Ogmion *
De sept à neuf du chemin destorner :
A roy de longue amy et † au my hom ‡
Doit à Navarre fort de Pau prosterner.

I propose here to make the meaning as clear as I can without a translation.

Napoleon III. (*le procrée*), the natural offspring of the French Republic (Ogmion), will turn from the right road for seven or nine years before his fall. Le Pelletier interprets otherwise. He says that the war in Italy began in the seventh year of the Empire, 1869, and from that date throughout the nine following years he changed his policy. I think the line

---

* Ogmion has been explained already to be the symbol of the French Republic.

† The *texte-type* reads *et amy au.*

‡ *My-hom,* Le Pelletier says, is *demy-homme,* a man of low birth, and Roy de *longue = de vielle race.* I prefer to read *de longue vie,* and understand the King of Prussia ; and *my-hom* I take to be the bivalve-man, or Bismarck.

means that from seven to nine years before the end of his reign he changed his policy. That is to say, from seven years previous to the close of his reign, when Charles August Louis, Duc de Morny, died, *i.e.* in 1865 ; and even for two years previously to that, things took a different turn. De Morny no longer exercised active control, and his was the head that had guided all along. When he died, all ran to distruction. The *roi de longue* and his friend *my hom*, Le Pelletier states to be Victor Emmanuel and Garibaldi ; one of long race and one of low birth, the tallow-smelter. I think it is Frederic William, *de longue vie*, and Bismarck, the *bi-valve* man, which it becomes, if we read it as *my-homme*. I have a great idea that *à Navarre* is a misprint for *le nepveu*. Whether *fort de Pau* may mean with his health re-established by staying at Pau or not, I cannot say. But, anyhow, I think that the two last lines are to be read together, and that he is to prostrate himself to the King and his friend. Louis Napoleon's whole reign must be represented as a failure, if you read it with Le Pelletier ; mine makes it a failure during the last seven to nine years. My King and friend bring about the catastrophe far below the date that his will do. My emendation to *le nepveu* certainly clarifies the meaning. The explanation of Pau is not quite so comprehensible as I could wish ; had *Ham* been a variant it would have spoken for itself.

The Quatrain 53 of Century VIII., which I have already explained as the flotilla of Napoleon Bonaparte, M. le Pelletier fixes as the ludicrous Boulogne expedition of Louis Napoleon, and the Italian campaign after he became Emperor ; but I think he entirely fails in reading the symbols.

Century V.—Quatrain 8. [I. 270.]

Sera laissé feu vif, mort caché,
Dedans les globes, horrible espouvantable,
De nuict a classe * cité en poudre lasché,
La cité à feu, l'ennemy favourable.

Translation.

Live fire, hidden death, shall be left
In bombs, a horrible and frightful thing :
By a band at night the city shall be fired with powder ;
The city seems on fire, it helps though intended to destroy.

Fulminating mercury (*feu vif*) in bombs in terrible explosion contains death hidden The city, Paris, will be startled with powder liberated (*lasché*, loosed) by assassins by night. The city will seem on fire. But the enemy (in spite of himself) will prove favourable to Napoleon. This, of course, is Orsini's attempt of January 14, 1858.

The next verse follows up the thread.

Century V.—Quatrain 9. [I. 271.]

Jusques au fond la grand arq † demolue ‡
Par chef captif l'amy anticipé, §
Naistra de dame front, face chevelue,
Lors par astuce duc ‖ à mort atrapé.

---

* Latin, *classis*, band ; à classe, by a band [sic ?]. It might be better here to render *classe* as " crash," κλασις, *brisure. De nuict la classe*, a crash by night.

† Latin, *arca*, chest, or dam.

‡ Latin, *demolitus*, demolished.

§ Latin, *antecaptus*, seized beforehand.

‖ Latin, *dux*, leader.

Translation.

When the peristyle is thoroughly demolished
By the chief prisoner, the friend being taken before,
A plot born of the woman, long beard and hairy face ;
Then by cunning the leader caught will be executed.

The peristyle (*la grand arq'*) of the opera shall be completely shattered. Pieri, the friend of Orsini, the chief captive, is seized beforehand by Hébert, head of the detective service, who recognized him in the crowd. The plot was conceived in the secret lodges of the Demagoguy [*de Dame*], whose members wear the beard and hair long. Orsini, the leader of the whole, will be surprised astutely by the confessions of Gomez at the restaurant Broggi, whither he had fled, and, being taken, will be sentenced to death.

I do not feel very confident as to this interpretation, but give it much as I find it in M. le Pelletier.

Century V.—Quatrain 10. [I. 272.]

Un † chef Celtique dans le conflict blessé,
Auprès de cave ‡ voyant siens mort abbatre,
De sang et playes et d'ennemis pressé,
Et secours par incogneus § de quatre.

Translation.

The Celtic chief is wounded in the strife,
Seeing death strike down his friends near the theatre,
Surrounded with blood and wounds and pressed by enemies,
He escapes the four ‖ assassins, by unknown aid.

The Emperor, slightly struck in the eye by a fragment of glass, shall see his people strewn in death

---

* Latin, *unus*, the first.
† Latin, *cavea*, theatre.
‡ Romance, *incogneus*, unknown
§ The four were Orsini, Pieri, de Rudio, and Gomez.

about the entrance of the Grand Opera. Pressed by the conspirators, four in number, he will receive unknown help ; whether of angels or pure spirits, M. le Pelletier cannot quite say. We now know that he had still to see Sedan ; but it would be curious if pure spirits had interested themselves greatly to protect the cold-blooded murderer of the Champs de Mars and Coup d'État.

Century VI.—Quatrain 4. [I. 273.]
Le second chef du regne D'annemarc,*
Par ceux de Frize † et l'Isle Britannique,
Fera despendre ‡ plus de cent mille marc, §
Vain exploicter voyage en Italique.

The second of the Napoleonic race in power will cause England and Hanover to expend 100,000 marks in fortifications and war material. Fearing invasion after the Orsini effort, he will then exploit the Italian campaign, though vainly, as he will not reap the results he looks for.

This corresponds so clearly with what happened that probably most will agree that it is a very remarkable forecast.

Century III.—Quatrain 37. [I. 274.]
Avant l'assaut l'oraison ‖ prononcée,
Milan prins ¶ d'Aigle par embusches deceus,**

---

* Greek, Δαν-ἀρχή, as we had it before (*v.* p. 289).
† *Frise,* Hanover.
‡ Latin, *dependere,* to weigh out, spend.
§ M. le Pelletier calculates that the golden mark was equal to 250 grammes, or 100,000 marks = 10,000,000 francs.
‖ Latin, *oratio,* harangue.   ¶ Romance, *prins, pris,* taken.
** Latin, *decisus,* cut off.

Muraille antique par canons enfoncée,
Par feu et sang à mercy peu receus.

Translation.

Before assault a harangue is pronounced ;
Lombardy is taken by the eagle, being cut off by ambuscade.
An ancient wall driven in by cannon,
Fire and blood, but little mercy shown.

Before the declaration of war, the Emperor will pronounce (January 1, 1859), in the presence of the diplomatic corps, a threatening discourse against Austria. Lombardy (Milan, part for the whole) will be ceded by Austria at the Treaty of Zurich (October 17, 1859) ; Austria, an old wall, will yield to cannon, fire, and blood.

Century V.—Quatrain 20. [I. 275.]

De là * les Alpes grande armée passera
Un peu devant naistra monstre vapin, †
Prodigieux et subit ‡ tournera §
Le grand Tosquan à son lieu plus propin.‖

Translation.

A great army will pass beyond the Alps,
A little before a prodigious scamp will come to power ;
He will drive the grand Duke of Tuscany
To his nearer home with astounding suddenness.

In 1859 Napoleon III.'s army will pass the Alps. A little before a prominent scamp will have come to the front, who will suddenly and in a most startling

---

* Delà, for *au delà.*
† Italian, *vappa*, scamp.   ‡ Latin, *subito*, suddenly.
§ *Il tournera,* for *il fera tourner.*
‖ Latin, *propinque*, at hand, near.

fashion drive the Grand Duke of Tuscany to seek refuge in Austria (*son lieu le plus propin*).

We have to note here that Nostradamus, whenever he emerges from the impassibility of the *secret estude*, it is to exhibit a profound hostility to the genius of Democracy and Revolution. There is therefore little doubt but that the powerful epithet here employed of the *monstre vapin* relates to the red-shirted Garibaldi.

We have now reached the point which covers the last of the Oracles of Nostradamus that commentary has yet been able to lay before the world with its meaning rendered transparent by the correspondence of interpretation with an event in history. The number of such correlations of occurrence with forecast falls immensely short of the number of the quatrains themselves. In fact, only about one hundred and fifty-one, out of a thousand. The rest give no scintillation as yet, but lie without sign of existence traceable, dead as a flint, till the iron stroke of Time's heel shall develop the spark. *Lateat scintillula forsan.* One or two Presages and two or three Sixains have been also resolved. Enough, we trust, has been opened up to show what a treasure-house it is that we have entered into, how rich in curiosity, if in nothing more. What may still lie perdu in the bulky remainder of eight hundred and fifty it is impossible to say; whether, though unidentified, they have been realized already, or are yet to bud in the future. If nothing more be ever done with Nostradamus than this book gives, still the work must for one reason or other hereafter stand out as the most wonderful book of its kind that was ever written or printed in this world. It has now to go forth and take its chance, good or evil, of notice or of neglect amongst the mass of printed matter, largely rubbish, that deluges our life. It is certainly calculated, so far as it can secure any attention whatever, to severely shock the prejudices now prevalent amongst mankind. The half-educated will find it troublesome to read, and disturbing, perhaps, to think about ; whilst the scientific may even denounce it as a locust-cloud of darkness mediæval in its tendency. Undoubtedly it must have the effect that Nostradamus in his preface to his son (see p. 50) says very graphically it will have, " que possible fera retirer le front à quelques uns." Although, as he says again, the forecasts may be clouded, they will be understood by men of sense, and they will grow clearer as ignorance dies out (see p. 54); which should be our care now.

To all objectors I rejoin, gentlemen, investigate, please, all the points in question as searchingly as you can; find every fault in my work, and in that of the other Nostradamic commentators, that you can; expose all that is weak or illusive, wherever you find it to be so. Let us see, then, how far all the learning and acuteness you can bring to bear, coupled with whatever established prejudice, and its rancour at being disturbed in comfortable somnolency, can suggest, to overthrow what other men heretofore, and I now, have taken so much pains to bring together and give shape to. Consciously I have not set down a single word with any other desire than that the truth should prevail ; and if your criticism can establish

the opposite, I shall still repeat, "Let truth prevail."
But I do not think you can do this : and if not, there is
only one other thing, open to the learned and the wise
that can be done,—that is, to rewrite their philosophies,
so as to make room for the reception of this rather
awkward piece of truth that has here got in the way
of our old theories, and cannot be got out of the way
again.   To the really competent and candid reader
I have nothing whatever to add beyond begging him
to refer back to the closing words of my preface, as
to him they will be found to contain my whole and
entire message.

APPENDIX.

Referred to at p. 178.

———◆◇◆———

The genuine and spurious portraits of Cromwell are numerous to such a degree, that they may almost be called innumerable ; for they can never be counted, as no one man can get at them all to reckon them up. Their main authority is said to depend upon the works of four artists, Lely, Cooper, Walker, Faithorne. Samuel Butler, the author of the ever-marvellous "Hudibras," is thought to have painted a likeness, but it counts for nothing, as it is not now to be identified as existing in any collection. The first-named three are painters, the fourth is a great engraver.

In all these, Mr. Frederic Harrison professes to discover "singular resemblance" ["Cromwell," p. 32,] but considers that Cooper's is the most successful of them all. I find the first to be a most misleading statement, and one that may be disproved by anybody who will compare Cooper's likeness, as given in Carlyle's "Cromwell Letters" with the picture by Walker in the National Portrait Gallery. They differ in every particular,—in character, feature, temperament, and conformation. Scarcely do they agree even in the wart. There is nothing to identify them as representing the same individual. Either Lely copied Cooper, or Cooper copied Lely, and they accordingly, of course, correspond with each other ; but truth is too much sacrificed to flattery by both these courtly painters, for us to suppose that their work corresponds very accurately with the sitter. Such examples of Faithorne as are readily accessible in the Print Room at the Museum convey no adequate idea of the man.

Neither do they resemble Cooper, Lely, nor Walker's work. There is a profile print by Houbraken, an excellent performance, which is interesting as showing that both the chin and forehead receded greatly. There is also a very peculiar engraving of Thomas Simon's medal, which is very beautiful as a work of art. But here again the facial angle is simply villainous, with very mean diminutive eyes, and the dress almost clerical. The engraving from the Cooper at Sidney College gives the wart on the left brow instead of the right.

From such discrepant things it seems to me next to impossible to derive any correct notion regarding the face of Cromwell, except that the facial angle of the side face must have been unusually bad. Yet Mr. Harrison is able to express himself as follows :—

"No human countenance recorded is more familiar to us than that broad, solid face with the thick and prominent red nose; the heavy gnarled brow, with its historic wart; eyes firm, penetrating, sad; square jaw, and close-set mouth; scanty tufts of hair on lip and chin; long loose brown locks flowing down in waves on to the shoulder. His whole air breathing energy, firmness, passion, pity, and sorrow." Carlyle's fancy version is given below.*

This being derived from a falsity, must itself be false. But is it not somewhat curious that friends and foes of Cromwell should alike sit down contentedly before this admirably executed miniature of Cooper's without devoting a second thought to its representative value as a portrait of the man in question?

---

* "Stands some five feet ten or more ; a man of strong solid stature, and dignified, now partly military carriage : the expression of him valour and devout intelligence,—energy and delicacy on a basis of simplicity. Fifty-four years old, gone April last ; ruddy-fair complexion, bronzed by toil and age ; light brown hair and moustache are getting streaked with grey. A figure of sufficient impressiveness ;—not lovely to the man-milliner species, nor pretending to be so. Massive stature ; big massive head, of somewhat leonine aspect, 'evident workshop and storehouse of a vast treasury of natural parts.' Wart above the right eyebrow ; nose of considerable blunt aquiline proportions ; strict yet copious lips, full of all tremulous sensibilities, and also, if need were, of all fierceness and rigours ; deep loving eyes, call them grave, call them stern, looking from under those craggy brows, as if in life-long sorrow, and yet not thinking it sorrow, thinking it only labour, and endeavour :—on the whole, a right noble lion-face, and hero-face." (Carlyle, "Cromwell Letters," ii. p. 435).

Its artistic felicity should be as nothing to the historical inquirer. Taken as a mere portrait, this Cooper is as valueless as Veronese's presentment of Alexander the Great ; or as any fancy portrait of Oliver would be, if sent in by some skilled modern hand to the next May show at Burlington House.

Our sense of surprise increases, when we come to remember that we possess an authentic original to go by, in the shape of a mask still extant that was taken at death. Historians draw up rigmarole pen-and-ink portraits of their own, but are all silent about this, or make only casual mention of it as "the mask at the Statuaries," just as though it corresponded in every particular with Samuel Cooper's exquisite pigment-figment. Romancists delight in coloured detail gathered from history ; and historians revel in romance when it saves them from searching into dry detail. In this case historical gossip slips in to illustrate the stringent veracity of Cromwell. When Lely was to take his portrait, he is said to have ordered him to be faithful in representing every blemish and defect, to paint warts and all, or he would not be paid. Lely knew what this meant, and acted accordingly. All portrait-painters flatter, they must to secure a practice ; but, they ought to select the best aspect possible, for so far it is what it professes to be, a likeness. Now the strong point with your court painter is, to throw in skillfully what is not there. In this Lely and Cooper have succeeded to admiration.

Walker, in his several portraits, gives us another set of varieties. His picture in the Portrait Gallery [Granger, "Biog. Hist.," iii. p. 290.] with Cromwell's son Richard as page tying on the father's scarf, has been finely engraved by Pierre Lombart. In this picture, which is a little wooden, we get an average-looking gentleman going to battle. A man we should have to look at three or four times before we should individualize him at all in the memory. Mr. Nobody riding to nowhere particular is the impression derived. Of the engraving, however, Evelyn says, and he knew Cromwell perfectly well, "that it gives the strongest resemblance of him." He therein physiognomically discovers "characters of the greatest dissimulation, boldness, cruelty, and ambition, in every stroke and touch." I can say nothing of this, for I have not seen the Lombart engraving. The picture does not convey the idea.

How pliantly subservient art was in those days, is well illustrated in another Cromwell engraving by the same Lombart. This artist had done, after Vandyke, a "Charles on horseback," from which he erased the face, and substituted that of Cromwell. The slender figure of the king had to do duty for the heavy-built brewer of Huntingdon. But times change, and we with them. So Peter reinstated the king. There must be impressions of this turn-face print in its three states; for no doubt copies were sold at every stage. The King is dead. God save the Protector! The Protector is dead. God save the King! The dead lion is never so good for the crowd as the live ass; irrespective of the latter creature being far more representative. A quality much sought after in modern governors.

There is a portrait of Cromwell affixed to Isaac Kimber's " Life of Oliver Cromwell," which he published anonymously [Granger, iii. 297]. This is pronounced in the " Letters of Mr. Hughes " to be most like the authentic family pictures of Cromwell. Vertue engraved it in 1724 for Rapin's " History of England," and when Granger wrote the picture was in the possession of Sir Thomas Frankland of Old Bond Street. I suppose this to be still in the hands of the Frankland-Russells of Chequers Court, who also possess a plaster cast of Cromwell's face. By the courtesy of the family I have been permitted to examine this; but it seems to me of no value, and it has no history.

We come now to the terra-cotta bust by Edward Pierce, which is in the National Portrait Gallery, said to be taken from life. Pierce was an artist in the second generation. His father, of the same christian name, was a painter, and assistant of Vandyke. Our Edward was trained for a statuary, and became the pupil of Edward Bird : he also acted as assistant to Sir Christopher Wren, and is said to have built St. Clement Danes under him. He did a bust of Wren, for the theatre at Oxford, and also one of Newton. He died at Surrey street in the Strand, and was buried at the old Savoy. This bust of Cromwell was, to all appearance, modelled by him from a cast taken from life, and must therefore, as to measurement and bulk, be of life size.

I was kindly permitted by Mr. George Scharf, of the National Portrait Gallery, to take the dimensions of this bust by measurement, but practically they are not very useful, inasmuch as the head has a great abundance of short curly hair, which of course in terra-cotta becomes perfectly solid, and thereby increases the circumference of the head by many inches.

The circumference, hair and all, at his brow is 28⅜ inches.

Nape of neck to frontal bone, where it unites
with nose ... ... 15¼ „

Breadth from ear to ear at level of the central
hole of each ear as near as can be approximated 6⅝ „

This last measurement is, I believe, correct, but it is a dimension that only a large forceps could take with perfect certainty. It is so small, however, that I feel sure that the other two dimensions must be very far from giving the true osseous formation, so that several inches will have to be allowed off them for the hair. Again, the measurement between the tip of nose and back of head (9⅝ inches) would also require that deductions be made for a wad of hair at the back. This measurement when reduced, and coupled with the third measurement given, indicates an undersized skull for a broad built man of five feet eleven in stature.

As for the physiognomy, the nose, though far from fine, is somewhat aquiline, and the best of all the features of the face. The forehead is low, ill-formed, and mean. The! mouth firm, cruel, deceitful. The jowl and chin sensual and gross almost to brutality. It is the face of a man of low passions, possibly ambitious, but of great duplicity, of a low-bred type, the type as of one sprung from a lower stratum of society than his history indicates him to have sprung from ; and you may readily suppose that in exchanges of course buffoonery with the roughest trooper of his corps, he would have been quite within his own province and at home. His mother's portrait shows her also to have been a very masculine coarse-featured woman.

It is well perhaps to mention here a bust that Grose in a letter to Granger in 1774, calls " a masterly and spirited bust of Oliver Cromwell by one Bannier." It was then in Mr. Gostling's collection. He says it is like that engraving given in Rapin's " History." I imagine it therefore to be a fancy rendering, and of very small historic value.

The expert historians, and of course the general public together with them, are perfectly satisfied with the Cromwell presented to them by Samuel Cooper. I confess that I think it a most laughable presentment, and of quite impossible credence. I do not think Pierce's bust to be satisfactory, but I most certainly consider that it is the only likeness I have had the opportunity of examining that conveys even a hint of what can be supposed to be the real appearance of the man. There is but one way now remaining to settle this question. It is very much to be regretted that, with so much pretence of a desire for historical accuracy, we should have allowed two hundred and fifty years to elapse without making the least attempt to settle this question.

We learn from Breval's " Travels " that at the Old Palace at Florence there is a cast preserved of Oliver Cromwell. The mould was obtained from Cromwell's face *a few minutes after his decease*, " through the dexterous management of the Tuscan resident in London." This, or a cast from it, ought immediately to be secured for our National Portrait Gallery. A copy of it would cost very little in either time, money, or trouble to secure ; and when secured three or four should be cast in bronze, and placed in different museums so that one fire could not destroy all of them at once.

I feel almost sure that it will be found to confirm the bust of Pierce, as being more like Cromwell than anything else that we possess. And further, as Pierce's work is by no means a grand achievement in the sculptor's art, I should hope to find in the Florence cast characteristic indications that are absent from Pierce's work. Grandeur of soul is incompatible with such a face as Pierce gives us. But I confess that I see no grandeur whatever that could be expressed by a man whose history is that of Oliver. His base success the world may worship if it will. I despise success if it must be obtained by Cromwell's methods. I observe that the great in history are always mean in fact ; and I well know that you must say to all the men who have been triumphant, let no probing moralist come near you. Pitiable and contemptible is the man who can envy the great in the greatness of their crimes. I do not expect that the cast, if procured, will make the reading any better for Cromwell; but, if it should, I am quite ready to give him all the advantage of it. At present I hold that the face is villainous, like the man.

"... ducitur unco,
Spectandus: gaudent omnes. Quæ labra? Quis illi
Vultus erat? Nunquam, si quid mihi credis, amavi
Hunc hominem."
                                    JUVENAL, x. 66.

Still, love or no love, we have reached the end ; and if we
should confirm Pierce, the flesh and bones of the man thus
revived will also confirm the epithets of Nostradamus, which
first induced me to enter upon this investigation.

"Sir, I perceive that thou art a prophet."—*John* iv. 19.

"Quod est ante pedes, nemo spectat : cœli scrutantur plagas."—Cic., *Divin.*, ii. 13.

This granted, a pig is nearest wisdom.

Μάντις ἄριστος, ὅστις εἰκάζει καλῶς.—Witsius, *Miscel.*, p. 14.

The best analogist is the best prophet.

"L'observation des analogies universelles a été negligée, et c'est pour cela qu'on ne croit plus à la divination."—Levi, *Clef des Mystères*, p. 216.

Μαντεῖον, ἐπὶ χείλεσι βασιλέως, ἐν δὲ κρίσει οὐ μὴ πλανηθῇ τὸ στόμα αὐτοῦ.—*Prov.* xvi. 10, LXX.

There is divination on a king's lips, and judgment fails not in his mouth.

INDEX.

" 'Tis the compass that you steer by through a book."—Obris.

2 B

ENVOY.

" He that knows anything worth communicating and does not communicate it, let him be hanged by the neck."—*Talmud, Sucah,* p. 58.

AR: 157° 30'

Natus.

Nostradamus. Dec. 24. 1503 (N.S.)

December 14. 1503 (O.S.)

Thursday, 11:03 a.m. : apparent time

ST. Remy, France

Lat 43: 48 N.

Long. 4: 51 E.

E 6° ✗ approx. = R.K.

☽ 15 ♏︎ 17

☉ 1° ♐︎ 33'

☿ 4 ♑︎ 24 ℞

♀ 2° ≈ S. ℞

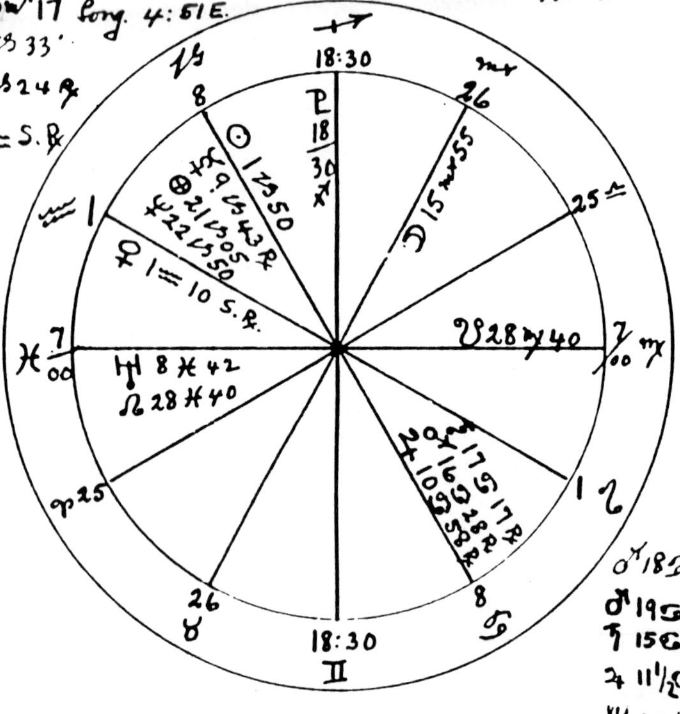

Inside the chart wheel (clockwise from top):

♐︎
18:30

♑︎ 8

☊ 26 ♏︎

15 ♏︎ 55 ☽

25 ♎︎

☊ 28 ♑︎ 40 ⚷ 00 ♍︎

≈ 1

♓︎ 7 00

♄ 8 ♓︎ 42 ☊ 28 ♓︎ 40

1 ♃

8 ♋︎

26 ♉︎ 18:30 ♊︎

♈︎ 25

♇ 18 30 ♐︎

☉ 1 ♐︎ 50

⊕ 9 ♑︎ 43 ℞ ☿ 22 ♑︎ 05 ♀ 22 ♑︎ 50

♀ 1 ≈ 10 S. ℞

Lower right segment:
24 ♋︎ 17 ℞
16 ♋︎ 15 ℞
11 ♋︎ 09 ℞
22 ♋︎ 28 ℞
8 ♋︎ 40 ℞

Right side listing:
♂ ✗ 18 30 ℞
♂ 19 ♋︎ ℞
♀ 15 ♋︎ ℞
♃ 11½ ♋︎ ℞
♆ 22 ♑︎ 42
♅ 8 ♓︎ 40

Chart Calculated by Ralph Kraum – Hollywood.

OTHER SUN BOOKS TITLES
you may find of interest:

AMERICAN INDIANS

BENEATH THE MOON AND UNDER THE SUN: A Re-Appraisal of the Sacred Calendar and the Prophecies of Ancient Mexico by Tony Shearer. The Sacred Twins, Tezcatlipoca - The Dark Lord, The Symbolic Glyphs, The 13 Sacred Numbers, The Dark House, Quetzalcoatl, The Prophecies Unfold, The Ceremony.

ASTRAL PROJECTION

THE PHENOMENA OF ASTRAL PROJECTION by Sylvan Muldoon and Herewood Carrington. Man's Spiritual Body, Multiple Bodies, Drugs and Anaesthetics, Accidents and Illness, Projections at the Time of Death, Experimental and Hypnotic Projections.

ASTROLOGY

ALAN LEO'S DICTIONARY OF ASTROLOGY by Alan Leo and Vivian E. Robson. Aaron's Rod, Casting the Horoscope, Disposition, Ecliptic, Equinoxes, Period of Sun, Objects Governed by the Planets, Mean Time.

THE ASTROLOGICAL GUIDE TO HEALTH FOR EACH OF THE TWELVE SUN SIGNS by Ariel Gordon, M.C. Information regarding the twelve signs of the Zodiac is taken from seven of the greatest authorities, past and present, on the different correspondences, as well as from personal experience, extending over many years of private practice.

ASTROLOGY: HOW TO MAKE AND READ YOUR OWN HOROSCOPE by Sepharial. The Alphabet of the Heavens, The Construction of a Horoscope, How to Read the Horoscope, The Stars in Their Courses.

THE DIVINE LANGUAGE OF CELESTIAL CORRESPONDENCES by Coulson Turnbull. Esoteric Symbolism of the Planets, Mystical Interpretation of the Zodiac, Kabalistic Interpretation of the 12 Houses, Evolution and Involution of Soul, Character of the Planets, Hermetic Books, Nature of Signs, Etc.

HEBREW ASTROLOGY by Sepharial. Chaldean Astronomy, Time and Its Measures, The Great Year, The Signs of the Zodiac, How to Set a Horoscope, The Seven Times, Modern Predictions.

THE INFLUENCE OF THE ZODIAC UPON HUMAN LIFE by Eleanor Kirk.
The Quickening Spirit, Questions and Answers, Disease, Development, A
Warning, Marriage, The Fire, Air, Earth, and Water Triplicities, Etc. (This is
an excellent book!)

**THE LIGHT OF EGYPT or THE SCIENCE OF THE SOUL AND THE STARS
by Thomas H. Burgoyne.** Vol. 1: Realms of Spirit and Matter, Mysteries of
Sex, Incarnation and Re-Incarnation, Karma, Mediumship, Soul Knowledge,
Mortality and Immortality. Basic Principles of Celestial Science, Stellar
Influence on Humanity, Alchemical Nature of Man, Union of Soul and Stars.
Vol. II: The Zodiac and the Constellations, Spiritual Interpretation of the
Zodiac, Astro-Theology and Astro-Mythology, Symbolism and Alchemy,
Talismans and Ceremonial Magic, Tablets of AEth including: The Twelve
Mansions, The Ten Planetary Rulers, The Ten Great Powers of the Universe,
and Penetralia – The Secret of the Soul.

MANUAL OF ASTROLOGY by Sepharial. Language of the Heavens, Di-
visions of the Zodiac, Planets, Houses, Aspects, Calculation of the Horoscope, Reading of a Horoscope, Measure of Time, Law of Sex, Hindu
Astrology, Progressive Horoscope, Etc.

**THE PLANETS THROUGH THE SIGNS: Astrology for Living, by Abbe
Bassett.** Includes chapters on the Sun, Moon, and various planets, and how
each one influences us through the different signs of the Zodiac.

**STARS OF DESTINY – THE ANCIENT SCIENCE OF ASTROLOGY AND
HOW TO MAKE USE OF IT TODAY by Katherine Taylor Craig.** History and
description of the Science, The Sun From Two Standpoints, The Moon and
the Planets. Astrological Predictions That Have Been Verified, Practical
Directions for Casting a Horoscope, Sample of General Prediction for a Year.

A STUDENTS' TEXT-BOOK OF ASTROLOGY by Vivian E. Robson.
Fundamental Principles of Astrology, Casting the Horoscope, Character and
Mind, Occupation and Position, Parents, Relatives and Home, Love and
Marriage, Esoteric Astrology, Adoption of the New Style Calendar.

WHAT IS ASTROLOGY? by Colin Bennett. How an Astrologer Works, Sign
Meanings, How Aspects Affect a Horoscope, Numerology as an Astrological
Aid, Psychology In Relation to Astrology, Etc.

ATLANTIS/LEMURIA

ATLANTIS IN AMERICA by Lewis Spence. Atlantis and Antillia, Cro-
Magnons of America. Quetzalcoatl the Atlantean, Stlantis in American
Tradition and Religion, Ethnological Evidence, Art and Architecture, Folk-
Memories of an Atlantic Continent, Analogy of Lemuria, Chronological Table,
Etc.

WISDOM FROM ATLANTIS by Ruth B. Drown. Being, Divine Selfishness,
Service, Nobility of Self-Reliance, Harmony, Divine Love, Principles of Life
and Living, Man's Divine Nature, Faith, True Thinking.

AUTOSUGGESTION/HYPNOTISM

MY METHOD by Emile Coué. Chapters include: Autosuggestion Disconcerting in its Simplicity, Slaves of Suggestion and Masters of Ourselves, Dominance of the Imagination over the Will, The Moral Factor in all Disease, Don't Concentrate, How to Banish Pain, Psychic Culture as Necessary as Physical, Self-Mastery Means Health, Etc.

THE PRACTICE OF AUTOSUGGESTION BY THE METHOD OF EMILE COUÉ by C. Harry Brooks. The Clinic of Emile Coué, A Few of Coué's Cures, Thought is a Force, Thought and the Will, The General Formula, How to Deal With Pain, Autosuggestion and the Child, Particular Suggestions, Etc.

SELF MASTERY THROUGH CONSCIOUS AUTOSUGGESTION by Emile Coué. Self Mastery Through Autosuggestion, Thoughts and Precepts, What Autosuggestion Can Do, Education as it Ought to Be, A Survey of the "Seances", the Miracle Within, Everything for Everyone, Etc.

CONSCIOUSNESS/MEDITATION

CRISIS IN CONSCIOUSNESS: The Source of All Conflict by Robert Powell. Chapters include: The Importance of Right Beginning, Zen and Liberation, The Worldly Mind and the Religious Mind, Repetition of the Pattern, Experience, Habit and Freedom, Can Illumination be Transmitted? The Equation of Unhappiness, Must We Have Religious Societies? Approach to the Immeasurable, Window on Non-Duality, Memory Without a Cause, Self or Non-Self? Common Sayings Revealing Uncommon Insights, On Contradiction, The Outer and the Inner, Etc.

THE FREE MIND: THE INWARD PATH TO LIBERATION by Robert Powell. Chapters include: Liberation and Duality, Crisis in Consciousness, Our Predicament, On Mindfulness, Living in the Essential, A Noncomparative Look at Zen and Krishnamurti, The Problem of Ambition, Only the Empty Mind is Capable of True Thoughtfulness, What Education Should Be All About, and What it Actually Is, If Awareness is Choiceless, Then Who is it That is Aware?, Free Among the Unfree, The Vicious, Vicious Circle of Self-Defense and War, Rflections on Causality: The Ultimate Failure of Metaphysics, Etc.

CONSPIRACY

THE ILLUMINOIDS – SECRET SOCIETIES AND POLITICAL PARANOIA by Neal Wilgus. Detailed picture of Weishaupt's Order of the Illuminati as well as other secret societies throughout history. Ties various far-reaching areas together including important information relating to the J.F. Kennedy assassination. "The best single reference on the Illuminati in fact and legendary" – Robert Anton Wilson in Cosmic Trigger.

CRYSTALS/MINERALS

CRYSTALS AND THEIR USE—A Study of At-One-Ment with the Mineral Kingdom by Page Bryant. Mineral Consciousness, Crystals and Their Use, Sacred Centers, Various Types of Crystals, The Anmethyst, Crystal Gazing.

THE MAGIC OF MINERALS by Page Bryant. The Inner Lives of the Mineral Kingdom, Megalithic Mysteries and the Native American View, The Healing Properties of Minerals, Psychic Influences in Minerals, Stones of the Zodiac, Crystals and Their Use, General Information on Selection, Use and Care of Minerals.

MAN, MINERALS, AND MASTERS by Charles W. Littlefield, M.D. School of the Magi, Three Masters, The Cubes, Initiation in Tibet, Hindustan, and Egypt, History, Prophecy, Numerology, Perfection. 172p. 5x8 Paperback.

PLANETARY INFLUENCES AND THERAPEUTIC USES OF PRECIOUS STONES by George Frederick Kunz. Includes various lists and illustrations.

EARTH CHANGES (Also See Prophecy)

CHEIRO'S WORLD PREDICTIONS by Cheiro. Fate of Nations, British Empire in its World Aspect, Destiny of the United States, Future of the Jews, Coming War of Wars, Coming Aquarian Age, Procession of the Equinoxes.

THE COMING STAR-SHIFT AND MANY PROPHECIES OF BIBLE AND PYRAMID FULFILLED by O. Gordon Pickett. God Corrects His Clock in the Stars, English Alphabet as Related to Numerics, Joseph Builder of the Great Pyramid, Numerical Harmony, Prophecy, World Wars, Star-Shifts, The Flood, Astronomy, The Great Pyramids, Etc.

COMING WORLD CHANGES by Curtiss. The Prophecies, Geological Considerations, The Philosophy of Planetary Changes, The King of the World, The Heart of the World, The Battle of Armageddon, The Remedy.

EARTH CHANGES NOW! by Page Bryant. Chapters include: The Earth is Changing: The Evidence, We Knew it was Coming!, The Sacred Covenant, The Externalization of the Spiritual Hierarchy, The Earth Angel: A Promise for the Future.

THE EARTH CHANGES SURVIVAL HANDBOOK by Page Bryant. Chapters include: The Emergence of Planetary Intelligence, Mapping the Earth, Earth Changes: Past and Future, Preparing for the Future, Walking in Balance, Etc.

ORACLES OF NOSTRADAMUS by Charles A. Ward. Life of Nostradamus, Preface to Prophecies, Epistle to Henry II, Magic, Historic Fragments, Etc.

PROPHECIES OF GREAT WORLD CHANGES compiled by George B. Brownell. Chapters include: World-War Prophecies, Coming Changes of Great Magnitude, False Christs, The New Heaven and the New Earth, The New Order and the Old, Etc.

ROLLING THUNDER: THE COMING EARTH CHANGES by J. R. Jochmans. The Coming Famine and Earth Movements, The Destruction of California and New York, Future War, Nostradamus, Bible, Edgar Cayce, Coming Avatars, Pyramid Prophecy, Weather, Coming False Religion and the Antichrist, and much, much more! This book is currently our best selling title.

UTOPIA II: AN INVESTIGATION INTO THE KINGDOM OF GOD by John Schmidt. Chapters include: Why Utopia?, Mankind's Past, Present, and Future, A Sociological Look, A Political Look, An Economic Look, A Spiritual Look.

GENERAL OCCULT

BYGONE BELIEFS – AN EXCURSION INTO THE OCCULT AND ALCHEMICAL NATURE OF MAN by H. Stanley Redgrove. Some Characteristics of Mediaeval Thought, Pythagoras and his Philosophy, Medicine and Magic, Belief in Talismans, Ceremonial Magic in Theory and Practice, Architectural Symbolism, Philosopher's Stone, The Phallic Element in Alchemical Doctrine, Roger Bacon, Etc. (Many Illustrations).

THE COILED SERPENT by C.J. van Vilet. A Philosophy of Conservation and Transmutation of Reproductive Energy. Deadlock in Human Evolution, Spirit Versus Matter, Sex Principle and Purpose of Sex, Pleasure Principle, Unfolding of Spirit, Marriage and Soul-Mates, Love Versus Sex, Erotic Dreams, Perversion and Normalcy, Virility, Health, and Disease, Freemasonry, Rosicrucians, Alchemy, Astrology, Theosophy, Magic, Yoga, Occultism, Path of Perfection, Uncoiling the Serpent, The Future, Supermen, Immortality, Etc.

COSMIC SYMBOLISM by Sepharial. Meaning and Purpose of Occultism, Cosmic Symbology, Reading the Symbols, Law of Cycles, Time Factor in Kabalism, Involution and Evolution, Planetary Numbers, Sounds, Hours, Celestial Magnetic Polarities, Law of Vibrations, Lunar and Solar Influences, Astrology and the Law of Sex, Character and Environment, Etc.

INFINITE POSSIBILITIES by Leilah Wendell. Chapters include: The Essence of Time, Time and Space, Inseperable Brothers, Coexistent Time, Traveling Through Time, Microcosmic Reflections, Cosmic Consciousness, The Universe in a Jar, Psychic Alchemy, Universality, The Divine Element, The Complete Whole, What Price Immortality?, Practical Infinity, Etc.

THE INNER GOVERNMENT OF THE WORLD by Annie Besant. Ishvara, The Builders of a Cosmos, The Hierarchy of our World, The Rulers, Teachers, Forces, Method of Evolution, Races and Sub-Races, The Divine Plan, Religions and Civilizations, Etc.

THE OCCULT ARTS by J.W. Frings. Alchemy, Astrology, Psychometry, Telepathy, Clairvoyance, Spiritualism, Hypnotism, Geomancy, Palmistry, Omens and Oracles.

OCCULTISTS & MYSTICS OF ALL AGES by Ralph Shirley. Apollonius of Tyana, Plotinus, Michael Scot, Paracelsus, Emanuel Swedenborg, Count Cagliostro, Anna Kingsford.

WHAT IS OCCULTISM? by Papus. Occultism Defined, Occult Philosophical Point of View, Ethics of Occultism, Aesthetics of Occultism, Theodicy – Sociology, Practice of Occultism, The Traditions of Magic, Occultism and Philosophy.

HEALING

DIVINE REMEDIES – A TEXTBOOK ON CHRISTIAN HEALING by Theodosia DeWitt Schobert. Fuller Understanding of Spiritual Healing, Healing of Blood Troubles and Skin Diseases, Freedom from Sense Appetite, Healing of Insanity, Healing of Insomnia, Healing of Poisoning of Any Kind, General Upbuilding and Healing of the Body Temple.

THE FINER FORCES OF NATURE IN DIAGNOSIS AND THERAPY by George Starr White, M.D. The Magnetic Meridian, Vital and Unseen Forces, Polarity, Cause of Un-Health, Colors, Magnetic Energy, Sympathetic-Vagal Reflex, Actions of Finer Forces of Nature, The Human Aura, Moon-Light and Sound Treatment with Light and Color, Etc.

HEAL THYSELF: AN EXPLANATION OF THE REAL CAUSE AND CURE OF DISEASE by Edward Bach, M.B., B.S., D.P.H. By focusing on the causes rather than the results of disease and thus allowing individuals to assist in their own healing, Dr. Bach shows the vital principles which will guide medicine in the near future and are indeed guiding some of the more advanced members of the profession today.

THE PHILOSOPHY OF MENTAL HEALING – A PRACTICAL EXPOSITION OF NATURAL RESTORATIVE POWER by Leander Edmund Whipple. Metaphysical Healing, Metaphysics Versus Hypnotism, The Potency of Metaphysics in Surgery, The Progress of the Age, Intelligence and Sensation, Mental Action, The Physical Reflection of Thought.

MEDITATION FOR HEALING by Justin F. Stone. Many Meditations—Many Effects, What is Meditation?, Different Modes of Meditation, Circulating the Chi, Breath, Way of Mindfulness, Chih-K'uan, Visualization, Tibetan Dumo Heat, Chanting Zen, Mind Control, Moving Meditation, Spiritual Side of Meditation, Etc.

THE PRINCIPLES OF OCCULT HEALING Edited by Mary Weeks Burnett, M.D. Occult Healing and Occultism, Healing and the Healing Intelligence. The Indestructible Self, Latent Powers of Matter, The Auras and the Ethers, Polarization, Music, Healing by Prayer, Angel or Deva Helpers, Thought Forms and Color in Healing, Magnetism – Mesmerism, Healing Miracles of the Christ, Etc

THE TWELVE HEALERS AND OTHER REMEDIES by Edward Bach. Chapters include remedies for the following: For Fear, For Uncertainty, For Insufficient Interest in Present Circumstances, For Loneliness, For Those Over-Sensitive to Influences and Ideas, For Despondency or Despair, For Over-Care for Welfare of Others.

HERBS

THE COMPLETE HERBALIST or THE PEOPLE THEIR OWN PHYSICIANS by Dr. O. Phelps Brown. By the use of Nature's Remedies great curative properties found in the Herbal Kingdom are described. A New and Plain System of Hygienic Principles Together with Comprehensive Essays on Sexual Philosophy, Marriage, Divorce, Etc.

THE TRUTH ABOUT HERBS by Mrs. C.F. Loyd. Chapters include: The Unbroken Tradition of Herbal Medicine, The History of Herbalism, The Birth of the Society of Herbalists, Herbs Cure-The Reason Why, The Healing Properties of Certain Herbs, The Effect of Herbs on Allergic Diseases, Herbalists' Fight for Freedom, Etc.

HISTORICAL NOVEL

CHILD OF THE SUN by Frank Cheavens. Alvar Nuñez Cabeza de Vaca was the first European explorer to cross the North American continent. His early 16th century wandering took him across Texas, part of New Mexico, southeastern Arizona, and down the west coast of Mexico into South America. His altruistic work and healing ministrations among the Indians of the Southwest drew to him multitudes of Indians who revered him as the Child of the Sun. Here, his story is told through the eyes of a deformed, itinerant Pueblo trader who joined him, studied with him, and witnessed the Great Spirit working through him.

HOLLOW EARTH

ETIDORHPA or THE END OF EARTH by John Uri Lloyd. Journey toward the center of the Earth thru mighty mushroom forests and across huge underground oceans with an entire series of fantastic experiences. A true occult classic! "Etidorhpa, the End of Earth, is in all respects the worthiest presentation of occult teachings under the attractive guise of fiction that has yet been written" – New York World.

INSPIRATION/POSITIVE THINKING

AS A MAN THINKETH by James Allen. Chapters include: Thought and Character, Effect of Thought on Circumstances, Effect of Thought on Health and the Body, Thought and Purpose, The Thought-Factor in Achievement, Visions and Ideals, Serenity.

CREATIVE MIND by Ernest S. Holmes. Chapters include: In the Beginning, Why and What is a Man?, The Law of Our Lives, Bondage and Freedom, The Word, The Power We Have Within Us, The Reason for the Universe, Mind in Action, Action and Reaction, Arriving at High Consciousness, The Perfect Universe, About Struggle Karma, Etc.

FROM PASSION TO PEACE by James Allen. Passion, Aspiration, Temptation, Transmutation, Transcendence, Beatitude, Peace.

FROM POVERTY TO POWER by James Allen. (Author of "As a Man Thinketh") Two books in one: The Path to Prosperity Including World a Reflex of Mental States, The Way Out of Undesirable Conditions, Silent Power of Thought, Controlling and Directing One's Forces, The Secret of Health, Success, and Power, Etc. and The Way of Peace including Power of Meditation, The Two Masters, Self and Truth, The Acquirement of Spiritual Power, Realization of Selfless Love, Entering into the Infinite, Perfect Peace, Etc.

HEALTH AND WEALTH FROM WITHIN by William E. Towne. Health From Within, Awakening of the Soul, Will, Love and Work, The Voice of Life, Non-Attachment, The Woman – The Man, The Supreme Truth, Power of Imagination and Faith, Practical Self-Healing, The Way to Gain Results, Lengthen and Brighten Life, Etc.

THOUGHT FORCES by Prentice Mulford. Chapters include: Co-operation of Thought, Some Practical Mental Recipes, The Drawing Power of Mind, Buried Talents, The Necessity of Riches, The Uses of Sickness, The Doctor Within, Mental Medicine, The Use and Necessity of Recreation, The Art of Forgetting, Cultivate Repose, Love Thyself.

THE SUCCESS PROCESS by Brown Landone. Five Factors Which Guarantee Success. The Process of Vivid Thinking, Tones Used in Persuading, Use of Action, Overcoming Hindrances, Developing Capacities, Securing Justice, Augmenting Your Success by Leadership, Etc.

KUNDALINI

AND THE SUN IS UP: KUNDALINI RISES IN THE WEST by W. Thomas Wolfe. Chapters include: The Hindu's View, The Esoteric Christian's View, The Professional Specialist's View, The Kundalini Subject's View, Physiological Effects, Spiritual Weightlessness, Emotional and Attitudinal Changes, Changed Dream Content, Event Control, The Reason for Summoning Up the Kundalini, Christ and the Kundalini, A Modern Parallel to the Second Coming, Etc.

LIGHT

PHILOSOPHY OF LIGHT – AN INTRODUCTORY TREATISE by Floyd Irving Lorbeer. The Ocean of Light, Sight and Light, Light and Perception, Some Cosmic Considerations, Light and Health, Electrical Hypothesis, Temperament, Beauty, and Love and Light, The Problem of Space and Time, Unity and Diversity, Deity, Soul, and Immortality, Light and the New Era, Etc.

LONGEVITY/SPIRITUAL ARTS/PROPHECY

FOREVER YOUNG: HOW TO ATTAIN LONGEVITY by Gladys Iris Clark. Chapter include: Ageless Symbology, Followers of Fallen Luminaries, Rejuvenation Practices, Youth in Age-Old Wisdom, Angelic Travel Guides, Longevity Begins with God Awareness, Coping with Realities, Non-Aging Techniques in Action, Musing on Transition, Cancel Out Negatives, Grecian Nostalgia, Sedona's Seven Vortices, Crystals, Etc.

MEDITATION

CONCENTRATION AND MEDITATION by Christmas Humphreys. The Importance of Right Motive, Power of Thought, Dangers and Safeguards, Particular Exercises, Time, Place, Posture, Relaxation, Breathing, Thoughts, Counting the Breaths, Visualization and Color, Stillness, Motive, Self Analogy, Higher Meditation, The Voice of Mysticism, Jhanas, Zen, Satori, Koan, Ceremonial Magic, Taoism, Occultism, Mysticism, Theosophy, Yoga, The Noble Eightfold Path, Etc.

NEW AGE

THE MESSAGE OF AQUARIA by Curtiss. The Mystic Life, The Sign Aquarius, Are These the Last Days?, Comets and Eclipses, Law of Growth, Birth of the New Age, Mastery and the Masters of Wisdom, Mother Earth and the Four Winds, The Spiral of Life and Life Waves, The Message of the Sphinx, Day of Judgement and Law of Sacrifice, The Spiritual Birth, The True Priesthood, Etc.

NUMEROLOGY

NAMES, DATES, AND NUMBERS – A SYSTEM OF NUMEROLOGY by Roy Page Walton. The Law of Numbers, The Character and influence of the Numbers, Application and Use of Numbers, Strong and Weak Names. The Number that Governs the Life, How Each Single Name Effects the Life, The Importance of Varying the Signature, How the Name Discloses the Future, Choosing a Suitable Name for a Child, Names Suitable for Marriage, How to Find Lucky Days and Months, Points to Bear in Mind.

NUMBER VIBRATION IN QUESTIONS AND ANSWERS by Mrs. L. Dow Balliett. Selections include: When Was Your First Birth?, The First Step in Reading a Name, Can the Name be Changed?, What Does the Birth Path Show?, The Numerical and Number Chart, Is an Esoteric Value to be Found in Gems?, Why Do We Not Add Either 22 or 11?, The Day of Reincarnation, Is Anybody Out of Place?, Are We Gods?, Of What Use is Prayer?, What Is the Soul?, Should Rooms be Furnished in our Own Colors?, What Months Are Best for Creation?, What Is Astral Music?, Where Should We Live?, Etc. Etc. Etc!

VIBRATION: A system of Numbers as Taught by Pythaforas by Mrs. L. Dow Balliett. Chapters include: The Principles of Vibration, Numbers in Detail, What Your Name Means (broadly speaking), Business, Choosing A Husband or Wife, Pythagoras' Laws, Your Colors, Body Parts, Gems, Minerals, Flowers, Birds, Odors, Music, Guardian Angel, Symbols, Etc.

ORIENTAL

THE BUDDHA'S GOLDEN PATH by Dwight Goddard. Prince Siddhartha Gautama, Right Ideas, Speech, Behaviour, Right Vocation, Words, Conduct, Mindfulness, Concentration, Resolution, Environment, Intuition, Vows, Radiation, Spiritual Behaviour, Spirit, Etc.

FUSANG or THE DISCOVERY OF AMERICA BY CHINESE BUDDHIST PRIESTS IN THE FIFTH CENTURY by Charles G. Leland. Chinese Knowledge of Lands and Nations, The Road to America, The Kingdom of Fusang or Mexico, Of Writing and Civil Regulations in Fusang, Laws and Customs of the Aztecs, The Future of Eastern Asia, Travels of Other Buddhist Priests, Affinities of American and Asiatic Languages, Images of Buddha, Etc.

THE HISTORY OF BUDDHIST THOUGHT by Edward J. Thomas. The Ascetic Ideal, Early Doctrine: Yoga, Brahminism and the Upanishads, Karma, Release and Nirvana, Buddha, Popular Bodhisattva Doctrine, Buddhism and Modern Thought, Etc.

SACRED BOOKS OF THE EAST by Epiphanius Wilson. Vedic Hymns, The Zend-Avesta, The Dhammapada, The Upanishads, Selections from the Koran, Life of Buddha, Etc.

WAY OF THE SAMURAI Translated from the classic Hagakure by Minoru Tanaka. This unique translation of a most important Japanese classic offers an explanation of the central and upright character of the Japanese people, and their indomitable inner strength. "The Way of the Samurai" is essential for businessmen, lawyers, students, or anyone who would understand the Japanese psyche.

THE WISDOM OF THE HINDUS by Brian Brown. Brahmanic Wisdom, Maha-Bharata, The Ramayana, Wisdom of the Upanishads, Vivekananda and Ramakrishna on Yoga Philosophy, Wisdom of Tuka-Ram, Paramananda, Vivekananda, Abbedananda, Etc.

PHILOSOPHY

GOETHE – WITH SPECIAL CONSIDERATION OF HIS PHILOSOPHY by Paul Carus. The Life of Goethe, His Relation to Women, Goethe's Personality, The Religion of Goethe, Goethe's Philosophy, Literature and Criticism, The Significance of "Faust", Miscellaneous Epigrams and Poems. (Heavily Illustrated).

PROPHECY (Also See Earth Changes)

THE STORY OF PROPHECY by Henry James Forman. What is Prophecy?, Oracles, The Great Pyramid Speaks, The End of the Age: Biblical Prophecy, Medieval Prophecy, Astrologers and Saints, Prophecies Concerning the Popes, Nostradamus, America In Prophecy, The Prophetic Future.

PSYCHIC ARTS

PSYCHIC GROWTH – DANGERS AND ECSTASIES by Kenneth Naysmith. Spirit of Mother Earth, Immortal Flame: Sex and Yoga, Some Psychic Dangers, Marriage, Duality, and Humility, Fall of a Titan, Splintering Souls, Possessiveness: The Beginnings of "Possession", Etc.

PYRAMIDOLOGY

THE GREAT PYRAMID. Two Eesays plus illustrations, one from The Reminder and the other from J.F. Rowney Press. Selections include: The Pyramid's Location and Constructional Features, Some of the Pyramid's Scientific Features, other Features of the Great Pyramid, Complete History of Mankind Represented in the Pyramid, The Shortening of Time, The Symbolism of the Passages and Chambers, Etc.

REINCARNATION

THE NEW REVELATION by Sir Arthur Conan Doyle. The Search, The Revelation, The Coming Life, Problems and Limitations, The Next Phase of Life, Automatic Writing, The Cheriton Dugout.

REINCARNATION by George B. Brownell. He Knew Who He Was, Memories of Past Lives, A Remarkable Proof, Lived Many Lives, An Arabian Incarnation, Dreamed of Past Life, Great Minds and Reincarnation, The Bible and Reincarnation, Karma, Atlantis Reborn, Thought is Destiny, The Celestial Body, The Hereafter, Etc.

REINCARNATION by Katherine Tingley. What Reincarnation Is, Arguments for Reincarnation, Supposed Objections to Reincarnation, Reincarnation and Heredity, Reincarnation in Antiquity, Reincarnation the Master-Key to Modern Problems, Reincarnation In Modern Literature.

THE RING OF RETURN by Eva Martin. Pre-Christian Era, Early Christian and Other Writings of the First Five Centuries A.D., Miscellaneous Sources Before A.D. 1700, A.D. 1700-1900, The Twentieth Century. In this book, Miss Eva Martin has brought together a most complete and scholarly collection of references to past, present, and future life.

RELIGIONS

NATURAL LAW IN THE SPIRITUAL WORLD by Henry Drummond. Biogenesis, Degeneration, Growth, Death, Mortification, Eternal Life, Environment, Conformity to Type, Semi-Parasitism, Parasitism, Classification.

PRINCIPAL SYMBOLS OF WORLD RELIGIONS by Swami Harshananda. Chapters include discussions of the symbols of these religions: Hinduism, Buddhism, Jainism, Sikhism, Shintoism, Islam, Christianity, Judaism, Zoroastrianism, Taoism.

THE RELIGION OF THE SIKH GURUS by Teja Singh, M.A., Teja Singh, formerly a professor of history at Khalsa College in Amritsar, outlines the foundation of history, tradition, ritual and principles which has kept disciples of the the Sikh religion strong and united into the present day.

SELF-HELP/RECOVERY

SO SPEAKS HIGHER POWER: A Handbook for Emotional and Spiritual Recovery by Dr. Isaac Shamaya. Addiction, stress and recovery, feeling, blame, anger, fear and pain, relationships, understanding, love, and Higher Power.

SOUL

THE HUMAN SOUL IN SLEEPING, DREAMING AND WAKING by F.W. Zeylmans van Emmichoven, M.D. Featured subjects include: What is the Soul?, How, by observing the phenomena of life, we can find the reality of the soul and its connections with the human organism. Man as a threefold being. Dreams. Psycho-Analysis. The awakening of the soul. Fears. Meditation, Concentration and Self Development. The counterforces that work against man's spiritual striving. Spiritual Science as a psychology of the living, developing soul, Etc.

TAROT

THE ILLUSTRATED KEY TO THE TAROT – THE VEIL OF DIVINATION by L. W. de Laurence. The Veil and Its Symbols, The Tarot in History, The Doctrine Behind the Veil, The Outer Method of the Oracles, The Four Suits of Tarot Cards, The Art of Tarot Divination, An Ancient Celtic Method of Divination.

THE KEY OF DESTINY by Curtiss. The Initiate, Twelve-fold Division of the Zodiac, Reincarnation and Transmutation, The Solar System, The Letters of the Tarot, The Numbers 11 thru 22, Twelve Tribes and Twelve Disciples, The Great Work, The Labors of Hercules, Necromancy, Great Deep, Temperance, Man the Creator vs. the Devil, Celestial Hierarchies, The New Jerusalem, Etc.

THE KEY TO THE UNIVERSE by Curtiss. Origin of the Numerical Systems, Symbols of the "O" as the Egg and the Cat, The "O" as the Aura and the Ring Pass Not, Symbol of the O, Letters of the Tarot, The Numbers 1 thru 10, The 7 Principles of Man, The 7 Pleiades and the 7 Rishis, Joy of Completion.

WESTERN MYSTICISM

BROTHERHOOD OF MT. SHASTA by Eugene E. Thomas. From Clouds to Sunshine, Finding the Brotherhood, The Lake of Gold, The Initiation, Memories of the Past, In Advance of the Future, Prodigy, Trial, and Visitor, The Annihilation and the King, The Lost Lemuria.

MYRIAM AND THE MYSTIC BROTHERHOOD by Maude Lesseuer Howard. A novel in the western mystic tradition.

THE WAY OF ATTAINMENT by Sydney T. Klein. The Invisible is the Real, The Power of Prayer, Spiritual Regeneration, Dogma of the Virgin Birth, Finding the Kingdom of Heaven "Within", Realizing Oneness with God, Nature of the Ascent, Reaching the Summit.

THE WAY OF MYSTICISM by Joseph James. God Turns Towards Man, The Unexpected, The Still Small Voice, His Exceeding Brightness, Man Turns Towards God, The Obstructive "Me", Where East and West Unite, Beside the Still Waters, Love's Meeting Place, Work – A Prayer, Every Pilgrim's Progress, Love's Fulfillment.

GENERAL NON-METAPHYSICAL

BEST ENGRAVINGS by Skip Whitson. One hundred twenty three beautiful steel cut and wood cut engravings from the nineteenth century.

THE LAND OF ENCHANTMENT FROM PIKE'S PEAK TO THE PACIFIC by Lilian Whiting. Chapers include: With Western Stars and Sunsets, Denver the Beautiful, The Picturesque Region of Pike's Peak, Summer Wanderings in Colorado, The Colorado Pioneers, The Surprises of New Mexico, The Story of Santa Fe, Magic and Mystery of Arizona, The Petrified Forest and the Meteorite Mountain, Los Angeles, The Spell-Binder, Grand Canyon, the Carnival of the Gods.